SAIL

AWAY

SKIPPER'S LIBRARY

Other books in the **SKIPPER'S LIBRARY** series

Short-Handed Sailing

By Alastair Buchan

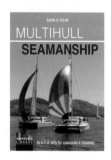

Multihull Seamanship

By Gavin Le Sueur

More to follow...

SKIPPER'S LIBRARY

SAIL

AWAY

HOW TO ESCAPE THE RAT RACE & LIVE THE DREAM

NICOLA RODRIGUEZ

SECOND EDITION

FERNHURST
BOOKS

This second edition published in 2019 by Fernhurst Books Limited

The Windmill, Mill Lane, Harbury, Leamington Spa, Warwickshire. CV33 9HP, UK

Tel: +44 (0) 1926 337488 | www.fernhurstbooks.com

First edition published in 2011 by John Wiley & Sons Ltd.

A catalogue record for this book is available from the British Library
ISBN 9781912177233

Front cover photograph © Don Hebert / Getty Images

Designed by Daniel Stephen
Printed in Czech Republic by Finidr

CONTENTS

Brutus:
There is a tide in the affairs of men.
Which, taken at the flood, leads on to fortune;
Omitted, all the voyage of their life
Is bound in shallows and in miseries.
On such a full sea are we now afloat,
And we must take the current when it serves,
Or lose our ventures.

Julius Caesar Act 4, Scene 3, 218-224 William Shakespeare

1
TURNING THE DREAM INTO REALITY

Why would you want to make a sailing boat your home and cast off to venture beyond the horizon?

Because it is an amazing experience on all levels and the best way to live life to the full – heading to the horizon in every way.

That's what my husband and I did. We wanted to have our adventure, our taste of paradise, in this life, not in the next. We set sail and lived the life we'd always dreamed of. Our four-day stay in magical Bimini slipped to four weeks. We spent five weeks anchored off the beach at Freeman's Bay, Antigua, one of the most beautiful anchorages in the world. Why? Because we loved it.

As a well-known pirate of the Caribbean once said: "What a ship is, what she really is... is freedom."

Freedom from the demands of work.

Freeman's Bay, English Harbour, Antigua, West Indies: one of the most beautiful anchorages

Freedom from the daily grind of office politics and social one-upmanship, schedules, the normal, the ordinary, school term times, the school run. Freedom from traffic and parking restrictions. Time out to explore on every level. Time out for yourself and your partner. Your boundaries will become the horizons you sail over; your perceptions will change with the tides. Teacher, gardener, lawyer and chef will all merge into a sailor of seas.

How much would you give for perpetual summer? To turn the cold rain and grey clouds into sunshine and blue skies, not for days but for weeks or months in the Caribbean or the Pacific. And then perhaps, having explored in t-shirt and shorts, you may want to go further, to the cooler waters of higher latitudes. The world really is your oyster.

While escaping the humdrum is challenging and doesn't mean a life of ease, even in the toughest times you'll be in a place that most call heaven on earth. For weeks on end you'll be somewhere that most people only visit for their precious fortnight's holiday and you'll have the luxury of not knowing which day it is, let alone which week. You'll be cruising, dropping in and out of the tourists' world as you wish: part local, part traveller. Or escaping the beaten path completely.

As JRR Tolkien wrote, 'Not all who wander are lost.' Whilst writing this book I delighted in emails from contributors starting: 'sorry for my delay in replying – we've been cruising among islands in the South Pacific where internet is pretty much non-existent even today...' or 'thanks for your SMS which was received in a very rare moment of mobile phone coverage in Alaska.'

One of the many joys of cruising is the unexpected pleasures – be it the thrill of discovering a stunning, uncrowded anchorage or the exhilaration of feeling free to go wherever you want.

Freedom doesn't mean release from stress, but it does mean stress on your own time, stress at your command. You will have to fix the boat, but you will be setting the agenda.

Hawksbill in the Bahamas

OUR STORY

I met John when I gate-crashed his party for top advertising clients in London's Soho. On our second date he said that he wanted to sail around the world one day and asked me to come too. John was in the process of buying a Beneteau Oceanis 311 Clipper anticipating coastal sailing for a few seasons. We named her *Serafina* in a force 10 gale. On our first sail, dolphins played around us – unusual off the Sussex coast. On our second sail on 5th November, in a force 3 with a harvest moon, we toasted hundreds of fireworks displays a mile off Sovereign Harbour.

A few days later John proposed, and we realised that the 'one-day' was now. But, we needed a blue-water boat. We began an extensive search for a suitable yacht for our trip. The Beneteau was sold. The day after we found *Moonshine*, a Westerly Corsair, everyone in my department was made redundant. The redundancy money paid for the refit. We married in May and sailed in July. 25,000 miles, eight years, two hurricanes and two sons later, I wrote this book.

John & Nicola Rodriguez

DECIDING TO GO

So, what does it take to sail over the horizon? The excuses and good reasons not to go are legion. In the end, it's about focus, chutzpah and sheer bloody-mindedness. It's a cliché but it's true: you have to make a commitment to follow your dream. Book after book, blog after blog, you read that once the decision had been made, the following one, five or ten years, was all about a focus on being able to cruise away, whether it's in a home-made boat or on a yacht bought with hard-earned money. You need to hold on to the dream day by day and not allow yourself to be distracted or persuaded that it's a mad idea.

Exploring the world from your own floating home allows for countless unforgettable achievements – those things that you want to do before you die. It is remarkable, having travelled thousands of miles, to sail into Manhattan or under the Sydney Harbour Bridge. Even crossing the English Channel and motoring down the Seine into Paris gives you a fantastic kick. Would you prefer to fly into Antigua and face the airport chaos or sail into English Harbour, one of the most beautiful anchorages in the world?

The first sight of land from the sea after a three-week passage is intoxicating. Equally, be it the Isle of Wight or the continent of the Americas, as the land slips away again, so do perceived problems and issues. The fascinations and concerns of the everyday world become more and more ephemeral the further and longer you sail away.

Many people are happy with a predictable life, year after year, TV series after TV series, football season after football season – for them that's life as it should be lived. For those who want to live a different life, it's about watching Spain versus Germany with the locals in Mallorca or England versus France with the locals in Martinique. How about following the English cricket tour of the Windies under your own sail, island by island? Perhaps you won't have all your family with you, but you can have your birthdays and Christmas on exquisite warm beaches, or spend New Year jumping around at Junkanoo, a carnival in the Bahamas. Every time you drop the lines there's a buzz of anticipation about where you are and what's next. You should be in control of your boat, but not necessarily in control of the life you're leading. You're looking for the new and unknown.

If that sounds like you, then this book will give you the information you need to make your life under sail a success. First, let's look at what you need to think about and know before you go.

Siesta time, Balearics, Spain

PRACTICAL ISSUES

As with all very big adventures, it's important to ask some fundamental questions, such as:

- What makes you think you can sail a boat for a year and a day, and another, and another? Do you have the aptitude, the knowledge and the skills? Are you physically and emotionally fit enough for the demands of life at sea?
- What about your job? Do you take time out when you're young and fit but risk your career in the process? Are you able to take a sabbatical and, if so, for how long? How will you feel if you have an amazing time, only to return and find yourself working for a junior you once trained? Have you considered the effect that leaving your job will have on your identity? Or do you keep climbing the career ladder, hoping for promotion and good investments to buy you expensive holidays for now, and the dream later?
- How are you going to pay for your travels? How much of your savings or inheritance can you spend? Would you be willing to go into debt?
- What about your current home? If you own your house, are you going to rent it out while you're away? If you come back early or for a visit, where would you stay? How long could you stay there before you and your hosts would be likely to fall out?
- Do you want to go as a family or just the two of you? If you are taking the children, when do you take them out of school? Are you willing to educate them yourself? If they are very young, are you willing to look after them 24/7, day after day, month after month?
- If you've waited until your retirement to sail away, will you cope? How good are you in high temperatures and high

humidity with no air conditioning? Are you fit enough to climb in and out of dinghies every day? Will you want to return to see your grandchildren growing up? How willing are you to be ill or require medical attention far from home?

- What plans have you made for living on land if you don't take to living on board? Even if things do work out, will you feel at ease with your landlubber's identity after a long time away at sea?

THE FOLKS BACK HOME

Obviously, as well as making the necessary practical arrangements for them, children, parents and possibly pets need to be cherished and cared for while you're away. Luckily, communications via mobile phone and email are increasingly good, even in remote places such as the Pacific, so you will be able to keep in touch.

Be prepared for negative reactions from some of those you leave behind. Not everyone will agree with your decision, nor will they be truly interested in your experiences. When you return home, whether for a visit or for good, people will listen for a few minutes and then begin to switch off, their eyes glazing over. You may have lost your connection with them because your experiences are so out of their world. People will eagerly tell you about their flotilla holiday, not realising that has as much to do with long-term cruising as rubber bands do with space flight.

One retired couple decided to leave the woman's elderly mother, who had severe dementia, in a good care home. When the old lady died, the grieving daughter flew home to be greeted by unsympathetic siblings. The couple had been in a remote part of the western Caribbean and had endured a dreadful time finding a safe berth for the boat, securing flights and making an arduous journey to the airport. The siblings who had remained at home vented their grief in the form of long-felt resentment of their sister's cruising lifestyle. They felt she had abandoned their mother, regardless of her condition and needs. They did not understand or care what stress on top of distress the couple had suffered en route home. They felt they deserved every mile of discomfort they had endured as penance for their selfishness.

Sometimes there will be news or pictures of a party or gathering that would have been fun to be at but was not worth the disruption involved in flying home. At other times homesickness or a temporary disappointment with cruising can make you find excuses to come back. One skipper was unimpressed with his new partner's trips home to mother their 19-year-old son who had just started at university.

Seraphim at anchor, Plana Cay, Outer Bahamas, on Easter Day

A LIFE CHANGE OR A STYLE OF LIFE?

There is a vast difference between those who are sailing away and changing their lifestyle completely, and those who continue to work and just take time out on their yacht. Which one are you? Think about how much you want to let go. How much you want to hold on to your career, or the reins of power if you are self-employed.

One workaholic executive who owned a superyacht with another wealthy friend came to deeply resent the fortune he was paying to maintain the boat and the crew, but without the benefits of lounging around his acres of teak deck. His friend viewed his investment differently and made time out from his hectic schedule to spend time indulging in what his hard work had brought him.

Some people argue that it's better to have a partial experience rather than none. Others claim that a clean break is essential to focus on the new life and that you're unlikely to fully grasp the cruising experience if you still have business interests at home.

A sad but true example is a successful businessman who set sail on a beautiful yacht, leaving his sons in charge of the thriving company. However, he did not want to let go completely and found himself being sucked back into running the firm. He flew back to the UK on business increasingly often and visits to his ocean-going yacht became rarer and shorter. The money wasn't the problem, he just couldn't let go. Unfortunately, a few years later the business failed, and he lost his boat as well.

A minority of high-powered business folk are able to manage their business from their yacht via wi-fi and satellite communication. They find that it works to their advantage that their employees never know quite where they are, or when they are online.

Unless you're already retired, do remember to think about what you are going to do for a living when you come back. Anne Hammick, a veteran cruiser who wrote *Ocean Cruising on a Budget*, remarked that 20 years ago it was easier for people in their mid-30s to sail away because they had the security of knowing they could find a job on their return. Financial times have changed, and the jobs market is less guaranteed. Many people face the problem not only of adjusting to sitting in an office on their return from the freedom of a boat, but of securing themselves a job.

DO YOU HAVE THE SKILLS?

It can take a lifetime to learn how to sail. However, you can learn the basics in just a few months. If you don't know how to read a chart, give coordinates (latitude and longitude), or understand that CD can stand for chart datum, then it's advisable for you to go on a course before you go off round the world.

COURSES

In the UK, sailing schools offer the Royal Yachting Association (www.rya.org.uk) courses from Start Yachting to Competent Crew, through Day Skipper, Coastal Skipper, Yachtmaster Offshore and Ocean. Don't forget that you can interview the school to find out about its staff and their teaching methods. You'll learn much more if you enjoy the company of the instructors. The UK Sailing Academy (www.uksa.org) is one of many organisations offering a 23-week course aimed at turning out fully qualified skippers with Yachtmaster tickets.

In the USA, a good place to start is US Sailing (www.ussailing.org), based in Portsmouth, Rhode Island. There you can find guidance on information and training all over the USA. The Seven Seas Cruising Association, based in Fort Lauderdale, Florida, was set up for cruisers using power and sail; you can find more information at www.ssca.org.

In Australia, Yachting Australia (YA; www.yachting.org.au) offers training schemes and courses, including those from the RYA. It also sells publications and provides information on regattas such as Sail Sydney in December in the Sail Down Under series (www.downunderrally.com).

In New Zealand, the Coastguard (www.coastguard.co.nz) runs Boating Education (www.boatingeducation.org.nz), with courses from beginner to professional.

International Yacht Training (www.iytworld.com) provide information on courses, worldwide. Their website claims that they are 'the global standard for maritime training and certification'.

If you're new to skippering, new to your boat or feel that the first leg of your journey is too much of a challenge, you could ask an experienced friend, or even hire a professional skipper and crew, to sail with you for a few weeks. You could view this as an investment, as an RYA-approved skipper can teach you about your boat and assist you in gaining your RYA Coastal Skipper or Yachtmaster certificate. Some new boat owners whose spouses don't want to, or can't spare the time to, be actively involved find two or three friends with whom to learn. Seek instruction, use your common sense, and also accept that you will learn quickly along the way.

Some of the most knowledgeable seamen have no qualifications at all. A piece of paper is not an absolute and experience can be just as valuable. There are also scores of books detailing how to be a good skipper and crew.

RESEARCH

If you're not sure where to sail to first, you could research destinations in sailing magazines, pilot guides, alternatively, experience the world through blogs, (blog.mailasail.com, www.sailblogs.com, www.getjealous.com), vlogs, YouTube, Facebook, Twitter, Instagram or the Ocean Cruising Club's *Flying Fish*, or Royal Cruising Club's *Roving Commissions*. Entering 'Sailing' on YouTube or 'Sailing' and 'Cruising' on Facebook will lead to numerous sites. A good site to guide you to a wide range of sailing blogs is: https://blog.feedspot.com/sailing_blogs/

At the end of this book is information on a selection of pilot guides that provide solid information on various destinations, offering expert advice on entry into ports, anchorages, marinas and much else besides. They cover your journey from the English Channel to the Baltic, the Mediterranean, the Atlantic, the Caribbean (east and west), the United States and Canada, the Arctic and Northern Waters, the Panama Canal, the Pacific, Australasia and the Far East.

For answers to a wide variety of yachting questions, and to feel part of the online sailing community, it's worth joining a sailing forum, such as those at Yachting and Boating World, www.ybw.com, www.allatsea.net, www.cruisersforum.com.

The Cruising Association (www.theca.org.uk), based in Limehouse Basin, London, provides information to sailors considering short or long-term cruises. Its illustrated talks, meetings and the members themselves are a fount of experience and information. The headquarters houses an extensive nautical reference library of over 10,000 volumes, and the organisation publishes a comprehensive handbook containing chart plans of harbours and anchorages, with sailing directions for the whole of the British Isles. The CA also runs RYA courses and a Crewing Service, which assists skippers looking for crew and vice versa.

The *Atlantic Crossing Guide* by Jane Russell is an essential reference book which we shall return to. Or for a glimpse of how the rich and famous live, take a look at the *Superyacht Services Guides* to the Mediterranean and Caribbean (www. superyachtservicesguide.com). As well as inspiring you, they will give you useful information to ground your dream.

HOW LONG & HOW FAR?

Do you actually want to go around the world? How much of your life are you prepared to invest? A circumnavigation can take 18 months on a World Rally, or 18 years at your own pace. Sir Francis Drake in the Golden Hind took two years, ten months 'and some odd daies beside'. In 1898 Captain Joshua Slocum completed a solo circumnavigation of 46,000 miles in three years, two months and two days. The present record (at the time of writing) is 42 days, 16 hours, 40 minutes and 35 seconds held by François Gabart in a 100-foot trimaran.

Many people who have completed a circumnavigation recommend eight years, which enables you to explore on land as well as taking trips home and allowing time for maintenance – and more maintenance. It also offers you the opportunity to take a berth for at least three winters, whether in New Zealand, Australia, the USA or Europe.

You may decide to opt for participation in a rally, on which there is more in Chapter

8. There are rallies that, for a price, can take you all the way around the world in 16 or 18 speedy months. There are also rallies for shorter distances, such as from the UK across the Bay of Biscay to northern Spain or Portugal. Others cross oceans, from the Canaries to the West Indies, through the Western Atlantic between the Caribbean and the USA, from the Pacific Islands south to Australia, from Australia through Indonesia, and so on into the Indian Ocean. Although you will be sailing by yourselves and you may feel alone, you will be sailing in company, even if the closest yacht is 100 miles away.

The end of our Atlantic crossing with Blue Water Rally

Cruising authority Jimmy Cornell, whose books *World Cruising Handbook* and *World Cruising Routes* are absolute necessities for long-term cruisers, started the website (now owned by World Cruising Club Ltd) , www.noonsite.com, that is full of information, including a comprehensive list of rallies around the world.

As a taster, you could attend one of the free seminars by the World Cruising Club held during various boat shows. They cover long-term sailing, giving information on the Atlantic and World rallies. They also suggest ways to raise money for your boat and equipment plus costs and routes. Previous rally participants speak of their experiences, and it is an easy way to gather information comparatively inexpensively.

For those who are serious about sailing away, once a year in March the ARC (Atlantic Rally for Cruisers) holds a more comprehensive, two-and-a-half-day ocean cruising seminar, for which there is a small cost. These are run in the UK and Annapolis, Maryland.

If you don't want to join an organised rally, you can be sure that if there is a route that has to be travelled at a particular time of year because of the winds – for example crossing the Atlantic in December because that is when the easterly winds blow you across – then there will be dozens of other boats with which you can form an informal rally. Local knowledge or cruising associations will give you good advice. Before you depart, check out whether your local yacht club has reciprocal arrangements with yacht clubs abroad, or perhaps join a club that has international connections.

The Ocean Cruising Club (www. oceancruisingclub.org) has a mentoring scheme that pairs potential blue-water sailors with experienced club members to advise on all aspects of preparation.

The course of numerous circumnavigators has been changed by the piracy situation in Somalia and the Indian Ocean. A British couple, the Chandler's, were kidnapped in 2009, a grim tale that ended after 388 days of captivity in their release in November 2010. In *Hostage: A Year at Gunpoint with Somali Gangsters*, Paul and Rachel Chandler recount their terrifying ordeal. In February 2011 four Americans on *SV Quest* off India were shot dead in a failed rescue attempt.

Some cruisers remain in the Caribbean and during their first hurricane season head north to the USA, in the following hurricane season travelling further north to Canada. Alternatively, they explore the western Caribbean, for example Colombia and the San Blas Islands (near Panama) or the ABC Islands (Aruba, Bonaire, Curacao: the Lesser Antilles). One long-term sailor recommended, Yansaladup, Eastern Lemmon Cay in the San Blas as one of the most beautiful anchorages in the world.

For those transiting the Panama Canal, some make an extended Pacific Circuit over two or three years. During the cyclone season, they stay in Australia or New Zealand, then return to the Pacific islands. A few remain in the cyclone belt, for example, in Fiji.

After exploring the Pacific islands, there is the choice of sailing home across the Indian Ocean through the Red Sea, and into the Med, or sailing via the Indian Ocean around South Africa and north into the Atlantic. Some ship their boat home from Australia or New Zealand or the Seychelles, which is an expensive option. Later we'll meet the Robinsons who spent seven years on the 'Pacific Eddy', commuting between New Zealand the Pacific islands and Australia, according to season. Another option is exploring the coast of India.

Two young adventurers, in their late twenties, Peter and Katharine Ingram took a year out. They flew to New Zealand, bought and kitted out a 38-foot yacht. They sailed to the Solomon Islands, Papua New Guinea, through the Federated States of Micronesia, the Philippines and Japan, up and round the Aleutian Islands to Vancouver. They then trucked the boat from Vancouver to eastern Canada and sailed her home back to Spain across the Atlantic.

In their early 40s, Al, an ex-skipper who

now runs ClearSphere, a home technology company in London, and his wife Mel, who danced for Ballet Rambert, and Madonna, and is now a choreographer, took the opportunity to take Al's parents boat *Troubadour* on an Atlantic Circuit. They made the decision, and the commitment, and they were off within months. *Troubadour* knew the way. Al's parents had made an eight-year circumnavigation with her. Al and Mel with their daughters, 9 and 6, sailed from the UK to Spain, to the Cape Verdes to Barbados, through the Caribbean. Whilst in this sailing paradise Mel discovered they were pregnant with their third child. Mel and the girls flew home from the British Virgin Islands (BVIs) and Al sailed *Troubadour* single-handed back to Falmouth, via the Azores.

The Gifford family from Washington, USA, spent eight years circumnavigating with their three children. We shall come back to them (along with Irenka and Woody and their three children who are starting their life aboard) in the chapter about children.

Ed and Megan Clay met through sailing and have both sailed since they were children. In their mid-thirties they gave up their jobs as an Operations Director and a corporate lawyer to take a year out. Their search for a yacht ended back at home, buying a half share of *Flycatcher of Yar*, an S&S Contessa 38 that belonged to Ed's parents. This gave the advantage of preparing a boat that they knew well so, while they replaced the mast and other major jobs before departing, they were confident in the boat.

Ed and Megan's voyage took them from Cobnor near Chichester to Falmouth, across Biscay to La Coroña, Spain, to Portugal and the Atlantic islands of Madeira and the Canaries. Untypically they did not head across the Atlantic from here, but, to West Africa where they explored the River Gambia. Then they went south to the Cape Verdes Islands, and across the Atlantic to Barbados from where they enjoyed Caribbean. Amongst their stops were the Grenadines, Grenada, Bequia, St Lucia, Antigua, Montserrat, St Kitts and Nevis, to the BVI's, and north to Puerto Rico and the Bahamas. They then chased the start of the hurricane season up the US Eastern seaboard from Charleston, through the Chesapeake and to New York, Long Island Sound, Boston and Maine. From here they did not take the 'usual' route home but went north to Nova Scotia, Newfoundland and Labrador, before heading to the West Coast of Greenland and up to the Arctic Circle. And then, with time against them, it was home to Falmouth.

The 'circuit' took 400 days of which 32% of the total time was spent sailing. They visited 246 harbours and anchorages and spent 79 nights at sea. On their return Ed returned to working for start-ups and Megan to working as a lawyer for ClientEarth. They would love to go on an extended voyage again, but the fact that they now have a daughter means they may need to go more slowly next time!

To read about their experience and see their beautiful pictures, look up www.flycatcherofyar.wordpress.com.

Suzanne Chappell and her husband David started sailing in their mid-forties, when the children left home. "Launching ourselves into this new way of life, we learned and studied everything we could, taking Competent Crew, Day Skipper, Sea Survival and Ocean Yachtmaster. We decided to change our lifestyle after surviving the Boxing Day Tsunami in Thailand where we were on a sailing yacht anchored in the Bay of Phi Phi. Since then we have sailed 55,000 miles and crossed the Atlantic twice, west to east, and east

THE INGRAM CRUISING DYNASTY

Before their worldwide cruising, Stuart and Annabelle Ingram sailed throughout their lives all over Europe and the Caribbean. They passed their love of sailing onto their sons who we meet in this book with their wives – Peter and Katharine, and Al and Mel. On the next page I describe some wives who sailed the Atlantic: they were led by Annabelle, encouraged by Stuart.

Stuart was a renowned anaesthetist. After taking early retirement, he and Annabelle commissioned eminent naval architect Michael Pocock to design a one-off 44-foot cruising yacht, which incorporated some unusual design features such as a music stand, reflecting their love of music. The yacht, *Troubadour*, was launched in Lymington, Hampshire. Stuart was appointed Rear Commodore of the Royal Cruising Club in the following year.

Their experience and skill ensured an eight-year circumnavigation, full of good times and safe passages, with minimal calamities. They were highly praised worldwide when, after a long and arduous passage to New Zealand, they turned around into a storm to rescue a yacht in distress. In Indonesia, again they stepped up, towing a disabled yacht 350 miles. They cruised throughout the Caribbean, the Pacific, Australia, New Zealand, South Asia. As Annabelle says, lightly, "We have sailed mostly everywhere including north of the Arctic Circle."

Stuart's thorough understanding of his travels, combined with his gift as a raconteur, come through in his knowledgeable and entertaining contributions to the first edition of this book, emailed from idyllic anchorages along their route from Australia to Thailand. Annabelle sent her delicious recipe, too.

On the insistence of their sons, *Troubadour* was shipped back to Turkey from Male by-passing the highly charged, politically-troubled waters of the Indian Ocean and Red Sea. It was here, on the final leg of their circumnavigation, that, on a dark pontoon in bad weather, Stuart, tragically, had an accidental fall. Four days later, he died from the head injuries he suffered.

Annabelle sailed *Troubadour* home to the UK with long time sailing friends. A year later her son and daughter in law, Al and Mel, with their two daughters, set off on *Troubadour*, on an Atlantic Circuit. Peter and Annabelle, brother and mother, worked tirelessly to help them 'sail away'.

At the end of this book, in the 'Thanks to Adventurous Sailors of Many Seas', I write of the 'earls of the ocean and queens of the high seas'. Amongst a few others, I was thinking of the Ingram families when I wrote this.

to west."

For those who really want to complete their circumnavigation, it is still possible to do so by sailing the 'old' way, around South Africa via the Cape of Good Hope. It is widely agreed that going via the Red Sea and the Suez Canal is not an option while the high levels of piracy continue.

Whichever way you go, it is important – and I repeat this for good reason – not to be in too much of a hurry. Weather, boat maintenance, bureaucratic delays, commitments at home, discovering somewhere gorgeous and wanting to stay longer or an unexpected fiesta – all of these can change your itinerary. Don't allow an artificially imposed deadline to deprive you of potential opportunities.

A RELUCTANT PARTNER

Most blue-water boats are crewed by a couple. But what can you do when one partner is set on sailing away and the other does not want to follow? Negotiate? Cooperate? Go it alone? Stay and be resentful?

Both a reluctant spouse and a sailor who will not take 'no' for an answer are challenges to the relationship. For 20 years, one spouse firmly believed that her husband would never get it together to sail away, but then he did. It caused a deep rift which they finally, after much trial and travail, accommodated by spending half their time ashore and half on the boat.

There are ways of making the situation work. Numerous spouses or partners and children fly out to the Caribbean in early December to celebrate and enjoy time on the boat that their partners have sailed across the Atlantic. A compromise would be to buy a boat in the Caribbean and divide your time between your boat and your home. (See Sue Bringloe's account, 'Best of Both Worlds', in the Chapter 9.)

Or you could follow the example of one crew of wives (mentioned earlier) who had sailed for years with their husbands. They then decided to have a sisters-are-doing-it-for-themselves ocean crossing, which proved a huge success.

Problems arise if the reluctant partner wants to meet the boat at regular intervals for a couple of weeks. This can cause stress for both: it puts pressure on the sailor to reach the destination (often risking a rough passage to arrive in time), and on the spouse to put their life on hold and make the journey to the boat. Does the boat remain in one place and the couple take shore excursions? Do they sail for a short time, with the return to the airport continually in their minds?

A dramatic change in one long-term sailing relationship was caused, ironically, when a reluctant spouse was forced by her husband's illness to take charge. The couple soon realised that she was the more competent skipper.

Another skipper bought a heavy-displacement yacht which could sail in local waters and oceans. Over a few years of sailing locally his wife fell in love with the boat, and with sailing away. The years gave her confidence in the boat and, critically, confidence in her sailing abilities.

The promise of beautiful anchorages, amazing places to explore or festivals such as Mardi Gras in Trinidad can tempt a reluctant sailor. As with all partnerships, understanding that 70% give, rather than take, on both sides helps soothe hardened attitudes. One skipper scuppered his chances by choosing a fast but uncomfortable yacht. Perhaps demanding Corian worktops is a fuss too far but including your partner in helping to fit out the boat can ease your reluctant spouse aboard.

Understand that, even if you feel exhilarated as the coast disappears over the horizon, your partner may be sick with fear. It's a natural survival instinct. Take it slowly, 'training' sail by sail, and edge towards the horizon.

Seasickness can be alleviated in numerous ways, and there is more on this in Chapter 5.

If you (or your spouse) needs a little further encouragement, consider the Chinese tale of the frog who lived in a shallow well. He proudly boasted to the sea turtle what a splendid place it was to live. The turtle looked down the well and thought for a while, then told the frog about the Eastern Ocean, which was thousands of miles wide and deep and how, even in times of drought and floods, the ocean remained the same. The turtle returned to the ocean. The frog reviewed his shallow well and was no longer quite so satisfied.

Jeanne Socrates is an inspiration, and a tour de force. I first met Jeanne when she was winning one of her awards from the Ocean Cruising Club. We subsequently met after she had completed another circumnavigation, at another awards ceremony at Southampton Boat Show. Jeanne's a lot of fun but, when it comes to sailing, there is a focus and steely determination which is the reason she has achieved her outstanding accomplishments. So far, she is the oldest (British) woman to sail a non-stop, single-handed unassisted circumnavigation three times.

Jeanne and her husband George learnt to sail, working their way up the RYA ladder. They took early retirement from their teaching jobs, and took delivery of a new Swedish boat a Najad 361. They named her *Nereida* and cruised for five years, with hopes of many more.

Sadly, George was diagnosed with cancer and died. Jeanne, who admits she was always the motivator behind the couples' cruising ambitions, decided to sail alone saying that the support of the cruising community helped immensely as she learnt, port by port, how to sail alone.

Jeanne encourages reluctant partners of keen sailors to 'jump in a dinghy, and learn to sail, and you'll get more into it. You'll know more about sailing and won't get worried in bad conditions. Once you've been up and down the Caribbean and been aboard for a time you'll know how things work. You'll be doing it as a couple.' We'll come across Jeanne later. Look her up on svnereida.com.

BEST BEFORE DATE

Like it or not, life has a best before date. We sailed away on a boat which had to be sold because the owner, despite his wife's best efforts, ignored his body's warning signs. Too late he realised that, while he could remain living ashore for years, he was not up to the physical demands of cruising. This is a book about escaping the rat race so beware: life throws curve balls and putting it off may not pay off.

Hunter S Thompson, who could be described as pushing the envelope on most of life, and who most readers will know from *Fear and Loathing in Las Vegas*, was twenty when he wrote a letter entitled 'Man has to be something; he has to matter':

I'm not trying to send you 'on the road' in search of Valhalla, but merely pointing out that it is not necessary to accept the choices handed down to you by life as you know it. There is more to it than that – no one HAS to do something he doesn't want to do for the rest of his life. But then again if that's what you wind up doing, by all means convince yourself that you HAD to do it. You'll have lots of company.

GETTING UNDER WAY

The following chapters in this book will give you numerous ideas on how to make it from dockside to worldwide under your own sail in do-able steps. 'Saving Up to Sail Away' and 'Choosing & Equipping Your Boat' cover the basics of saving up to make the dream happen, how to choose the right boat and what you need to equip it for your voyage.

Not surprisingly, this leads us into 'Children on Board', in which we encourage you to think about who you want – and don't want – on board, such as children, pets and guests.

The adventure begins in 'Time to Go' and 'Life Aboard'. Having set off and learnt the mechanics, electronics and histrionics of living on your boat, you can move on to 'Deciding Which Way to Go', on the options for major cruising routes. 'Blue-Water Sailing' provides a timetable of routes showing when to cross which ocean, what equipment you will require, and how best to prepare yourself and your boat for an ocean crossing.

Before aiming to sail to the Caribbean you may consider sailing north, perhaps to the Baltic or the Western or Eastern Mediterranean? High and low latitudes are becoming popular exploration grounds. In this edition I have include information on sailing in Greenland and the North West passage.

Having gained your Atlantic stripes, you'll be ready for 'Cruising the Caribbean'. Do you explore the eastern and western Caribbean and go northwards, or do you have a quick tour of the eastern Caribbean and head home back across the northern Atlantic?

For those who decide to stay in the hurricane belt, 'Hurricane Season' is a discussion on hurricanes, the bad and the ugly. The good part is exploring north through the Bahamas chain to the USA, even the Canadian Maritimes. From there it is either 'High and Low Latitudes' or 'The Pacific and Beyond', through the Panama Canal, the Pacific, Australasia, the Far East and the Middle East, and back to Europe. By that time, you will have circumnavigated or completed your voyage and be 'Sailing Back' to life ashore, to readjustment and thinking about starting again.

If you do decideto go on this journey the experience will be life changing. Fellow *Skippers Library* author, Alastair Buchan

(*Short-Handed Sailing*), summed this up when he said:

Memebership of the blue-water cruising tribe is for life and there will be ever present knowledge that all you have to do to reach Narnia is steer for the wardrobe.

Seraphim under sail, Bay of Alcudia, Balearics, steering for the wardrobe

2

SAVING UP TO SAIL AWAY

Once you've made the decision to sail away, you need to work out how you're going to finance your trip.

The experience of sailing has been likened to standing under a shower tearing up £10 notes.

Sailing can certainly be expensive, but there's a solution for nearly every budget and a great deal can be achieved with leg work and ingenuity.

In Alan Sefton's book *Sir Peter Blake: An Amazing Life*, Peter Mazany talks about building up Blake's Team New Zealand, which won the America's Cup in 1995. He said that the cost / benefit trade-off meant that money was put only into areas that really mattered. Where there was an alternative method that would give 95% of the benefit at 10% of the cost, it was always taken. This also resulted in greater overall focus, since scarce resources tend to make one focus only on the most important issues.

What are your most important issues?

SALE AWAY

Chapter 3 explains how to choose the right boat, but first you need to know how much money you're likely to be able to raise. In addition to the basic cost of your boat, you must pay for her upkeep. Most yacht owners estimate on spending 10% of the value of the boat each year: for example, if your boat costs £100,000 then you will probably spend £10,000 per year on berthing and equipment. For those who race, the costs can be significantly higher.

There are almost certainly tax implications involved in receiving or spending large lump sums, so ensure that you fully comprehend the tax regulations or consider consulting an accountant before buying your boat.

The best-case scenario is that you have, or inherit, a fortune or receive a massive bonus. For the rest of us it's hard graft, but you do have options depending on the assets you already own.

SELLING UP

Selling your home to finance your boat is an option, but it's a serious decision and should be made over time. A jolly lunch in

POSTCARDS FROM THE KEDGE

Graham and Tanya Leech both grew up dinghy sailing. They've cruised the Mediterranean, Caribbean and Pacific in their Westerly Corsair, which was sadly lost in a fire in New Zealand. An RYA Yachtmaster Ocean, Tanya was awarded the OCC Water Music Trophy and, when not sailing, runs her own interior design business, Curtains by Design, in Cornwall, UK.

Dear Nicola

Our top five anchorages:

- Baie de Vierges on the island of Fatu Hiva – the tall, sheer cliffs of dense greenery encircling this safe anchorage would, on their own, rank this anchorage highly. But the fact that one arrives after a typical passage of three weeks from the Galapagos adds to the drama.
- Minerva Reef (lies between Tonga and New Zealand) – a complete contrast with Fatu Hiva, as there is absolutely no land to be seen at all, just a submerged reef – a surreal experience of mid-ocean anchoring!
- Pedi, on the NE corner of the island of Symi in the Dodecanese in Greece – I fell in love with cruising and Graham and I fell in love with each other while cruising Symi 17 years ago.
- Little Harbour on Peter Island in the BVI – a Caribbean anchorage that is reminiscent of Mediterranean anchoring – drop a bow anchor and tie to the rocky shore. A quiet little place with nothing ashore.
- Scotland Bay in Trinidad – wonderfully protected and surrounded by thickly wooded slopes that echo to the sound of howler monkeys, this anchorage provides such a welcome respite from Chaguaramas.

Nicola Rodriguez
The Yacht Moonshine
Cameret
North West France

Best wishes
Graham & Tanya

the bar at a boat show may sow the seeds of the idea, but weeks and months are then required for you to think it over – and over. If you do have to sell your property to buy your boat, be sure that you really are committed to the sailing life, and that in six months' time you're not going to regret your decision and long for your land-based home.

Yacht brokers have a tendency to mentally dismiss buyers who say they have to sell their house before buying their boat. There are too many variables in house sales and it's too close to wishful thinking for a yacht broker to take you seriously. Once you've sold the house, put the money in the bank, and then buy the boat.

An alternative or halfway measure is to sell your house, buy your boat and purchase a small flat as well. In the final year while you continue to work and refit the boat, you can live in the flat. This has sharpened the appetite of many cruisers. When you leave, the flat can be rented out to cover the mortgage or provide income for your trip. If you prefer to keep it as your own space, it can be used to store your belongings and as a sanctuary during visits.

USING YOUR EQUITY

When house prices are high, you may be willing to take the risk of borrowing against the equity in your house and using it to buy a boat. Remember, this is a hazardous option. You're taking out a loan, so you have repayments to meet; interest rates may go up, meaning that you might not be able to pay for both your boat and your home. House prices may also fall, in the worst-case scenario leaving you with negative equity, where you owe more than your home is worth.

RENTING OUT YOUR HOME

If you already own your sail-away boat, if you can afford to buy the boat without selling your home or if selling up is too big a step, especially if the house sales market is flat, then renting your property out is a good option. However, it is essential to find both a good tenant and a good friend to watch over your property. Bad tenants can become a blight on your cruise, since what is a minor problem at home can become a major one at a long distance. Who wants to have scraps about rent payments when they could be snorkelling in clear water? Management companies don't come cheap but using a recommended one could be a wise investment.

REMEMBERING STORAGE

If you are selling or renting out your home, think about the possessions you still want to keep. Storage can be expensive. Sell or give away as much as you can and consider asking friends and relations to find room for the furniture and treasures you cannot let go. But do remember who has what and where it is.

If you are storing belongings in a room or storage unit, make a detailed list of the contents of each box, stick one copy on the box and keep another copy in a master file. As you are filling the room, draw a map of where each box is located. The least important stuff goes in the first box in, therefore at the back of the room. The box you will need the most goes in last, and thus is the most accessible. For example,

if the first things you think you will need when you get back are warm clothes, a radio and your bank statements, put those in the last box.

Try to have contingency storage in case friends want to return your chattels while you are away. Also, although they are just boxes to your friends, they are part of your life. It is worth pointing out (with a bottle of their favourite) that the way the boxes have been left is how you expect to find them. This should be obvious but, take it from bitter experience, it is not.

Norma and Trevor have sailed extensively around the Caribbean and the eastern USA. They said that after nine years: "One of our neighbours asked if we wanted the stuff that was in his basement – we had actually forgotten that we had anything there. We almost told him to give the lot to charity, but we went to have a look and one thing turned out to be a beautiful chest that we both thought was in our own attic. We thankfully moved it to our store."

SELLING YOUR COMPANY

If you own a business or shares in one, you may be able to raise enough money for your boat by selling all or part of your investment to someone else. One cruiser signed away the final rights to his company, walked along the pontoon, stepped aboard his boat and literally sailed into the sunset. Another entrepreneur sold greater percentages of his company the longer and further he was away.

Some executives with shares in a company are still negotiating final terms in the first few months of their cruise. Some feel that at least they have made the break from the business and that the separation gives them better insight, and a stronger negotiating position. Others

Travelling light in North Bimini, Bahamas

regret not completing the arrangement while in situ because, once they left the office, their colleagues used their absence to manipulate their hard-won agreements.

TAKING OUT A MARINE MORTGAGE

When taking out a marine mortgage, the boat acts as security for the loan. The mortgage is on the boat, not on your home, and needs to be registered in accordance with the Merchant Shipping Act 1993. The loan can be for up to 80% or even 90% of the value of the boat. If you default on the mortgage you lose the boat.

If you intend registering a marine mortgage against the boat in the UK, generally, the boat will need to be on Part 1 of the UK Ship Register. For more

information on this, see the Registering section on www.gov.uk/owning-yacht-sail-boat-motorboat.

In order to secure the mortgage, the boat must be surveyed out of the water to ascertain the state of the hull. The survey also covers the superstructure, equipment and interior. (There is more on surveys in Chapter 3.) The boat will then be valued and insured. Your insurers must be kept informed concerning the mortgage held on the boat.

As with any mortgage or loan, it is wise to be truthful with yourself about how realistic the payment schedule is in relation to your income, particularly after you set sail. How much do you want a more expensive new boat, versus being able to sail away in a refitted older one rather sooner? If you take on a marine mortgage, how many years will your departure be delayed because you are paying off the boat? If interest rates go up, can you afford your home mortgage, your boat mortgage and your other commitments? Do you want the responsibility of more debt if you are aiming to be debt-free when you sail away?

RELYING ON CREDIT CARDS

As with a mortgage, how much can you afford to put on a credit card and how soon can you pay it off? Remember that interest rates on credit cards are normally very high, so this is not a long-term solution. While cruisers find that credit cards are helpful to pay for big-ticket or unexpected items such as a piece of equipment or an air fare while they're away, the money to pay it off should be taken out of the cruising fund immediately or as soon as possible thereafter.

SHARING

Sharing a boat is also an option for enabling the acquisition. This is okay for holidays but becomes unrealistic when you are leaving for a considerable length of time.

Let's also remember that you're sharing with your partner or spouse, and the ugly reality is that not all couples who start out on the dream together make it to the end – or even the true beginning. One couple we know separated after five years of planning, one year away from the dream becoming reality. The wife kept the house and the husband retained the boat. In most similar situations it is usually the boat, and all that goes with it, that is sold.

SELLING YOUR CAR

The last possession to be sold should add vital top-up money to the kitty. If you're not selling your car, be sure that whoever is looking after it does drive it regularly and treats it with the same care and attention you do yourself. Will the car be easily accessible when you return home? How much will it cost to travel to your car? How much will it cost to keep it on the road? Perhaps it would be best to rent a car or borrow one when you come home for visits.

MAKING BOATING PAY BEFORE YOU GO

There are various boat-related ways of earning money to pay for your boat or fill your sailing kitty before you go.

TAKING A SABBATICAL

A popular way to take time out without burning your work-related boats is to take a sabbatical. Your company may prefer to lose you for a year of sailing than to lose you for good to a competitor.

Remember, though, the main problem with a sabbatical is that after months or a year of cruising, knuckling down to your job again can be a challenge.

Bob Parr, a long-term cruiser, takes two or three months away from sailing to work and earn some money. For example, he may fly from the Caribbean to the Far East, to work on a TV series and then return to his wife Nicky, who has stayed with the boat. They can continue cruising with funds replenished.

CHARTERING

Once you've bought a boat, you may help pay off any loan or top up your cruising budget by chartering out your floating home. Again, this sounds a good idea, but is rarely a good reality.

If you feel you do want to entertain and take care of paying guests, then, for a start, make sure that the boat is 'coded'. Is it properly equipped, certified and does it meet the standards of compliance set by the relevant authority, such as the Maritime and Coastguard Agency, www.gov.uk/government/organisations/maritime-and-coastguard-agency? Does it meet the requirements of the Code of Practice for the safety of small commercial vessels (under 24 metres)? To find out more, go to the www.rya.org.uk website, search for the 'Five minute briefing – MCA Coding'.

A few questions to consider before you decide to charter out your boat:

- How official is your set-up? Do you fully understand all the tax, legal and liability implications?
- Are you sufficiently insured?
- Are your guests paying friends, acquaintances, or even strangers who are paying? How much do you charge each category?
- Are you breaking any local laws and regulations?
- What will happen if you step on established local charter companies' territory?
- Are you ready to smile as your guests trample sand into your newly cleaned boat, and then clean up after them all over again?
- Do you know where to buy provisions if the usual supermarket has run out? How do you stop the lettuce from wilting when you can't get to the shops?
- Are you happy to cook the food that they, not you, want to eat?
- Are you prepared to miss some islands because you have to stay on board and work, or stand watch?

POSTCARDS FROM THE KEDGE

Jonny and Kate Harrison are now living in Australia. Jonny works for an international accountancy firm and Kate is a maths teacher. They took time out to sail from Newcastle upon Tyne to Australia on *Newtsville*, a Colvic Countess 37.

Dear Nicola

Our top five anchorages:

- Manihi, Tuamotu, French Polynesia – our favourite because it was quiet, with stunning scenery, amazing snorkelling, friendly locals, and great French bread delivered fresh to your boat!
- Petite St Vincent, Caribbean
- La Pedro Gonzalez, Las Perlas Islands, Panama
- Graciosa, Canary Islands
- Bandeup, Holandes Cays, San Blas Islands, Panama

Best wishes
Jonny & Kate

Nicola Rodriguez
The Yacht Moonshine
La Coruña
C/O Real Club Nautico
North Spain

RACING CHARTERS

diYachting: from a Sigma 33 to a Bordeaux 60 to organising the chartering of over 15 crewed boats between 60 and 85 feet now

diYachting (diyachting.co.uk) was originally set up by Matt and Lizzie Abbiss as a charter yacht catering for cruising but also set up for clients who wanted to race. They launched with a Sigma 33, racing in the Solent and then to the Caribbean. Then came the Beneteau First 47.7 which went to the Caribbean every winter. Sailors racing *Disco Inferno* mounted the winning podiums in the Grenada Sailing Festival, Heineken Regatta (St Martin), USVI Rolex Regatta, BVI Sailing Festival, Antigua Race Week and Galway.

Lizzie says, "From racing our way around the UK, Europe & the Caribbean we slowed down and managed a Bordeaux 60-foot yacht built by CNB with 1 or 2 regattas a year and focussed on luxury crewed yacht charter. We did this for 6 years but, as we got older, we realised

we were ready to move back home. We chose Southend as that's where I grew up and is by the sea, although leaving life on the sea we still have to see it every day! We set up diYachting to help owners with 60-foot yachts that didn't really need a full-time crew but did need help with the maintenance and servicing of them.

We did a bit of charter as well. 4 years on, we manage 15 yachts, 60-85 foot some with full services: financial, crew & technical services, and some just for charter. We are a team of 8 and will be expanding again this autumn when we move into our larger office. Do we still race? Of course! We went to the CNB rendezvous last weekend and won the under 70ft on the brand new CNB66 and we have our Sandhopper at home and do club racing when we have time…"

WALKING THE DOCK

You may decide to 'walk the dock' in search of temporary work as crew. If you want to earn money, see exotic places and fill your own cruising kitty, crewing on large vessels is one way to go. It is hard work with long hours and you'll be living in close quarters in shared accommodation. Although you might be living on a luxury yacht, you will not be in luxury; you're more likely to be polishing hand rails in the hot sun or loading bags on epic supermarket shops. After the guests have had fun on jet skis, you'll be the one hoisting them in and maintaining them.

Still keen? *Dockwalk*, a monthly magazine for superyacht crews and skippers, has advertisements for crew agencies in the back. Keep an eye out for vacancies in the back pages of the yachting press as well. The PYA, Professional Yachting Association (www.pya.org) 'exists primarily to represent the interests of professional yacht crew'. A useful place to seek advice. Similarly, the worldwide organisation, International Yacht Training (www.iytworld.com).

I have not included a list of agencies as they can vary widely, and their personnel can change with the seasons. Agencies can be useful. However, 'word of mouth' is equally important. I have spoken with numerous crews, all starting out with sailing qualifications, who say that they found their first jobs by taking on a day here, a day there, on superyachts and working up their contacts until they had a week, a month and upwards of work. This chimes with the words of friends who have worked their way up over the years to being superyacht skippers and engineers.

If you are an experienced skipper and can live abroad for months at a time, you could apply for a job running flotilla holidays such as those run by Neilson, Seafarer and Sunsail. The requirements for a skipper are at least Yachtmaster with a year or more experience. For those with less experience, for example as a hostess on a yacht, you would need to be qualified to Competent Crew level.

Twenty years from now you will be more disappointed by the things that you didn't do than by the ones you did do. So, throw off the bow lines. Sail away from the safe harbour. Catch the trade winds in your sails. Explore. Dream. Discover.

Mark Twain

TWO TO CREW

Experienced sailors Mark and Charlie Durham, a couple in their 30s with sailing experience and qualifications, crossed the Atlantic on a Contessa 32, in the Blue Water Rally, in the hope of finding work with Moorings, a charter company in Antigua. On their arrival they were offered plum crewing positions on an Oyster 66, *Miss Molly*, owned by David and Linda Hughes. After eight years as a skipper and hostess, they came ashore to work successfully in the sailing industry in Palma de Mallorca. They are now settled on the island with two children.

Mark and Charlie Durham crewing on Miss Molly off Moorea, Society Islands, French Polynesia

STAYING CASH NEUTRAL

During the two years before her retirement from the RAF, Cally Logston considered her options. With years of catering experience in the RAF and 10,000 miles clocked up 'sailing around the cans' in races, she decided to combine her love of sailing with adventure and work her way around the world. She headed to UKSA (www.uksa.org) to gain, among other qualifications, her Yachtmaster and Power Boat 2 qualifications. The MCA AEC (Approved Engine Course) was also useful.

Cally described her three-and-a-half years sailing around the world, working on ten different international yachts via the Caribbean, Tahiti and New Zealand as 'cash neutral', because she only spent what she earned. And she didn't stop there – she arrived home on a Thursday and by the following Monday was working for an international rally company.

SAIL FOR A LIVING

If you have useful qualifications, opportunities can arise as you are cruising. For example, Hazel Teale, an experienced British nurse found work in a hospital in Gibraltar while wintering there. Marine engineers, riggers, shipwrights, varnishers, hairdressers and cooks can all find work – but remember: don't step on local toes, or to use a yachting expression, 'leave a clean wake'. As Sue Bringloe sails through the Caribbean chain she does 'pop up' yoga classes on the beach, for cruisers and locals: win win. (See Chapter 9, 'Cruising the Caribbean'.) Cruisers' nets on the VHF radio from George Town, Exuma in the Bahamas south through the Caribbean chain are used as platforms to advertise the skills of cruisers. Sue Pelling's book, *Sail for a Living*, also gives information concerning working and sailing.

KEEPING THE DREAM ALIVE

As with all commitments, it is easy to become disheartened about your ability to reach your goal unless you keep focused. Try putting pictures of your dream on the fridge or laptop or the back of the office door. Set yourself a deadline – an immovable, non-negotiable deadline that you can't squirm out of – to help tighten the budget and rein in your expenditure.

Set a timeline of, say, five years before you depart and gradually squeeze your savings harder and tighter the closer you come to the date. Two years away, perhaps think again about an extra pair of shoes, eating out so often or having takeaways. Make small economies such as buying own label items or large sacrifices such as giving up a second holiday to work on the boat. Buy judiciously at online auctions or boat jumble sales. Invest any bonuses or dividends from investments in the cruising fund. You could also think about obtaining extra income from your home, such as renting out a room or garage, offering bed-and-breakfast facilities or selling at car boot sales or on eBay, Gumtree, or such sites.

In the last year, with the deadline approaching, if time and energy around boat refitting allow, explore the possibility of taking on a part-time job, preferably in a chandlery or marina. An American cruiser was glad to give up her job as an accountant and worked in a chandlery for the final year. Babysitting is less strenuous than boat cleaning, but either way, every little helps.

Although moorings are cheaper, in the year to six months when you are having the boat refitted, it is much more efficient to be in a marina.

You can draw up a chart showing precise details and prices of what needs to be bought for the boat. Gradually, as you acquire the chart plotter, the boat's kettle, and so on through the long list, item by item, the dream gradually becomes a reality.

The more time you spend living aboard, the more you will appreciate what cruising is truly about. The bills for landlubber items and the standing orders for life ashore will diminish. Christmas and birthday gifts can be boat orientated, although I don't recommend the anchor chain that one Swiss skipper gave his wife. Our wedding list helped to equip our sail-away boat.

At this point it's a good exercise in maintaining hope over stress to imagine what you'll be doing six months ahead, or where to go for hurricane season.

If you have seen the film *Finding Nemo*, you will have come across Nemo's friend, Dory who insists that when life is tough, 'Just Keep Swimming'. All the people featured in this book have encountered problems and overcome them.

Jacqui and Freddie Rose, on *Shavora*, a Moody 39, persevered through several trials before they set sail. Their first attempt

ANTIPODEAN ADVENTURES

There are many examples of people who have taken a job in Australia benefiting from the opportunity to sail instead of fly across, pursuing their dream on the way:

Jonny, an accountant, was offered an opening in his company's Australian office. He and his wife Kate, a maths teacher, took a year off and sailed from Newcastle in the north of England to Sydney, Australia on *Newtsville*, their Colvic Countess 37.

A communications executive and her family sailed to Australia to take up a new post there. En route the children were home schooled. At the beginning of September, their first day of home school was a field trip to Santiago de Compostella, a mediaeval city and site of pilgrimage in northern Spain.

With their three children under 7, teachers Gerald and Monica sailed *Clarabella*, a Nicholson 35, from Bristol, England to New Zealand. Once they'd arrived Gerald secured a teaching post in Christchurch, at a school that was remarkably similar to the one he had taught at in Bristol.

Nick from New Zealand and Blue from Australia just missed buying the boat of their dreams. However, they suggested to the person who did buy the boat that he use their house in Australia while they took a year to sail the boat from England to Australia.

John Rodriguez (right) with Jonny and Kate Harrison in Marin, Martinique en route from Newcastle, UK to Australia – Jonny and Kate were one of John's first blue-water brokerage clients

to sail away failed. A year later they set off again. On arrival in the Caribbean they found water under the floor boards, four times. They kept going. Jacqui found work evolved as they became part of a community in Carriacou, in the Grenadines, north of Grenada. Jacqui has turned her sewing on her domestic sewing machine on board into an income – dinghy covers, fixed sails. She and Freddie work in a sail loft and have saved enough for a Mikado 56, a ketch which they are rebuilding. This led to work renovating two more Mikados plus finding crew. From this Jacqui set up a Foundation 'to help people help themselves in raising funds to pay for medical procedures', and Freddie spends nearly all of his time, rebuilding boats.

CALCULATING YOUR KITTY

As well as knowing how money much you need to buy your boat, you need to have a figure in mind that you have to amass as a kitty for living and maintenance expenses while you're away. Cruising full time is hard on a boat, and its crew. Being flexible and expecting the unexpected, as well as being financially prepared, is all part of cruising.

CUTTING YOUR SAIL TO FIT YOUR DREAM

Where you are going to cruise and when will affect the amount of money you require. For instance, Turkey is much

The author working on an article on Moonshine, a 35-foot Westerly Corsair, off Honeymoon Beach, George Town, Exuma, Bahamas

cheaper than France. The Spanish Virgin Islands are much cheaper than the British or US Virgin Islands. While French Polynesia is expensive, experienced sailors say that, if you shop smart and provision well, it is charmed sailing.

Planning your route around your budget makes the voyage go further without imposing too many limitations. For example:

- Do you intend to anchor everywhere or stay in marinas? (In Europe it is not safe to live aboard in winter at anchor.)
- Will you winter in a marina in Europe, which will cost approximately £5,000, or anchor around the Caribbean?
- Is it better value to keep the boat in a hurricane cradle in St Lucia in the West Indies, or ship it from the US Virgins to Genoa, Italy to a marina for the summer?
- At the end of your Caribbean season will you sail home to the UK or lay out the £10,000 required to ship her home?
- If you are going to sell your boat at the end of your voyage, do you intend breaking even? Are you prepared to take a loss?

BEING INVENTIVE & KEEPING A SPARE

With knowledge and experience some corners can be cut to save costs, but not at the risk of safety. Safety equipment is expensive and may well not be used, but you still need it on board. So, when budgeting, allow a large margin for extras relating to safety equipment and rudimentary medical training.

Creativity and ingenuity are a bonus, but don't be too clever. On one rally, rumour had it that the windows on a certain home-built boat came from police riot shields, and the lead in the keel from the local church.

Cost cutting can come back to bite you. Re-cutting ageing sails can push the budget a little further but will affect your sailing. Distances will take longer and, in the tropics, the sails will be subjected to intense UV rays. How soon will they begin to disintegrate and when might they tear? If your rigging is over ten years old, you must consider having it replaced. Don't forget that rigging disintegrates from the

---

BOUNTY-FULL

At the start of our adventure we had a little wedding present money which we used on bounty. A set of cups (buckets) we bought in Portugal travelled over 25,000 miles with us. Mine is in several photos in various anchorages (e.g. on p31).

It is worth saving for the gifts which at the time seem too expensive but carry so many memories. The wooden fish bought in Antigua for John's birthday, the picture and drum bought for my birthday in St Lucia, the posters bought in Norfolk of the mermaids, the Cats in the Catskills and Lighthouses of the US East Coast.

When you return home, print your favourite pictures of the boat at anchor onto large canvases. I can lie in the bath dreaming of our weeks anchored in English Dockyard, Antigua or our Easter on Plana Cay.

One of the precious gifts was made by a friend we were sailing with across the Gulf Stream from Marathon Cay to Nassau, Bahamas. We rafted up to them overnight. On Christmas morning at 5am we exchanged gifts. Our friend Phyllis made us oven mitts with our boat name *Moonshine* on them.

The lighter items can be posted home to stop the boat becoming… bounty-full.

inside out, so by the time you see rust, you're in big trouble.

When cutting your equipment list to suit your budget, remember that life on shore is different to life on a boat. Although spares seem expensive and space consuming, they are always useful. Invariably it is cheaper and easier to have a spare on board. It will cost you time and money waiting for your particular boat part to be shipped in. You may be in a beautiful ria in Galicia, northern Spain and a local holiday causes more delay, but you have a great experience with the locals at the fiesta – or you might be in an oily harbour being rolled in the wake of hostile fishermen. Try to avoid becoming one of the dozens of frustrated skippers on hot buses searching for chandleries, knowing they've just missed a weather window and then squealing at the price of a spare part.

And do remember that, as with everyone, when sailors mature in years, their strength and stamina decrease. If you are older, this should be reflected in the equipment on your boat such as electric winches, which do not come cheap. Think realistically about what you need to make your life comfortable aboard, because little compromises to save a few pounds during the fit-out can become big problems once you are living full time on the boat.

THE FIRST YEAR IS THE CHEAPEST

The first year after sailing away tends to be the cheapest. Most of the equipment is new or at the top of its productive life.

The worst can happen, though. One new boat had to have a new engine in Gibraltar, and a new generator in Antigua. The yacht had been built around the engine, so the engineers had to cut through the cockpit to do their work – you can imagine the expense.

From alternator to radar to winches, you will spend more money each year you are out. If the sails do not need attention after an ocean crossing, after a year or two in the tropics the UV strip will need replacing. The sun protection from your bimini may not be sufficient, and you may have to have a new one made. The fridge that was efficient when the boat was surrounded by temperate waters may not cope with hot, tropical waters. You may accidentally slice the dinghy open on sharp oyster shells growing on the docks in Beaufort, North Carolina. Or during the night the rope attached to the second anchor may chafe badly so that you cannot raise it in worsening conditions and have to cut it loose. (The ending to that story was a happy one: Spanish yachtsmen saw the incident off Bini Becca, dived on the anchor and followed us to Mahon, where they returned it.)

As time goes by, perhaps you decide to head for the Pacific where anchorages are deep, and you need to buy more anchor chain: a great deal more. You won't be shopping in your local chandlery or using West Marine vouchers, so be prepared to pay the full, sometimes very high, price. It's the same when it is time to haul out and anti-foul: you will have to look around. Most cruisers wear their clothes to the last threads, but after a while you may need to replenish deck shoes or replace worn foulies. After about two years you may want or be forced to take a visit home – what will that cost?

Just bear in mind that once you have left, the bills keep coming and growing. This is a reality check, not a reason to pocket your dreams.

To give some perspective, Ed and Megan Clay set off in what some cruisers would consider a very basic boat. However, they completed an extended Atlantic Circuit which included exploring the Gambia River and Greenland and found themselves remarkably comfortable. Ed writes:

Flycatcher started life as a race boat and is pretty simple, particularly down below with a Taylors paraffin hob / oven for cooking, a paraffin heater we used in the Arctic and a Blake's head. She has no refrigeration, freezer or watermaker and the shower is a bucket. She carries 150 litres of fresh water and 50 litres of diesel. With a Monitor wind vane her power demands at both sea and anchor are low, meaning we used a small solar panel and a tow generator on passage when the sun didn't shine.

Some would think her too spartan for long-distance cruising, while others might think her Dyneema halyards and radar unnecessary. We found her well suited to our style of cruising as she sails beautifully and can take much worse weather than we can. The main advantages of relative simplicity were more time to explore and things being simpler to solve when they did break.

KEEPING IT SIMPLE

The KISS rule, Keep It Simple Stupid, applies to financial arrangements while you're away. It is not always easy to sort out your investments when aboard, or over the internet, whatever the claims that are made when you are setting up internet banking and investing. It is best to presume that you will have to write letters and post (or courier) them in order to change arrangements, or, as often happens, clarify arrangements that were already agreed. Every cruiser can tell you the problems of finding someone who understands the situation over the phone, let alone someone who can act on your instructions without written confirmation. Banks and variations on the theme of incompetence have long been sources of frustration in calm, sublime anchorages.

Incidentally, if you do use a credit card while you're away, be alert for credit card fraud. Some sailors have had problems, and the subsequent discussions with your bank can be long and tedious.

CHECKING UP BEFORE CHECKING OUT

Finally, you don't just need a boat that is ready – you should be as fit as possible yourselves. Accidents may occur en route, and dental work or old injuries can be exacerbated by boat life and may require medical attention. At the same time as you are prepping the boat, review your health with a view to long-term sailing.

Health insurance for cruisers is a complex area. It is possible, but not easy, to obtain and is often expensive.

If you are a citizen of the European Union, you can carry a European Health Insurance Card or EHIC. At the time of writing, the websites www.ehic.org.uk and www.nhs.uk/ provide information, how to apply and instructions for use of the card. After Brexit, you may need to consult other websites.

It is still strongly advisable to have medical insurance. The card gives access to state-provided medical treatment only, and the service of the country in which you are ill may be better or worse than in your home country.

Another website for British travellers giving information concerning medical facilities is www.nhs.uk/nhsengland/healthcareabroad.

Bear in mind that, if you sail away, you

CLEAN WAKE

The literal meaning of this phrase is becoming essential. In your research for boat equipment, try to give time to finding a way to contribute to clearing up the oceans, for example www.sailinggiventime.com organised by yachtswoman Sarah Connor. Her mission statement is:

We are the lead vessel in a collaborative marine ecology research project, which will see the cruising community work hand in hand with the global scientific community. We are creating a global network of resources for marine expedition research – a first of its kind mission of 'Exploration through collaboration' – not crowd science but 'fleet science'!

Dee Caffari (MBE) was the first woman to sail solo, non-stop around the world against the prevailing winds and currents. Caffari skippered a boat in the Volvo Ocean Race called *Turn the Tide on Plastic*. Caffari says: "I have seen first-hand the sad reality of our ocean's health. Now, having been part of a team collecting micro-plastic data for the first time around the world, we know the issue is much worse than we all initially thought." (www.deecaffari.com)

Other sites at the time of writing include:
- Ocean Futures Society founded by Jacques Cousteau (www.oceanfutures.org)
- The Ocean Research Project (ORP) based in Annapolis (www.deepseanews.com)
- theoceancleanup.com
- 4Ocean.com which sells bracelets from recycled materials to fund beach clear up
- www.reefcheck.org
- www.theyachtmarket.com/oceansaviour

must be able, whether by credit card or cash, to leave your boat in a marina and fly your whole family home from wherever you are; be prepared to pay for a transatlantic Medivac as well. In an emergency you must be able to fly the patient to a good hospital, not leave them to fester in an island clinic where the treatment and hygiene may be so poor that their smashed-up leg, or even their life, is in danger.

If you are sailing offshore, check how far you are allowed to go by your insurance policy. If you break a leg, say, how far offshore are you covered? If you need a helicopter, will the insurance company pay? What is the definition of pre-existing medical condition and does this cause you any problems?

Certain health insurance policies require an annual visit home, which may or may not work for you. At the time of taking out the policy this may seem like a good idea however, as the year progresses, and a trip home becomes a major inconvenience, you may regret it. The number of days you are allowed to visit the UK may not be sufficient, or a limit on your time at home may not be practical if an elderly relation becomes sick.

Don't forget to check the terms of your life insurance as well. Does your insurer agree to cover you while following 'dangerous sports' such as sailing an ocean?

Sailing into the Caribbean sunset

SAFE IN SPAIN

Our son James, who was 18 months, and had a febrile convulsion in Mallorca. Thankfully, we received excellent treatment. The medical care and an overnight stay were paid for by the insurance, although the company did insist that we carry an EHIC. We were assured by the medics that they saw febrile convulsions twice a week and James would be fine in a few hours. Our Spanish was not up to the job, but several of the doctors in the hospital spoke fluent or good English. In a few hours James was fine.

If you are sailing with children, be certain that one of the parents is insured to stay or travel with a sick child. When James was ill, good and supportive friends came to our aid and helped a shaken John sail the boat back to Palma while James and I gathered ourselves together.

3

CHOOSING & EQUIPPING YOUR BOAT

I want a boat that drinks 6, eats 4, and sleeps 2.

Ernest K Gann

Bernard Moitessier, the accomplished French circumnavigator, writer and free spirit of the seas, recommends being careful in your choices and not falling in love with a boat. He says: 'It blinds you at first, only to leave you unhappy and at a loss aboard a boat that doesn't in the least match your real hopes.' This sentiment has been echoed by many yachtsmen. You may be in love with a Hallberg Rassy 43, but you may have to work your way up, learning as you buy, sail, sell, buy, sail, sell – until you come to the boat that best suits your needs.

What are your needs? Let's say the boat should sleep at least four. Where are you going? Let's say at least across the Atlantic. Then discussions can begin concerning whether a good second-hand, heavy-displacement boat is better than a new, modern production boat. (Or in a phrase coined by writer Dick Durham, 'an average white boat'.) For now, we will say

you want a boat made from GRP (glass-reinforced plastic, or fibreglass), or steel, or aluminium, not wood or ferro-cement. (Ferro-cement is cheap, but you must know what to look for.)

WHAT ARE YOUR OTHER CRITERIA – QUALITY, SPEED, LEVEL OF COMFORT?

Do you want a centre cockpit? (If you're not sure what that means, you must do some chartering to discover.) How many cabins – two doubles or a double and two singles? A pilot berth and two doubles? How many heads (lavatories)? Most boats under 40 feet only have one. In-mast furling? Slab reefing? If you're not hugely experienced, do you really want to cling to the mast fighting sails and battens screaming directions to your spouse / crew who is white-knuckled at the helm in a force 7? What about power winches?

Do you buy an older, more traditional production boat that is stronger and heavier with superior fixtures? Choices could include Amel, Bowman, Bristol, Colvic

Countest, Contessa, Contest, Formosa, Halberg Rassy, Hylas, Island Packet, Moody, Mystic, Nauticat, Nicholson, Nord West, Oyster, Rival, Rustler, Southerly, Swan, Tartan, Tayana, Voyager, Warrior, Wauquiez, Westerly.

Or do you buy a modern, high volume production boat but upgrade some of the standard equipment. Here you might decide from Bavaria, Beneteau, Catalina, Dehler, Dufour, Elan, Gibsea, Hanse, Jeanneau. All these are monohulls and are the most common type of cruising boat.

These lists are far from exhaustive but will give the novice sailor an idea of what boat to look for. For more detailed information on selecting the right boat, read *The Insider's Guide to Choosing and Buying a Yacht* by Duncan Kent.

A discerning owner gave a brief for the perfect blue-water cruiser to the renowned naval architect and designer Michael Pocock: 'capable of sailing to windward properly while making long-distance passages and being self-sufficient while cruising in remote areas.'

A POSSIBLE WISH LIST

This is a list from a potential cruiser with many sailing miles under her keel. It won't be perfect for everyone, but it is a sensible example of where to start and the factors that should be considered.

Budget
Cash buyers – £80,000 – ready to sail. Therefore, a boat that requires TLC (tender loving care) / new rigging / sails etc. or does not include blue-water kit (SSB / wind generator / solar power, watermaker, wind vane steering, holding tank, autopilot, inverter, smart charging, LED lighting, bimini, etc.) would need to be appropriately priced.

Want
- 36-40' yacht (ideally less than 12m)
- Wheel steering, but still with excellent feel of helm (i.e. no hydraulic steering)
- Decent-sized steering wheel
- 35% ballast-to-displacement ratio
- 20 Ted Brewer comfort motion
- 6'2" head room in saloon and galley
- Two sleeping cabins
- Good access from cockpit to side decks
- Good sea-keeping qualities, but still an excellent sail

- Well-respected manufacturer for durability and strength
- Slab reefing
- Inline spreaders
- Good water and fuel storage
- VAT paid
- Shaft drive

Ideal
- Encapsulated keel
- Skeg-hung rudder
- No teak decks
- Water / keel-cooled fridge
- Cutter
- Aft cockpit (but some centre cockpits will be considered, good looks and stability being the core reasons for preferring the aft cockpit)

Do not want
- Wheelhouse
- Bilge keel
- Multihull
- In-mast or in-boom furling
- Sail drive

Prefer not to have
- A traveller that crosses access from the companionway
- Swept-back spreaders

NEW OR OLD?

Let's remember that this isn't a trailer-sailor we're discussing: you're aiming to cross oceans. The choice lies between buying a new ocean-going boat that is fully equipped or purchasing a cheaper, second-hand boat that you spend months or years fitting out. Somewhere in the middle of these scenarios will work for most people. You must also seriously consider whether you perceive the boat as a lifestyle choice or you hope for a return on your investment.

There is, of course, a balance to be struck, with pitfalls on both sides. Don't underestimate the costs of buying all the kit that comes with a used boat, nor the likely expense of having to re-wire, re-rig or re-engine it.

In conversations around the anchorages you'll discover that most people have been working up to their present boat for years. They start with a second-hand, 20-foot weekend boat, then save up and move up to a 32-foot family boat, then a 40-footer and so on. Each boat grows with your experience. Determined cruisers have gone around the world in 25-foot boats – slowly and not very comfortably, but they have circumnavigated. The point is that they've done it in what they could afford when they were ready to go.

Over the years of buying and selling, owners discover what they require of their boats, and themselves, guiding them to wiser choices as the boat grows in size and the equipment grows in sophistication. And remember that the larger the boat, the larger the berthing bills, fuel bills, all bills. Yacht brokers see boat size in terms of a lifetime – their size grows as the sailor grows in confidence and family size, but then decrease again to a small, manageable single-hander in which their owner can potter around familiar waters.

Even if you build your boat yourself – which many people have – it's not going to be perfect. Rather than hoping for a 60-foot gem, it's better to buy a second-hand, 35-foot boat, refit her yourself as much as you can – and then go. If you keep prevaricating, your dream will slip away.

David Hughes and his family circumnavigated on a 44-foot boat and decided that they wanted to go around again. They returned home, worked hard and started once more on a 66-foot Oyster with a crew. Some sailors whose finances and energies are stretched by young children sell their yacht and buy a Boston Whaler or RIB, then ten years later return to sailing en famille with older children who can be a help, not a hindrance. Whatever the variation, a love of sailing and exploring will keep you wanting more.

Some inexperienced sailors buy a bigger boat, believing that the boat will keep them safe. If you do not know how to handle a yacht, selling your 30-foot boat and buying a 40-footer is irresponsible and will only put you and those around you in jeopardy. If you do not know how to sail, learn; and be aware that the bigger the boat, the more complicated the systems and the greater the loads on every sheet, halyard and winch.

Lin and Larry Pardey's 'Go small, go simple, go now', is laudable. They circumnavigated, eastabout (the difficult way), in a 24-foot engineless cutter for 11 years. They were purists, and most cruisers are not. There is a balance between losing good cruising years as you save up to buy a luxurious gem and sailing away on a packing crate with a tea towel and high hopes.

Sailing guru Tom Cunliffe describes his requirements for his kind of boat in *Topsail and Battleaxe*: 'For a combination of seaworthiness, comfort, reasonable speed, affordability and that indefinable but vital extra, beauty, it had to be a pilot cutter.' A pilot cutter won't be everyone's choice, but you can't fault his wish list (www.tomcunliffe.com).

Would you prefer to buy a boat that has already circumnavigated and carries all the equipment; or even better, one that is about to set off and the skipper has been forced to abandon the dream? If you are buying second-hand, how old is too old? Remember, if you are going to live and cruise on a boat it will be subjected to a great deal more wear and tear compared to a boat on a mooring or in a marina used at weekends and holidays.

Moonshine, a Bermuda-rigged yacht

MULTIHULLS

Do you want a boat with one hull or more?

A trimaran has three hulls and, although speedy, is considered uncomfortable for long-term cruising, unless you buy a very large one.

A catamaran has two hulls. The name comes from the Tamil *katta*, to tie, and *maram*, wood. Makes include Bahia, Fontaine, Fusion, Jaguar, Jeanneau, Leopard, Perry, Privilege, Prout, Sunreef and Voyage.

Fans of catamarans will tell you that they provide a good floating home that is sea kindly, viewing monohulls as cramped and uncomfortable. A catamaran provides more space and remains comparatively flat in the water. Some sailors prefer to feel the motion of the sea, heeling over in monohulls; some crews on catamarans complain that the cockpit floor seems to 'ripple' when slamming into big seas.

In marinas, a catamaran – if there is room for it – is charged between one-and-a-half times and twice as much as a monohull, because it is perceived as taking up one-and-a-half to twice the amount of space. Catamarans can sail in shallow waters, making them ideal for anchoring close to the beach or sailing in areas such as the Bahamas. The problem that monohull fans are quick to point out is that, unlike a monohull, which is designed to take a 'knock down' and right itself, once a catamaran flips over in a big sea, it stays that way.

A catamaran on the ARC World Cruise, Hout Bay

BOAT CLASSIFICATIONS

How do you know whether the yacht you are considering has been designed to cross oceans? For boats in Europe, the following are the definitions of seaworthiness as laid out in Annex II of the Recreational Craft Directive (RCD):

- Ocean: Classification A: Designed for extended voyages where conditions may exceed wind force 8 (Beaufort scale) and significant wave heights of 4m and above, and vessels largely self-sufficient.
- Offshore: Classification B: Designed for offshore voyages where conditions up to, and including, wind force 8 and significant wave heights up to, and including, 4m may be experienced.
- Inshore: Classification C: Designed for voyages in coastal waters, large bays, estuaries, lakes and rivers where conditions up to, and including, wind force 6 and significant wave heights up to, and including, 2m may be experienced.

In the USA and Australia there are similar categories.

Yachting Australia recommends that, if you want to differentiate between a cruising boat for inshore or offshore, you should refer to ISO 12215 for design and construction, and ISO 12217 for stability and buoyancy. Hull construction standards are guided by OSR 3.03. The website www.yachting.org.au has more information on technical regulations.

There is much discussion concerning the numerous variables during the building of a boat that affect whether it justifies a Category A classification. There are boats built before the regulations and outside Europe that are not classified but are capable of sailing across oceans. The directive should be taken as a guide and not a rule. If you find a yacht broker, marine surveyor or boat builder whom you trust, it is worth discussing their take on which boats are truly seaworthy for blue water. The Yachting and Boating World forums at www.ybw.com have continuing threads on this complex and subjective issue.

HULL & KEEL

Are you comfortable with a keel that is bolted on? Or would you prefer to spend out on an encapsulated keel that forms part of the boat? On rare occasions keels that are bolted on have been known to fall off, for example in a grounding.

At its most simple, the shape of the hull comes down to speed versus stability. Most racing boats that have speed as a priority have fin keels or a fin with a bulb at the base. The other essential is the rudder, usually a 'skeg hung' or 'spade', which will affect the drag in the water.

Cruisers who are racing are inclined choose a lighter, fin-keeled yacht. Others, who put seaworthiness and stability as a priority, choose a classic long keel, or a long fin, which is a compromise, and perhaps the most popular choice. (There are also keels that act as legs, self-supporting, twin-bilge keels on which the boat can sit upright in shallow or tidal waters, but these are unlikely contenders for blue-water boats.) The chances of a knock down in heavy seas are greater in a fin-keeled boat than in a long-keel one.

Some cruisers opt for swing or lifting keels, which can be raised and lowered to allow the yacht to sail in shallow waters or even sit on its cast-iron grounding plate on the beach. Builders such as Southerly and Ovni argue that this gives cruisers a wider area and more choice to explore: a deep keel for oceans, and a shallow keel for inland waterways and tidal areas. Detractors say that the mechanism and housing for the swing keel takes up space in the interior of the yacht.

Yacht with a fin keel

YACHT BROKERS

There are scores of yacht brokers with different specialities. Hopefully you will find a proactive professional who really works hard and diligently for his or her fee. Look for an accredited broker, a member of either the British Marine Federation (BMF) or ABYA (Association of Brokers and Yacht Agents).

Jane Gentry, Chief Executive and Company Secretary of ABYA writes:

The Association of Brokers and Yacht Agents is the UK-based professional association for those who sell both new and second-hand boats. With members around the UK and other locations across Europe, we can help you sell or buy ensuring the correct title documentation is in place and your money is protected. Our members submit documentation for scrutiny before they can become members, so you can be sure they are knowledgeable and will provide you with a professional service.

With over 100 years of experience behind the association, we pride ourselves on bringing the best service to our boat owners.

In the USA and Canada brokers are divided into different areas, for example the Florida Yacht Brokers' Association, or the Yacht Brokers of British Columbia. For surveyors looks for SAMS, The Society for Accredited Marine Surveyors (www.marinesurvey.org).

In Australia the Boat Industry Association (BIA, www.bia.org.au) is a good place to start.

While searching for your boat, make sure that you get to grips with the tax and legal implications, especially if you are buying a boat abroad. The situation is complex and important to understand. In the UK, can your broker competently explain VAT and any Recreational Craft Directive regulations for which you may be responsible? The Royal Yachting Association (RYA, www.rya.

org.uk) is a good source of advice.

My husband John is a yacht broker (www.JRYACHTS.com). He has served as both Deputy and Chairman of ABYA. The JR Yachts' website contains the following guide to the buying process:

When purchasing a used boat, it is important that the legal and financial processes are handled correctly.

ABYA member yacht brokers are professionally qualified and, as a requirement of membership, must also carry Professional Indemnity Insurance, operate specifically designated client accounts and follow the ABYA Code of Practice.

Unlike a property transaction, where an agent will market the property and then hand over to conveyancing solicitors after acceptance of an offer, the ABYA yacht broker continues with the conveyancing until completion.

He or she will ensure the distribution of final funds are handled correctly and that the boat's title history, record of mortgages (if part 1 registered) and RCD and VAT status evidence have been requested, as well as administering the sale and purchase contracts and legal transfer of title.

The purchase is made by using a Sale & Purchase agreement. Buying a yacht this way can be less stressful than the current English system of property buying, as everything is agreed in writing at the beginning. Once an offer is accepted and a deposit is paid, the yacht is then essentially off the market. At that point, no other offers can be accepted whilst the agreement is in place.

An unconditional sale means the boat is sold 'as is, where is' without any other inspection other than the buyer's own inspection. A conditional sale usually means the buyer will commission an independent surveyor to survey the yacht prior to purchase.

The usual sequence of events for a conditional sale are set out below:

- The boat is offered for sale and an offer is received 'subject to survey' and accepted.
- The seller and buyer enter into an agreement drawn up by the yacht broker. A 10% deposit is taken and held in an independent designated client account. The deposit protects the seller if the boat is damaged during the survey or if any associated lift out / yard bills are not settled by the buyer. It also gives the seller reason to accept no further offers whilst the agreement is running.
- The buyer is protected as the seller is now agreeing to sell to only that buyer at an agreed price and within an agreed time frame. The seller cannot change his / her mind or sell to a higher bidder whilst the buyer is spending money on a survey and the agreement is in place.
- As we are dealing with the sale of second-hand goods between two private individuals that are not warranted, having a survey gives the buyer independent knowledge of what he / she is buying.
- It is also possible to insert an optional sea trial clause into the agreement.
- The agreement allows the buyer to re-negotiate the price or have his deposit refunded if the survey shows the boat to have serious or unexpected defects. In the unlikely event of an agreement not being reached within 7 days of notification of any such defects, the contract may be automatically rescinded, and the buyer's deposit refunded. The boat is then free to be re-marketed.
- However, it is important to remember that a used yacht will not survey like a brand new one. The survey will almost

certainly have a relatively long list of recommendations for repairs and upgrades that are non-structural, or safety related and form part of the on-going maintenance of a used yacht. Your surveyor will advise.

- The buyer pays for the survey and any associated lift out or yard costs etc. and the seller may no longer use the vessel until the agreement is completed.
- After the survey the boat sale moves to the completion stage.
- Once the sale is agreed, the balance payment is made to the yacht broker's client account.
- On agreement of sale and receipt of funds to the protected client account, the yacht broker executes an MCA Bill

of Sale in the name of the new owner. He then collates the paperwork and title documents to hand over with the newly executed Bill of Sale, whilst simultaneously transferring the funds to the vendor.

It all works very well for both parties. The seller knows he / she has a committed buyer and financial protection. The buyer has time to find out exactly what he / she is buying and the knowledge that any money spent on surveys will not be wasted by the boat being sold elsewhere during the process. There is a clear written framework, with a professional yacht broker as a third party to administer it, and a safe method of distributing the funds.

SURVEYS

A survey is essential when buying a second-hand boat. It must be an out-of-water inspection to check the hull primarily for osmosis, but an out-of-water survey will also reveal evidence of hard grounding, plus the condition of the rudder, keel and propeller. If you do your survey yourself and get it wrong, you have only yourself to blame.

In the UK, the Yacht Designers and Surveyors Association (YDSA, www.ydsa.co.uk), and in the USA, the Society of Accredited Surveyors (SAMS, www.marinesurvey.org), can provide lists of qualified, experienced professionally accredited surveyors.

The YDSA states that a marine surveyor's report will:

A yacht needs to be lifted out to be properly surveyed

Outline the extent or limitation of the inspection. This is followed by a full description of any defects found, together with graded recommendations for remedial action indicating how urgent the repair is. It generally includes the following main areas as appropriate:
- Hull underwater
- Machinery
- Keel
- Skin fittings
- Rudder
- Deck fittings

- Stern gear
- Mast, boom and rig
- Topsides
- Gas installation
- Deck, coachroof and cockpit
- Water
- Steering
- Fuel
- Hull internal
- Electrical installation
- Bilge
- Anchoring and mooring
- Hatches and doors
- Sails
- Windows and portlights

Julian Smith, of Hamble Yacht Surveys, is an internationally renowned surveyor. Here is his view:

Whether a surveyor is brought in to provide re-assurance during a pre-purchase scenario, or if you choose to employ a surveyor as part of the preparation for a blue-water cruise, choosing the right surveyor is critical.

Their accreditation is your first consideration. In the UK two principal organisations provide memberships and support for marine surveyors. These include the Yacht Designer & Surveyors Association (YDSA) and the International Institute of Marine Surveying (IIMS). Members are graded based on their experience and they have to provide evidence of insurance and keep up to date with their Continuous Professional Development (CDP). By choosing a qualified surveyor who is a member of one of these organisations you can normally be reassured that the surveyor is who he says he is.

Depending on the nature of the survey, your insurance or finance company may stipulate the expected contents of the survey report, and minimum membership level of the surveyors in one of the above-mentioned organisations. So, when looking to appoint a surveyor for a Pre-Purchase Survey or Insurance Survey, make sure they meet the required standards.

Your next consideration is the surveyor himself. A recommendation from a fellow yachtsman goes a long way. Always ask for a sample survey report to check on style of reporting.

Most surveyors charge based on the length of the vessel and prices range from £12-18 per ft LOA. Some surveyors will be VAT registered. Be aware that travel charges may be included or charged separately.

Whether you are purchasing a yacht to go blue-water cruising, or you own a yacht already, surveyors can play a critical part in your preparation. Many have vast experience not just on the vessel itself, but on the equipment installed including navigational, safety and electrical systems. Many yachtsmen find an independent approach to checking a vessel by a surveyor is beneficial as one can become blinded by falling in love with a potential new purchase.

A surveyor will inspect all areas of your yacht

INSURANCE

With two hurricanes and a storm in the Atlantic under my keel, I would absolutely advise on taking out suitable insurance. For those with marine mortgages it is a requirement. Most sailors with boats over 30 feet do pay for insurance, which varies between 1% and 2% of the boat's value, depending on variables such as age and size, sailing grounds and additional equipment.

Some long-term cruisers feel that the risk is outweighed by the expense, hoping that their 'self-insurance fund' or contingency (about 1%) will cover any catastrophes. If you choose to go this route, are you sure that your boat and your sailing abilities will keep you out of trouble? What about the other crazies? Mistrals? Mistakes? Lightning?

If you have put all your money into your boat and have no safety net, where and how are you are going to live if you lose her? What if you have everything right but hit a sleeping whale, or a container?

There are various factors to bear in mind when choosing and specifying insurance. Are you coastal sailing or blue-water? How far offshore can you go with this particular insurance? Which latitudes and longitudes are your borders? When do these borders come into effect, for example: cyclone or hurricane season? Where are the edges of your insurer's world? How far east of Turkey can you sail towards Syria and the Middle East? If you change your mind and route, and decide to head to cooler climes such as Chile or Alaska, are you still insured? If you are sailing in the Indian Ocean and the Red Sea, will your insurer cover you? If so, how long does your insurance company give you to traverse these risky seas? Can you do it in the time it allows?

Does your replacement figure correspond with the one the broker sets? You're going to insure the boat and what else – equipment, personal belongings? When choosing a policy, think carefully about the 'deductible' or no claims clauses. How much are you willing to lose before you claim? Be sure that this is reflected in the policy. Remember that what you feel you need at home maybe not be the same when you are away. You may feel you can row to and from the dock if your outboard gives up – but can you do that every day, in every weather, with a load of shopping and laundry, and a passenger? That's hard work.

Where is the dividing line between equipment failure and problems caused by wear and tear? On one Atlantic crossing, many satellite phone hours were exhausted arguing with an insurance company that claimed that the loss of the rudder (that is, the ability to steer) was caused by a failure of the boat manufacturer and therefore was not its responsibility. Finally, after several valiant attempts to fix the rudder, the crew and a few belongings transferred to another ocean-crossing boat and their yacht was scuppered. The insurance reluctantly paid out.

Do not underestimate how hard and complex an insurance claim can become. Your idea of 'total loss' and the underwriter's concept of 'repairable' could well differ. Who can prove that a boat was dropped heavily in the boatyard or en route to a boat show if the manufacturer claims it was not? The insurer may perceive that you can have your boat fixed in situ, while all you see is a wrecked yard, without the facilities or experts, let alone the atmospheric conditions, to carry out the work.

If you're buying a second-hand boat,

check at what age your insurer stops insuring boats of your type and class. Some older, heavier-displacement boats can be insured for longer than lighter, production boats.

It is not just the age of the boat, but of those on her, of course. Whether the skipper and crew have RYA Competent Crew, Day Skipper, Coastal or even Yachtmaster qualifications is factored into most good policies. Insurers usually demand that at least three crew, including the skipper, are on board for an Atlantic crossing.

When you are away cruising, try to be sure that you have your next insurance payment paid in good time, just in case the insurers require documentation to be posted or couriered, or you need (or want) to change insurers because of unexpected problems. The SSB radios in the Caribbean were ablaze from St Maarten to St Lucia

with angry cruisers comparing insurance companies because one firm had decided to double the insurance premium and reduce their cover, no longer insuring against damage caused by named storms (hurricanes) even if yachts were out of the designated hurricane belt.

It may seem like semantics but beware of clauses distinguishing whether you are 'living aboard' or 'live-aboards'. Live-aboards can be a pejorative term, referring to those who live on their boat while working ashore. They are found in marinas all over the world. Clarify how your policy defines living aboard, since some policies can be tricky. If the boat is your primary residence, will the insurers quibble? How long are you allowed to live on your boat in one marina? Some marinas do not allow living aboard, and this is reflected in the insurance.

EQUIPPING YOUR BOAT

After many discussions with scores of long-term cruisers, meaning those who have been living and travelling on their yacht for over four years, the following is a collation of many 'wish lists' concerning equipment for long-term cruising:

- Solar panels
- Wind generator
- Forward-looking echo-sounder
- Wind self-steering
- Watermaker
- Generator
- Autopilot
- Dinghy davits

GRAB BAG

First, let's consider what goes in your grab bag or panic bag: what you grab just before you get into the liferaft. (The blood-

run-cold fact that most people take from a sea survival course is that you step up to the liferaft – the boat should be going down.) When sailing offshore in blue water, these are suggestions for what you should have in that bag. It's a two-tier list of what you require to survive and other things that it would be good to have, depending on how long you have. Your own list may be slightly different, but this is a start.

Must haves
- ❑ EPIRBs
- ❑ Hand-held VHF
- ❑ Iridium phone (incl. antenna & MRCC telephone number)
- ❑ Water (20-litre container & drink extra before leaving) & food
- ❑ Flares
- ❑ Lifejackets

☐ Strobe, whistle etc. from dan buoy (or whole dan buoy set-up)
☐ Fog horn
☐ Signal mirror
☐ Bucket
☐ Spectacles
☐ Medicines (vitamin pills & antibiotics)
☐ Clothes
☐ Hats & sunglasses
☐ Fishing gear
☐ Multi-tool
☐ Torches & batteries
☐ Sun cream

If you have time
☐ Large plastic bags (clear & black) & zip-lock bags
☐ Charts, pilot books, log, hand-bearing compass, pencils & notebooks
☐ Zippo lighter & fluid
☐ Penknives, machete & sharpening stone
☐ Twine, string & rope
☐ Duct tape & seizing wire
☐ *SAS Survival Handbook, The Ship Captain's Medical Guide*
☐ Dinghy & oars
☐ Dry bags
☐ Money
☐ Passports & yacht documentation
☐ Precious items (e.g. photo cards, jewellery, logbooks)
☐ Laptops

OTHER EQUIPMENT

Now that you have your grab bag, what other equipment do you need? Here's a start, and then some further lists in particular categories.

Deck Equipment
☐ Anchors – How many? Why? Do you have space? Where can you make space, safely, on the deck or guardrail? Some prefer a Bruce anchor, others a Danforth, some a combination of CQR & Kedge. The new anchor from New Zealand, the Rocna, is also becoming popular.
☐ Anchor chain – The amount of chain in length depends on the size of boat & anchor
☐ Anchor markers (showing 5, 10, 20 metres of chain)
☐ Solar panels – Are you hanging them on a gantry ('goal posts') or on the push pit? Can you angle them easily?
☐ Wind generator – How are you mounting it on the boat?

Rutland wind generator on 2-metre-high stainless-steel post bolted to the deck with light rigging and wire shrouds and a solar panel

A sturdy anchor is essential

Sails

- ☐ Spinnaker or cruising chute for light airs
- ☐ Trisail & storm jib
- ☐ Twin luff groove or second forestay – For trade wind sailing which enables the skipper to run with two headsails that can be simultaneously furled or dropped (sometimes referred to as 'goose wing' on a downwind run)
- ☐ Two spinnaker poles
- ☐ Sailors' palm, waxed thread & sail repair kit
- ☐ Some people opt to carry a spare mainsail & genoas

Cockpit Equipment

- ☐ Canvas bag for cockpit debris
- ☐ Cockpit cushions
- ☐ Cockpit seat for long passages
- ☐ Cockpit speakers for the party boats
- ☐ Cockpit tents – Provide an extra room when wintering in temperate climes
- ☐ Command mic (a means of operating VHF from cockpit)
- ☐ Drinks holder
- ☐ Diving knife – Strongly attached to compass
- ☐ Winches
- ☐ Winch handles

Typical sail plan for a trade wind Atlantic crossing from late December to March from the Canaries to the Caribbean

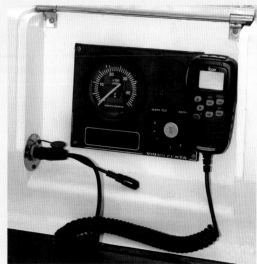

VHF command mic in the cockpit

Rowan Wood in the shelter of a cockpit tent – #MotherShipAdrift

Cabin Equipment

- ☐ Duvets
- ☐ Pillows
- ☐ Pillow cases & sheets
- ☐ Thin covers
- ☐ Fans strategically placed for cooling
- ☐ Mattress – Make sure it is really comfortable. Consider having one specially made for your berth. Or Bedflex, special slats for extra comfort.
- ☐ Mosquito nets
- ☐ Mosquito screens for windows & hatches – Make sure they fit properly
- ☐ Nets to help with stowage – For fruit & vegetables the larger holes will help air circulate. Smaller-holed nets can stop bottles falling out of cupboards in a storm. When hanging your nets, try to imagine the boat rolling at sea; heavy nets swinging across the cabin can be dangerous. 'Death by cantaloupe' was a joke on our Atlantic crossing as we ducked the fruit & veg laden nets. Three days out into the Atlantic, one of our crew heard running water. We finally tracked the noise down to scores of rustling onions. The backs of lockers in the galley or bathroom are useful nooks for nets.
- ☐ Stowage – How much is there? Is what you need every day accessible? Keep a book – not on the laptop, a small book that you can lay hold of any time – & draw a map of what is where.
- ☐ Ziplocks – Large bags with strong zips in which to store spare sheets / duvets in the tropics. Make sure that you squeeze as much air as possible out of the bag. These are also good for clothes, pillows, books, pretty much anything that will turn mouldy when you are away from the boat. Some people swear by tightly wrapped clingfilm for duvets.
- ☐ Windscoop – To scoop the air into the boat & cool it

Fans are essential in warm climates

Netting for storage as pointed out by Emony Nicholls – one of our crew for the Atlantic Crossing

Galley Equipment

- ☐ Barbeque – On the aft rail
- ☐ Bread board – A plastic bendy one
- ☐ Cake tin & cupcake tin – Silicone 'rubbery' tins are easily stored
- ☐ Captain's kettle
- ☐ Casserole dish with lid – Two if possible
- ☐ Colander
- ☐ Corkscrew
- ☐ Cutlery for table & kitchen (e.g. knives, forks, spoons, spatulas, wooden spoons, garlic crusher, knives, potato masher, egg whisk)
- ☐ Dust pan, dusters, mops, sponges
- ☐ Favourite herbs, spices, condiments, drinks & treats
- ☐ Fridge – Will your fridge that is efficient in temperate waters be able to cope in the tropics?
- ☐ Gas for cooking – Check the fittings. You may need one for Europe & one for the Caribbean.
- ☐ Kitchen towel holders / kitchen towels
- ☐ Liquidiser (12 volt)
- ☐ Marker pen – For writing on the tops of tins, if you are going to look at them from above when they are stowed
- ☐ Melamine or plastic plates
- ☐ Microwave (12 volt)
- ☐ Mixing bowls
- ☐ Non-stick frying pan

The galley

- ☐ Oven gloves
- ☐ Pressure cooker
- ☐ Recyclable bags for shopping – Strong enough to withstand many dinghy rides
- ☐ Saucepan (small, stainless steel)
- ☐ Sieves (large and small)
- ☐ Sinks (two if possible) – One more sink makes three times the difference
- ☐ Spatulas & wooden spoons
- ☐ Storage boxes for flour, sugar
- ☐ Tableware (plates, glasses, cups)
- ☐ Tea towels
- ☐ Towels
- ☐ Vacuum cleaner (12 volt)

Communication Equipment

- ☐ Mobile phone & various SIM cards for your location – Be sure about the real range of your SIM card, not just the sales person's claimed range
- ☐ Apps for your mobile phone – There are numerous Apps which become outmoded and updated within the life span of a monthly magazine let alone a book!
- ☐ EPIRB (Emergency Position Indicating Radio Beacon) – Both on the yacht & hand-held for the grab bag
- ☐ GPS (Global Positioning Satellite)
- ☐ Laptops – See main list below
- ☐ Personal GPS
- ☐ Skype – Cheap for phone calls home, gives the joy of inconsequential chatter
- ☐ SSB radio (single-side band radio)
- ☐ Satellite phone
- ☐ VHF Radio with Digital Selective Calling (DSC) – With command mic in the cockpit
- ☐ Handheld VHF radios – Waterproof with strap to secure to user, e.g. over shoulder
- ☐ Walkie-talkies – For close range, boat to shore (beach) communications (e.g. extra shopping, dinghy pick-up from the beach)

Electronic Equipment

- ☐ AIS (Automatic Identification System)
- ☐ Chartplotter – Will you have it routed from the navigation station up to the cockpit?
- ☐ Forward-looking echo sounder
- ☐ Radar
- ☐ Depth, log & wind instruments

Navigation station including radar, chartplotter, PC navigation, Navtex and VHF radio

Electrical Equipment

- ☐ Batteries – For torch, camera, head torches
- ☐ Crimpers
- ☐ Crimps
- ☐ Distilled water for batteries
- ☐ Electrical tape
- ☐ Electrical wiring – Different colours
- ☐ Fuses (various)
- ☐ International plug for Europe / USA
- ☐ Light bulbs (spare) – Check throughout the boat. LEDs if possible.
- ☐ Light / fluorescent tubes – Crack them & a fluorescent light shines
- ☐ Vaseline (for battery terminals)
- ☐ Volt meter
- ☐ WD40

Safety Equipment

See also the grab bag list.

- ☐ Bailing pump
- ☐ Bungs (seacock plugs)
- ☐ Danbuoy
- ☐ Deadman rope – Trailing from the back of the boat
- ☐ Fire blanket
- ☐ Fire extinguishers – For cabins, galley, engine & saloon
- ☐ Flares (e.g. Paines Wessex Offshore or ORC (Ocean Racing Club) kits)
- ☐ Fog horn
- ☐ Hand-held torches
- ☐ Harness lines – Strong webbing with a quick-release stainless steel clip, attached to harness & jackstays
- ☐ Harnesses for adults & children (e.g. Crewsaver) – Your life could depend on them, so choose well
- ☐ Head torches
- ☐ Hydrostatic release units on liferaft & EPIRB
- ☐ Jackstays / lifelines – For easy movement around the deck your life could depend on them. Be absolutely sure that the ties holding the jackstays to the deck are super-strong.
- ☐ Lifebelt with self-igniting light
- ☐ Lifejackets with crotch straps
- ☐ Liferaft

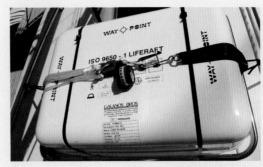

This liferaft is secured with a hydrostatic release unit: when the unit is immersed to a set depth, a release mechanism is triggered and the liferaft will float free – even if the yacht sinks

- ❏ Man Over Board (MOB) alert & position devices
- ❏ MOB life tags recovery equipment
- ❏ Radar reflector
- ❏ Rope ladder – For the first in the liferaft to secure & throw out for assistance to others to climb in
- ❏ Smoke alarms
- ❏ Strobe – Personal strobe attached to lifejacket
- ❏ Torch – 1000 candle, waterproof

Safety equipment

Tool box
- ❏ Allen keys
- ❏ Blocks and tackle
- ❏ Drill
- ❏ Drill bits
- ❏ Hack saw
- ❏ Hammers
- ❏ Saw
- ❏ Screws
- ❏ Screwdrivers
- ❏ Shackles
- ❏ Spanners
- ❏ Wrenches

First Aid Equipment
BASIC MEDICAL KIT from the third edition of *The Pacific Crossing Guide* published by the RCC Pilotage Foundation. This may cover more than you require for an Atlantic passage, but it is better to have, just in case.

Equipment
- ❏ Cotton wool
- ❏ Crepe bandages
- ❏ Plasters, rolls of adhesive plaster
- ❏ Sterile gauze & dressings (e.g. Melolin, tulle gras)
- ❏ Tubigrip bandages
- ❏ Thermometer
- ❏ Eye bath & pads
- ❏ Steristrips
- ❏ Plaster of Paris
- ❏ Scissors, forceps, needle holder
- ❏ Syringes, hypodermic needle
- ❏ Needle & suture, sterile gloves
- ❏ Scalpel & blades
- ❏ Dental kit & oil of cloves

Preparations for the Skin, Ears & Eyes
- ❏ Dettol, chlorhexidine, Savlon
- ❏ Neomycin & bacitracin
- ❏ Silver sulfadiazine cream (Flamazine)
- ❏ Calomine lotion
- ❏ Antihistamine cream (e.g. Phenergan)
- ❏ Suncream, lip protection
- ❏ Insect repellent
- ❏ Eye drops & ointment: chloramphenicol
- ❏ Ear drops
- ❏ Isopropyl alcohol (Auro dri)
- ❏ Steroid & neomycin (e.g. Betnesol-N, Neo Cortef)

Drugs Taken by Mouth
- ❏ Antitihistamine
- ❏ Lomotil
- ❏ Loperamide (Imodium)
- ❏ Laxative
- ❏ Kaolin mixture

❑ Propantheline (Pro-Banthine)
❑ Antacid
❑ Anti-sickness
❑ Malaria prophylaxis
❑ Vitamins & water-purifying tablets
❑ Painkillers (e.g. paracetamol,
  paracetamol + codeine (Solpadol))
❑ Ibruprofen (Nurofen)
❑ Naproxen (Naprosyn)
❑ Tramadol (Zydol)
❑ Antibiotics (e.g. flucloxacillin)
❑ Co-amoxiclav (Augmentin)
❑ Metronidazole (Flagyl)

Doctors who have sailed in the Caribbean and Pacific emphasise the importance of insect repellent and cleaning wounds.

The Pilotage Foundation's *The Atlantic Crossing Guide* covers numerous medical problems. Their *The Pacific Crossing Guide*, of course, has a more extensive list reflecting the area it covers: for example, dengue fever, sea snakes, ciguatera. (In extreme: www.wildmed.com/wilderness-medical-courses)

The *Ship Captain's Medical Guide*, Harry Leach is essential. Also refer to the Safety and Medical information on Noonsite (www.noonsite.com/General).

Sun protection
❑ Aloe vera in
  cream & spray
  – For sunburn
❑ Bimini top –
  For covering
  the cockpit
  in tropical
  climates
❑ Cotton hats &
  thin long-sleeve
  tops
❑ Hats & t-shirts –
  For swimming
❑ Sunscreen

Dinghy Equipment
❑ Anchor
❑ Bailer
❑ Cover – In the tropics UV light can take its toll
❑ Davits – How are you lifting the outboard from the dinghy to the deck? Davits on the aft deck? Stainless steel swing-arm davit? Are you rigging a halyard to lift the dinghy & heavy shopping aboard?
❑ Dinghy repair kit
❑ Oars
❑ Outboard – Remember it will have to be lifted aboard, & the bigger the engine, the heavier. Have numerous practice runs so the less strong members of the crew have the 'pull' power to start it & newbies have the confidence to 'park' the dinghy at the dock & beside / behind the boat.
❑ Petrol can
❑ Solar-powered light – Used on pontoons fixed to the outboard engine
❑ Strap for hoisting dinghy outboard motor
❑ Umbrella – Useful for rain & shine and acting as a spray hood in the dinghy
❑ Waterproof bag – For keeping vital documents dry when dinghying to customs.

A well-equipped dinghy is essential – here in Eowyn, Grenada on the ARC World Cruise

Land Equipment – Getting Around Ashore

☐ Bicycles – Fold-up if possible, for shopping & exploring
☐ Granny or shopping trolley
☐ Hiking boots
☐ Passarelle – A gangplank used from the bow or stern to the dock, usually in the Mediterranean
☐ Rucksacks

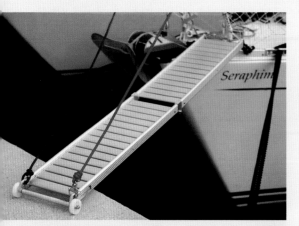

A passarelle

Other Basic Equipment

Let's say that since you're aiming for a good cruising boat, not a weekender, you already have a head (lavatory), a fridge, a basin in the head and a sink in the galley, and a shower with hot and cold water. I would also say that heating is a must.

Other equipment you may want to consider could include:

Boat Equipment
☐ Anchor black ball – To show at anchor
☐ Autopilot
☐ Binoculars (two pairs) – Preferably one pair of offshore binoculars with internal compass
☐ Boat hooks – Extendable & fixed
☐ Ensign with flag pole
☐ Fenders

☐ Flags – Code & courtesy flags for each country / island out of the EU. Also Q flag (quarantine flag), the yellow flag that should be flown instead of the courtesy ensign until your yacht has been properly cleared by customs & immigration.
☐ Harness lines – Strong webbing with a quick-release stainless steel clip
☐ Holding tanks – Where are they going to be fitted? They are a requirement if not a legal necessity in some cruising grounds.
☐ Hose & various attachments for different marinas
☐ Fuel cans
☐ Impellers
☐ Rigging screws
☐ Ropes / lines / warps – Lots of these, for extra lines, anchors, tying down
☐ Topclimber bosun's chair – To assist in climbing up the mast
☐ Windlass for the anchor

Clothing
☐ Gloves
☐ Hats against the sun (e.g. Tilley) – Straw is pretty but is wrecked after a few trips in the dinghy, & often flies off, gets soaked or sinks
☐ Sunglasses – Polarising with 'granny holders'
☐ Swimming costumes – It is worth having at least two, one for everyday swimming in the sea / pools & one for 'best', or when you don't want to get into a wet costume
☐ Thermals
☐ Warm gloves
☐ Waterproofs
☐ Wellington boots

Books & Stationery
☐ Address book / contacts
☐ Books – To be read, then swapped
☐ Bubble wrap for fragile 'bounty'

- ☐ Diary
- ☐ Dictionaries (English, French, Spanish)
- ☐ File with plastic leaves – To keep clippings & mementos in
- ☐ Logbook for recording nautical details – The log is for the boat, the diary is for you
- ☐ Map of land – If you are in a large country, e.g. America
- ☐ Navigation charts (paper, e.g. Imray)
- ☐ Photo frame with montage of loved ones
- ☐ Pilot books
- ☐ Tourist books (e.g. those issued by Lonely Planet)

Fernhurst Books' Logbook for Crusing Under Sail

Electrical & Other Items

- ☐ DVD player & DVDs / CDs / memory stick
- ☐ Fans for heating / cooling run from shore power – See also Wind scoop
- ☐ Generator – Hand-held
- ☐ iPod
- ☐ Kindle (for reading eBooks)
- ☐ Laptop (with case to protect against sea air & water)
- ☐ Laptop only for navigation – Several cruisers have recommended having a laptop which is only used for navigation & weather. They like to keep it 'clean' without too much memory or applications to clog up space. A dedicated laptop avoids any unregulated downloads.
- ☐ Memory sticks
- ☐ Navigation charts (electronic, e.g. Navionics)
- ☐ Radio for use in aft cabin – If you cannot or do not want to hear the yacht stereo
- ☐ Sewing machine – If you think the use is

worth the space it takes up
- ☐ Solar-powered lights for anchor lights in rigging in anchorage
- ☐ Solar shower to hang from spreaders or on mast – Make sure the water does not become too hot in the tropics!
- ☐ Scales for weighing yourself – An unorthodox addition, but tapas & rum punches make for a jolly but rolly crew
- ☐ Wind vane
- ☐ Washing machine – Manual, if the use is worth the space taken up
- ☐ Watermaker & watermaker chemicals – Safely stored

Electronic charts

'Household' Goods & Equipment

- ☐ Babywipes – Non-scented for quick washes if water is short or you're sticky
- ☐ Brushes for washing the deck
- ☐ Buckets – Pack-away bucket (folds up) & ordinary bucket with glass bottom for looking at fish
- ☐ Cans for carrying extra water and fuel on deck – Make sure they are UV resistant & different colours for water & fuel
- ☐ Hot water bottle to heat & cool
- ☐ Lighter
- ☐ Matches

- ☐ Methylated spirits
- ☐ Nappies – For oil / water spillages
- ☐ Picnic kit (e.g. light tarpaulin, sandproof bag & Tupperware for food & drink)
- ☐ Sponges – For washing the boat
- ☐ Surface cleaner with antibacterial agent
- ☐ Thermos flask
- ☐ Washing-up liquid bottles cut up – To prevent rats climbing lines (ropes)
- ☐ Water containers – As UV proof as possible

Tools & Equipment
- ☐ Axe
- ☐ Bolt croppers – Heavy duty
- ☐ Cable ties
- ☐ Diver's knife
- ☐ Duct tape / sticky tape
- ☐ Epoxy – For drying both in air & in seawater
- ☐ Gaskets / gasket sealant
- ☐ Jubilee clips
- ☐ Leatherman / multi-tool – Remember to pack it in the suitcase, not walk through security with it. Security in Palma Airport, Mallorca regularly send skippers back to repack their luggage.
- ☐ Nets for extra stowage in galley & cabins
- ☐ Nets for rescuing objects that have fallen overboard
- ☐ Octopus bungees – For extra strength in tying down bicycles, fuel cans, dinghy, granny trolley, surf board
- ☐ Oil extractor
- ☐ Pegs for wet clothes / swimming kit – Some say these should be stainless steel
- ☐ Plastic hose for protecting lines (ropes/ warps)
- ☐ Plunger for blocked drain
- ☐ Push-fit connectors for plumbing hot & cold water
- ☐ Self-amalgamating tape
- ☐ Stern gland packing – To go around the shaft of the engine where it enters the back of the boat. Only attempt to repair

this if you are sure what you're doing or have an expert on hand.
- ☐ Superglue
- ☐ Whipping twine

Tools & equiment are always neede for repairs

Other Sports Equipment
- ☐ Canoe / kayak / surf board
- ☐ Diving equipment
- ☐ Fishing gear (rods, hooks, lures, gaff, cheap alcohol to pour into the gills to 'anaesthetise' the fish)
- ☐ Flippers / goggles
- ☐ Inflatable rings & bananas etc – For towing behind dinghy
- ☐ Sports equipment (tennis racket, golf clubs, yoga mat)

Other Items
- ☐ Hammock(s)
- ☐ Luxuries, such as a special scent
- ☐ Tarpaulin
- ☐ Whistle – Some have thermometers and compasses

LITTLE LUXURIES

Jason has crossed the Atlantic twice and sailed to Australia on *Trenelly*, an Oyster. He and his wife Fiona met the author in Antigua. We danced on their aft deck on New Year's Eve! Jason says:

Top of our list is AIS. We only have a receiver, but it is good to see exactly which of a dozen targets are on a collision course. Usually they will alter course for you, but you will know when that happens too.

Our Honda 3kw generator has been great too. It sits on deck and enables us to have fridge and freezer on 24/7 with no problem. Next time I would make a small, tilting box to protect it from the seas and to help soak up the big heel angles when sailing to windward. It has an ignition cut-out if its oil dips below a certain level so, when we heel over too much, it will stop.

He adds: 'The most important thing about the generator is that we can use it to make toast in a domestic toaster – luxury.'

Of his Autohelm ST7000 he comments: 'Any weather, for as long as is needed. Like having a bionic extra crew member with a serious love for helming.'

And on his dinghy davits: 'They are wonderful. Not for long-distance transport but, if you're cruising in a small area for a while, they are perfect for pulling your favourite tender up to safety each night and then moving to your next spot.'

TOP FIVE 'HIS' AND 'HERS'

Clive Woodman and Angela Lilienthal have sailed extensively in the Baltic, Caribbean, the US and Canadian east coast, the Great Lakes, St Lawrence Seaway, Labrador, Newfoundland, Northwest Greenland, US Northwest, Alaska on their boat *Cosmic Dancer*. When they emailed this, they were 'at anchor in Hoonah, a small Tlingit Indian settlement on the edge of Glacier Bay' (Alaska, where the internet is intermittent).

This is the list of their favourite pieces of kit (but in no special order):

Angela:
1. iPhone with a waterproof case and topped with a full store of Navionics charts, music & audio books
2. Dubarry Goretex sailing boots
3. Rab down jacket for wearing below decks to supplement the cabin heater in cold places
4. A small bottle of Maggi sauce (a German cannot go sailing without this condiment on board!)
5. A bottle of Ungave (Labrador) gin for celebrating arrivals in remote anchorages (particularly good if drunk with lump of glacier ice in it)

Clive:
1. As for Angela's number 1 but with a stock of BBC podcasts rather than audio books to help pass the night watches
2. Same as Angela's number 2
3. A Buff facemask / head over
4. As many packs of smoked bacon as we can fit in the fridge to make bacon sandwiches for those early morning watches
5. A bottle of Famous Grouse whisky for making wobbly coffees to celebrate a dawn arrival in harbour after a long, cold overnight passage

TOP 5 'HERS'

Al and Mel sailed an Atlantic Circuit with their daughters Ayla (9) and Molly (6). Mel's Must Haves were:

1. Large tubs of green and red Thai curry paste
2. Face spritzer: aromatherapy oils & water
3. Music playlists / films / books
4. Polaroid sunglasses
5. Cushions

TOP FIVE 'HIS' AND 'HERS'

Mike and Devala made a nine-year circumnavigation spending seven years in the Pacific.

Devala:	Mike:
1. Dust buster	1. Teng TM029 1/4-inch Bits Box Drive
2. Knee pads	2. Overboard rucksack
3. Marmite	3. Head torch
4. Kindle eBook reader	4. Underwater camera
5. Moisturiser	5. Stainless-steel insulated cafetiere

POWER AFLOAT

Even when plugged into shore power, there never seems to be enough power onboard a boat. Power management is often dealt with by a generator. It is better to rely on a wind generator and solar panels, particularly if voyaging to the Pacific where generator parts can be hard to find. It's time to forget the hair dryer and think 12-volt plug – not a lot of power.

TOP ITEMS

Loraine and Graham are sailing with their young son on their catamaran in the Pacific. Lorraine, says, 'My beanbag from Lazy Bones. Love it, picked up in Antigua, made out of Sunbrella, so water runs off it. Can put it anywhere on the boat, take to the beach etc., it is so comfortable.'

Iridium phone. Great for downloading GRIB files or emails at sea plus, if you need to talk to someone in the middle of the ocean, you just dial, so you are always contactable.

iPod Touch. Great for night watches, also can get web access, Skype, email, GPS from it, plus you can play movies while in the bar, for your child, or on night watch and, of course, it plays music.

WHAT DOCUMENTATION DO YOU NEED ON BOARD?

1. Certificates – ICC (International Certificate of Competence), RYA or other qualification certificates. Copies of birth & marriage certificates.
2. Yacht documentation, including ship's registration & insurance.
3. Full paper driving certificate, not just the plastic card.
4. Visas – if you think you are going to spend hurricane season in the USA (or Canada), sort out your visa before leaving the UK. It can save sailing (into the Easterlies) to Barbados or the expense of flying & staying in Barbados / Trinidad. Research the Australian, Galapagos & Indonesian visa requirements as well.

These long and daunting lists should get you thinking. No wonder Americans say that 'boat' stands for 'Break Out Another Thousand'. Of course, one can simplify things a great deal.

Anne Hammick in her book *Ocean Cruising on a Budget* quotes Jerome K Jerome's *Three Men in a Boat*: 'George said, "You know we are on the wrong track altogether. We must not think of the things we could do with, but only of the things we can't do without."' That's still very true.

BOAT SHOWS & JUMBLE SALES

Boat shows attract bargain boat outfitters. Shows to look out for include:
- UK – Southampton in early September.
- USA – Annapolis (sail) in early October; Miami in February; Newport Boat Show in September in Rhode Island; Seattle in late January.
- Australia – the Australia Marine Exports website, www.aimex.asn.au, lists numerous international boat shows around the world. Australian shows are in Brisbane in mid-April; Melbourne in early February; Perth in early April; Sanctuary Cove Queensland in mid-May.
- Canada – Toronto in early January; Vancouver in mid-February.

The Boat Jumble Association (www.boatjumbleassociation.co.uk) lists boat jumble sales around the UK. While you're on the web, keep checking on eBay and looking at other sites for used gear, including that at www.worldcruising.com. When berthed in or near a superyacht marina, it is always worth digging around in the nearby skips.

FOR WETTER OR WORSE

We sailed away just after we got married. Our wedding list was at a chandlery, which helped hugely with equipping the boat.

Eight inches of tube to fix the engine in a force 8... was not on the list. 37 knots across the deck it was the only wedding present I wanted. Didn't have to be wrapped, just had to be in some deep recess of the Bukh 36 horsepower engine. Somehow in gale conditions it wasn't going to happen. Heavily reefed we had set sail, at the sound of the gun, at 11am precisely, from Torbay on the Blue Water Biscay Triangle Rally, the first day of our circumnavigation. After eight hours of a sloppy force 6 with the wind rising, we decided to turn on the engine and punch through to the blue skies on the horizon and some way beyond France. The engine overheated. We turned back. After 57 miles of sailing via the mid-channel blow, a mere 8 land miles on, all shook up, we moored in Dartmouth where our crew jumped ship. Two days later we received a text declaring neither we nor *Moonshine* were ready...

Two drifters off to see the world... there's such a lot of kit to buy and the shake-down cruise in a rattle-and-roll sea revealed a whole lot more. We realised that the seemingly endless re-fit list required to bring the 19-year-old yacht up to top condition for safe world cruising was only the beginning. Planning a world cruise and a wedding in five months is a one-off lifetime experience, with the added spin that we had only met five months before. Nevertheless, compensation came in the form of the wedding list, which helped towards readying *Moonshine*, our home, a 36-foot centre cockpit Westerley Corsair, and us for several years of cruising. The initial perceptions of absolute necessities changed as the rally deadline sped towards us. After we dropped out, the 'deadline' became when we and the boat were ready.

My mother, 'Shore Support', controlled the master wedding list and Port Solent Marina gamely dealt with bemused enquiries. The first pages included... Liberty photograph frames – I had given descriptions of the anticipated contents, 'Landfall in Antigua' and 'Crossing the Equator'. These were followed by two pages of kitchenware – so far, so comparatively ordinary. And then, six pages of 33 gifts ranging from six-man liferaft to teak trays... Most of our guests were amused, confused and intrigued. Most bottled and sent overly-generous cheques, but others set forth to that mysterious place, a chandlery. We gratefully put the cheques towards the budget busters in the 'Contributions Towards' section – the EPIRB, SSB radio, digital camera and my will-not-go-without-it, a forward-looking sonar. To our surprise and delight the marine microwave, Iridium phone, Offshore 54 binoculars with internal compass and handheld GPS were one-off gifts. The first aider and his wife who gave us the Offshore First Aid Kit supplemented it with a day's course in first aid, which really instilled in us the potential dangers on the yacht. Mind you, putting your lover in the recovery position in the tight confines of the passage between the engine and pilot berth can be quite a hoot.

The SOS grab bag did not go. No one wanted to be associated with the last snatch as we leapt. And no one contributed to the holding tanks! One couple felt that if they gave us the Henderson bailing pump, the wooden plugs were a must too. The code flags, the yachtsman's heavy kettle, Captain Currie's knife and various manuals, *The Pacific Crossing Guide*, Jimmy Cornell's *World Cruising Handbook*, were snapped up. One friend who regularly flies across the Atlantic chose *The Atlantic Crossing Guide*, so she could think of us from her club-class haven. The Pratique flag, the Firefly Plus personal strobe, and Maglite torch were the late-comers' choices, but, welcome any time...

After the list had been sent out we realised that we had forgotten some essential gifts and thankfully channelled non-specific cheques to the marine barbecue, now on the guardrail, and a new hatch for our cabin. Every morning we are glad that we did not compromise, and squint at the blue skies through the mass of crazing and cracks. I added *The Care and Feeding of Sailing Crew* by Lin Pardey, which is expensive but is packed with years of worldwide sailing experiences and knowledge. I refer to it often. A razor-sharp, professional mandolin for slicing vegetables is kept safely under the oven...

The wedding, of course, reflected our imminent circumnavigation. The marquee poles were dressed in hessian with palm leaves and (Tesco's) coconuts sprouting from the top. John's first boat, *First Steps*, decorated with exotic Caribbean flowers, was 'moored' to one of the 'palm trees'. In front of a huge photograph of *Moonshine* in full flight, beside a map of our anticipated route and a chart of Biscay, sat the cake – a small replica of *Moonshine*, sails and all. In the evening pirates, mermaids, castaways, even a ship's cat attended our Seven Seas Party. And the first dance?... *Moon river*... two drifters off to see the world... there's such a lot of world to see... avoiding low pressure.

Source: Yachting Monthly.

4
CHILDREN ON BOARD

Most cruisers agree that children thrive on board. The best age to cruise with children is when they are between 5 and 11 years old. They will remember the time aboard, they can be useful, and they can return to formal education and friends in time for secondary school.

Time aboard with children is hard work but is priceless at whatever age. It is time as a family unit away from the pressures of everyday life. The amount of time you spend together on a boat is concentrated, so one year on a boat is the equivalent of four years of shore-life, four years equates to sixteen.

This chapter contains some hints and tips for the family on board, starting at the very beginning.

We sailed in company with several families. We met the Dutch Berendsen family in Alcudia, Mallorca and sailed with them from the Caribbean to the USA. Sergej and Isabelle Berendsen described the time on board with their son and daughter, "Amazing. I found that our trip has unbreakably bonded us as a family."

Jack, aged 4, on his own private beach, which came and went with the tide: Waderick Wells, Exuma Land and Sea Park, Bahamas

PREGNANCY

If you find you are pregnant, it is best not to cross an ocean. Risks include ectopic pregnancy, pre-eclampsia and early labour. It is better to be somewhere near good medical assistance in case of an emergency.

The basic dos and don'ts for pregnancy are similar living aboard as living on land. Do not lift heavy items such as buckets of water or shopping. Do not work the winches. Be careful on the companionway and climbing up from the dinghy. Be careful walking in the heat of the day and then going into air conditioning and out again – this can cause fainting and squeezes (mild contractions), which are most alarming.

Also, be aware of how debilitating morning sickness can be. I was fine for my first son. We sailed from the Bahamas to Grenada from where we flew home for the birth. But, I was flattened with morning sickness with my second son. We had to take a marina berth for two weeks.

Half way through sailing an Atlantic Circuit, Mel discovered she was pregnant with their third child. Mel recalls, "Early

The author, five months' pregnant, after a very wet dinghy ride looking over Admiralty Bay, Bequia, the Grenadines

pregnancy in the Caribbean is not advisable if you ask me. I suffered from the heat, the smell of the diesel, rubbish, heads and my family! Early stages are brutal enough and the constant movement from the boat forced a normally non-vomiting mother-to-be to stay in her bunk for days at a stretch. No fun!!! Don't let me put you off though, we did survive!"

Think very carefully about where you want to give birth. You have to be realistic. Babies are enchanting, but births can turn ugly. If you are considering an overseas birth, can you speak the language sufficiently well to understand the medical language in an emergency? How do doctors in that country control pain? Do you trust the medical team? In the trauma of a bad labour, do you want to risk being there? Can you afford to have a baby in the chosen country or island? Does your insurance cover it?

Most airlines prefer not to fly pregnant women long haul after 28 weeks. With a doctor's letter they may extend this time to 35. If you do decide to come home, start preparing to return home by the end of 28 weeks, which means finding a marina and arranging for the boat to be put to bed.

If it is your first pregnancy, the birth, and the 'babymoon', are a special time for you and your family. When the baby is born you will want everyone to meet and enjoy your new child. Don't be in too much of a hurry to return to the boat. It is worth waiting at least six months, until all the vaccinations are completed, and you are totally over the birth. The change from pregnant-sailing woman to new mother can swing your emotional compass wildly. Postnatal depression can start up to six months after the birth, and it is no fun suffering from this on a boat away from family and support groups.

JASON & FIONA'S STORY

After many trials and tribulations and two Atlantic crossings, Jason and Fiona made it to the Pacific for the second time. Jason wanted to sail under the Sydney Harbour Bridge on his 40th birthday and perhaps arrive in time to be anchored in the harbour for the world-famous New Year's Eve fireworks. However, their best-laid plans changed when he discovered that he and his wife were expecting their second child. They were in the middle of the Pacific with several thousand miles to go, so Fiona sailed over 1,000 miles from Fiji to Opua, New Zealand with Dylan, aged 2, and a bump of seven months. The baby was born safely in New Zealand.

CHILDREN

Whether on land or sea, adding a child into the family equation alters the balance. With one child it's not so much, but with more than one it's a lot, and on a boat, this is amplified. On land you have doctors, supermarkets, nurseries. There is support from friends, mothers, child carers and later pre-school and school. On a boat you make your own infrastructure.

As a cruising couple, teamwork is second nature. As a cruising family, the dynamics change that much more. The father (usually the skipper) finds himself single-handing while his partner does mother-watch. Fathers can miss the help of their partner; mothers can miss the sailing and sometimes resent having to look after the children. Fathers can resent having to sail, maintain the boat and then take the children off the boat because their mother is shattered. One exhausted mother slept through her toddler raising the US Coastguard by playing with the EPIRB. If you need a sleep, make sure that a responsible adult is in charge who can stay awake and watch the child. It is unlikely there will be babysitters, so a night on the town is one that includes the kids.

So realise that living on board with children will be a life less ordinary and full of wonder, but it will be a life where you have to work together, 24/7.

IS IT BETTER TO WAIT?

We had sailed for two years before children and took a year off for each child, starting again when they were 8 months old. We are hugely grateful for the time and experiences we had with our young children as we travelled – they were priceless and unmissable.

However, we would not recommend sailing long term with children under 5. Whether you find a new home en route or return home and start again, more than two children under 4 is too much. If you all want the best benefits from cruising, it may be advisable to wait a little.

BABIES AND TODDLERS

Although very young children may not remember their experiences on board, you will, and, on numerous levels, the child will benefit from the extraordinary. It is a time of rapid growth, both mentally and physically. The baby or toddler will be open to all kinds of unusual stimuli that, osmosis-like, they will soak up. They are too young for school and, so long as they are with their parents, they are happy. They develop social skills as you travel and mix with other families. Although visits with grandparents may not be as frequent, when they do see them the 'quality time' will be longer.

The pressures, exhaustion and frustrations of parenthood are magnified on a boat. With babies and toddlers, the confinement of a cabin helps, and the 'bumbo' seat keeps them in place. It is

Jack, aged 7 months, in his restaurant seat on his first outing on Seraphim, on the Round the Island Race (Isle of Wight, UK)

when the child starts walking that the challenges really begin. When they're young, a seat used in restaurants can be secured in the cockpit. As they grow older, a car seat can be used in the cockpit and, of course, ashore when hiring cars.

'Entertain and contain' will be your motto. As at home on wet days, imagination and silly games are important, particularly with little balls and bricks. The game of 'empty the cans from the locker and put them back again' is fun, although it could encourage curious forays into secret hidey-holes. The locking devices on lockers are the perfect deterrent to small hands – but do remember to lock them. Sugar all over the galley floor and baby sunscreen massaged into the carpet and

upholstery are among the penalties for forgetting. Tools must also be kept safely stowed, since hacksaws seem to be a draw to investigative toddlers. One child lost beach time for cutting the wires on his father's multi-meter.

Blowing bubbles is a giggle and keeps them happy, if not for ever, at least for half an hour. Do be careful where you put the bubble mixture, though. When they are too young to fish for real, fishing for magnetic fish is a hit. Little children think it's a laugh to unclip clothes pegs and pull them apart but seeing your favourite dress or tea towel or swimsuit floating or, worse, sinking far below is not funny.

Even with all the games, for long-term cruisers with children a DVD or access to a ton of downloads, is essential, and it's fun for the adults too. But for preservation of life and sanity, have at least two portable DVDs, just in case one is broken, and a large DVD library.

Jack & James with a coconut boat made by John – many fathers make these

CHILDREN 5 UPWARDS

Children raised on boats become incrementally more useful as they, literally, learn the ropes.

Teenagers will require different 'entertain and contain' boundaries. By thirteen they should be useful members of the crew taking watches, being involved with the navigation and fixing the boat. Just as on land teenagers can be toxic, so too on a boat. But they will still be on a boat exploring the world.

They could make weekly YouTube videos of their trip. Researching the next port could be part school project, part information for 'vlog'. Once 'ashore' there is swimming, surfing, kayaking and hikes. They can also be allowed more freedom such as their own dinghy in which to explore the anchorage. The jury is out on tablets and laptops however, as on shore, these can be used as incentives, and good ways to stay in touch with friends at home. Depending on your inclination, friends from home could visit…?

PACIFIC BIRTH

Sailing on a Crealock 44, John and Sara Coxon joined the Blue Water Rally Circumnavigation with Sara's 10-year-old daughter Charlotte. In Gibraltar, Sara discovered she was pregnant. Their son was born during a coup in Fiji. John, a paediatrician, takes up the tale.

Sara went into labour a day out, so I gave her some drugs to calm down the uterus and, although she arrived safely next day, still in labour, the contractions were a bit stop, start for a few days. The coup took place just after we were downwind of Niue and, as it was force 8-9, we could not really get back there, so chose to go into Savu Savu.

To get a curfew pass I had to make a formal request to the chief of police and, as all chiefs have to be real chiefs, this involved the cava ceremony. After I had been formally introduced and drunk my cava, I was summoned to join the chief under the tent and the minions were dispatched to check that there really was a foreigner about to give birth in the local hospital. So, he said in his best Sandhurst accent, "You need a curfew pass so that, if you have a boy, you can go and visit him?" "No, I need the pass to be there at the

birth." Not the Fijian way, it seems.

The midwives were fantastic, but after a week got a bit bored so we were transferred to the district hospital in Lambassa. An hour in a Landrover over dirt-track roads worked wonders and out he popped on arrival. It was too late to return, so we stayed overnight and returned in the same vehicle next day (and Sara managed all of that on two paracetamol!).

The tradition in Fiji is that the middle name is given by the village and parents have no say. Lots of suggestions all too long and ending in -onga, but when we got back the harbour master came to see 'the baby George'. Like Harry, the coup leader, George Speight, caused lots of problems and would not come out (of the Parliament building). We had already picked Harry as a boy's name, Harry George does not sound right, so he is Henry George Coxon on the birth certificate. And it was only after we got back to the UK that I found out his great-great-grandfather was... Henry George Coxon.

The update to this story is that ten years later in May 2011 they set off again with Harry aged 10.

THE BABY'S CAUL

A 'caul' was once hugely valuable. Midwives would sell them to sailors who believed if they wore one (in a locket) it would protect them from drowning. (The caul is part of the amniotic sac which can still be wrapped around the baby at birth. We still have my eldest son, Jack's, safely.)

A slightly more extreme version was practiced by the Woody and Ivanka presently exploring in the Eastern Med. "We took the placenta of each child out to sea and ritually sacrificed it to over the side to Poseidon with a drop of rum along with our hopes to the future."

ACCIDENTS

Vigilance, a berth with high-sided netting, children's harnesses and swimming lessons can keep the fear of drowning at bay. Babies cannot climb up the companionway. Most toddlers and children living aboard understand the dangers and obey the rules. When Jack and James fell in they were fooling around and forgot the rules. Both times an adult was in the water rescuing them before they sank. It is important to make the child know that they must not fall in again without making them fearful.

If small children are in the cockpit, the situation can be dangerous if small fingers are caught in the running rigging (ropes). Children should only be allowed on deck, if at all, when the boat is anchored. (Think of the damage a clew or flapping sail can do to an adult.) But if they are supervised, learning the ropes can be great fun.

Even safety equipment can become hazardous, for example small hands find the firing pins of fire extinguishers secured at table height extremely tempting. It is revealing to crawl around the boat at your child's height.

In Mahon, Menorca I was complimented by a mother who saw me helming with one hand, holding Jack in the other. Little did she know that Jack had squirmed out of his cockpit seat as we were anchoring, so I was just keeping him in one place.

Remember that children become used to their own boat: the companionway, the ankle and head knocking dangers. When they are on another boat, they may not know the dangers. Jack lived aboard from 8 months old. At 2½ he fell down a friend's companionway and bounced two more steps, because three parents missed catching him. Half an hour of ice packs and howling, and a large egg on his head, and he was fine. He was kept awake for another two hours to check he was fully compos mentis. Vigilance, always, all ways.

Realistically, with children, accidents do happen. You have to do your best with what you have at the time. Graham and Lorraine have been cruising on a catamaran with their son Lucas. Lorraine says: "Lucas jumped on a beanbag in Virgin Gorda and cracked his head on the side of the seat. Lots of blood, he needed stitches, but we just strapped it up. It healed up okay; will always be a little scar, but I am sure if he had stitches, it would have been the same outcome."

ILLNESS

Illness in babies and toddlers can become serious fast – though they can recover quickly too. If you are in an isolated anchorage you will have to rely on your own knowledge and medical supplies.

As a mother who has seen her child suffering the consequences of severe overheating, I recommend fans around the

FIVE USEFUL TIPS FOR PREPARING A BOAT FOR CHILDREN

1. Netting around the boat.
2. Wrapping the bottom of the travel cot around the companionway stops a child climbing
3. A 12-volt DVD player is a godsend
4. Sunscreen (at least factor 50) with a hat
5. Car seats for securing in the cockpit, cabin or car

Jack fascinated by dolphins off Ibiza holding onto the netted guardrail with his harness

boat, particularly above their bed, and cold flannels or dunks in the sea to keep them cool.

Do not underestimate the effect of heat and humidity on yourself and your children. Holidaying in a hotel or villa with air conditioning and a swimming pool is entirely different from living on a boat with wind scoops and fans. Keep everyone hydrated. If anyone starts seeing stars, make them drink more.

Incidentally, it is often those working on the boat who sweat hard as they fix batteries in the aft cabin or windlasses in the heat on the deck who forget to drink. Be aware of your own limitations. You may be in paradise, but the heat, looking after the children and helping with the boat can lead to breathing difficulties and palpitations. As parents you have to remain fit and proactive. If one of the parents becomes ill, the cruise unravels because a sailing boat and young children together are too much to handle safely on your own.

BERRIES & BEASTIES

As at home, children have to be warned about eating berries. In the tropics this

is particularly true. For example, the manchineel tree with its yellow-green apples grows on beaches. After a rain storm, the water falling from the tree is poisonous and causes blisters. Have a good look at the manchineel so as not to confuse it with the harmless sea grape.

Beware of snakes too. While in Oriental, South Carolina I was shocked when the dock master confirmed that the area around the walkway from the dock to the mainland had become the perfect breeding ground for water moccasins, deadly (for children), and rattlers, although it seems the rattlers were not so aggressive or deadly. I began to hear hissing in my head and every shadow coiled into a deadly reptile. I renamed the path to the dock Snake Alley. The children were ordered to walk in step with me or be carried.

If the children are rummaging in tropical undergrowth, be aware that they may come across beasts or plants that are poisonous or at least unfriendly. There's no use becoming paranoid, you'll see a rock fish in every pool. Just take care and be aware. You want to teach them about the Bimini Boa, a rare gem of a snake, but you don't want to breed too much familiarity.

BABY ON BOARD – OUR STORY

We set sail from Southampton, when Jack was exactly eight months old, armed with our top four baby books: *The Great Ormond Street Baby and Child Care Book, What to Expect in the First Year, The Haynes Manual: Baby: Conception to Two Years* and Annabel Karmel's *New Complete Baby & Toddler Meal Planner.* Just before leaving we also squeezed in a first aid course. Dr Gotham, our GP, and Caroline, the health visitor, were full of encouragement and advised on problems to look out for.

Once in the English Channel the fears I had sitting in friends' kitchens diminished. As a skipper and father John is far more cautious. On the trip across the Channel we made it easy by having two friends to help John. I could focus on Jack, literally 'mother watch'. Each time we sail offshore for the first 20 miles both John and I feel uneasy, even though we know the what-if scenario inside out, and are fully confident in the yacht, and each other. In conditions over a force 5, rocking and blustery, Jack's cabin is padded with a duvet or cushions.

I soon discovered that breast feeding a baby in his bulky lifejacket is a problem. I breastfed until Jack was one. Since I do not suffer from seasickness, I happily sat below with Jack, without his lifejacket, breastfeeding, sometimes at an angle of 45 degrees! By the time we left I did not need to steam sterilise. I used bottled water for the formula. My bulk buy of HIPP organic milk ran out after two months when I found alternatives in French and Spanish supermarkets. I took a Helios Homoeopathy basic kit, and extra chamomilla for teething. However, halfway through France during the eruption of some really mean molars I bought industrial-strength gel. Gesticulations and pointing to my howling son filled in where my dodgy French failed.

Although I am sometimes reduced to jars of baby food, I try to make Jack's food myself. I used a low-wattage, lightweight whizzer via our 300-watt inverter. Sadly, the bowl cracked. So I ground away with a manual mincer, bought in a French market. Unfortunately, Mr Mincey rusted and it was back to Mrs Fork-and-Elbow-Grease, until the purchase of a new sturdier low-wattage whizzer. Favourite whizzed yums have included nectarine baby rice, banana and chicken, red peppers and humous, mushrooms in milk and butter, and mashed potato with cheese or chicken. When I have the luxury of shore power in a marina I use the blessed microwave. When feeding Jack downstairs, I used the bumbo seat until, at about four months during a particularly energetic splatter fest, Jack twisted out of it. Since a high chair is impractical, he has a seat that attaches to the table.

With a little savvy and nouse many household items can be adapted. A blue, plastic storage box was a cheap answer for a bath. The garden spray hose attachment was a surprise bath time hit. Before he could walk the bouncer was a favourite, either hung from the boom or on the salon hatch in bad weather. His changing mat doubled as a cushioned floor. Items such as the camera and mugs of tea are kept out of range. Whether in port or at sea, if on deck Jack is secured to the yacht in his lifejacket or harness. A parasol is essential in the sun, either clamped above his seat in the cockpit, or ashore on the buggy. One very windy day did for our first parasol. Now, when it's blowing, we attempt the battle of hat and sunscreen.

On rainy days, just like at home, imagination and silly games are the only real answer to keeping Jack entertained – but a ball goes a long way. The bag of toys is constantly recycled, with forgotten toys re-appearing as 'new'. (An exasperated friend and yachtswoman claimed that an aircraft carrier would not be large enough to carry her daughter's clutter.) Space is at a premium, but *Seraphim* keeps revealing new crevices in which to store Jack's kit and toys, although I have to remember where I have put them... Everyday items also become toys – melamine plates, egg boxes and, top of Jack's list, four kitchen rolls in their plastic cover...

Eleven-month-old Jack made five 120-mile passages from Spain's Costa Brava via the Balearics to Gibraltar. Jack sleeps better on passage, otherwise up to a year old he would often wake at about 2 and 6am. On night watch we took turns, three hours on, three hours off, three hours on, then cat napping when we needed the next day. Including Jack in the night-watch-rest equation is difficult and exhausting, because the sleep catch-up time during the day is baby-watch time. In our semi-conscious state, we found songs went a long way, such as our version of One Man Went to Mow or Baby Jack went to sea, went to sail the Med, Baby Jack, Daddy-Mummy-lifejacket-winches-sails-liferaft...

To celebrate his first birthday and second Christmas we took two months out at home to visit grannies and friends. Since Jack did not have too many open places on the yacht to cruise, he climbed. His balance was amazing. Jack quickly realised that Granny's house did not rock, and he was up and away. Not toddle toddle bump, but walking.

On our return the netting across Jack's bunk had to be raised. He also had to relearn one hand for the yacht and one for you, which means putting down his bottle or toy. January on a yacht being buffeted against a dock in high winds and rain with a toddler is a challenge. Now Jack is older we have established the 'naughty spot' in the forward cabin where he sits for 30 seconds if he has committed a serious misdemeanour such as climbing out of the cockpit without his harness.

Jack washes the decks, aged one, Gibraltar

John and I know we made the right decision to set off again. With Jack our precious cargo, we are looking forward to a new and different adventure. Gradually we figured out a balance between baby, yacht, exploring and work. Cruising with Jack is a joy if we take our time.

To us Jack seems more alert and curious on the yacht. In Gibraltar he stood on the deck waving at the planes that landed 500 yards away. While sailing he can clap for the dolphins swimming beside us, or watch dazzling sunsets or squawk pointing at fish in clear waters. The yacht is Jack's home where, like any adored child, he has security and routine, and the love of his parents. In addition, we hope he will grow by being exposed to ever-changing surroundings, tastes, smells, languages and sights.

Source: Practical Parenting

'I DON'T LIKE IT'

That's a whine to drive parents mad, whether they're on a boat or on land. Children may have eclectic palettes and eat olives, clams and sugar cane, but sometimes even their favourites are rejected. They won't starve themselves, but they could cause their parents unnecessary angst.

It will help make life easier if, when provisioning, you can find tins that are a guaranteed favourite to help the first course go down. My bribe was Ambrosia custard; other mothers swear by baked beans or scrambled egg on toast. A two-in-one activity is making a cake with the children, which is fun and gives them the anticipation of cake after supper.

Be wary of barbequed food, which can be unpalatable for youngsters. Sitting at anchor with a pile of what they perceive as cremated chicken, wishing you'd cooked fish fingers (again), is not a happy place to be.

SAILING NANNIES

If you are missing the support network of friends and mothers you had at home, and if you have a spare berth, you could take on a sailing nanny. When Jack was 1 year old, and we were considering our sailing options, Stella, a trained nursery nurse and daughter of an RYA instructor, was keen to join us for experience plus bed and board.

Two years later when Jack was 3 and James 1, Elise, a student and skilled sailor, came to my exhausted aid as we were sailing around the Balearics. It worked well. She was on her father's boat and we were sailing in company. A few conversations with fellow yachties or sailing folk back home will find a keen youngster ready to join the family.

Crew agencies can supply nannies, but they will be more geared to superyachts. The Cruising Association (www.theca. org.uk) can advise members on potential crew or nannies. Both sides should agree on what is expected and who will pay for things like airfares and meals ashore; in both cases this will probably be you, unless an arrangement is made with the nanny's parents. You may only take a nanny on for a few weeks, but it could make the difference between finishing your cruise early and achieving a circumnavigation.

SCHOOLING

Between the ages of 5 and 15 is the best time to cruise with children, but it is also when their education begins in earnest. Are you going to be able to teach them?

Home schooling is an option, but it isn't the only one. From Antigua to the USA to Australia, cruisers often take a break for the winter or a term and put their children aged from 2 to 12 into school locally. If you can afford it, an international school is another possibility.

If your children have already attended school, their teachers may be willing to help with long-distance lessons. At least six months before departure, discuss your plans with the school and establish which home school system you believe works for you and your child.

If you're leaving from the UK there are many useful government services and information websites such as www.gov.uk/ home-education, www.gov.uk/national-curriculum and www.gov.uk/government/ organisations/department-for-education. Enough digging around on www.gov. uk could lead you to some ideas. Other helpful suggestions and pointers can come from the Home Education Advisory Site, www.heas.org.uk, or other sites including www.ahomeeducation.co.uk and www.

oxfordhomeschooling.co.uk.

In the USA, www.calverteducation.com and www.kidsource.com are popular sites for home school information.

In Australia, start with the Department of Education on www.education.gov.au, www.homeschoolingdownunder.com, www.hea.edu.au, www.aussieeducator.org.au.

In New Zealand, Te Kura (formerly The Correspondence School) (www.tekura.school.nz) provides distance education from early childhood to adults following the New Zealand Curriculum. For general enquiries, or more information on courses, enrolment and fees, email info@tekuraschool.nz.

In some countries, for example the Netherlands, it is a legal requirement to seek permission from the local Education Authority to remove your children from school, and you have to prove that they are being educated.

Teaching a child to read and write is not easy, but you get a hell of a kick when you both discover that from 'a' to 'c' and 'up' to 'down', the child is now reading *The Cat in the Hat*. There are numerous books to assist pre-prep school and early-years readers. It can be a challenge when one child is 5 and starting home school, and the other is a crazy-making 3. Either Daddy or the DVD should be employed to entertain and distract the younger child.

Some mothers like to be called 'Mrs...' during school hours to maintain discipline. It is not easy to instil a school environment on a boat in the tropics, so don't be surprised if your child is restless and wants, for example, to do lessons upside down. If you are cruising with other families and the children are of similar ages and mother tongue, and given the right mix of talents or knowledge, one parent can teach maths, another English and so on. If not a full-time routine, it can be a treat. Usually the children are keen to learn, or at least to finish lessons because they can then go to the beach or on an outing. An empty sandy beach helps the education go down easily. Sitting with children from three or more boats comparing reference books and discussing which type of whale, dolphin, fish or bird you have seen is one of life's most simple and amazing pleasures.

Although you need to ensure that your child keeps up academically, there should be a line between a rigid timetable and seizing the day. Perhaps an event ashore beckons, or the weather and tide are right for a dinghy ride to an unusual cave that by the afternoon will be inaccessible. Don't chain a child to their lessons.

When cruising, children will meet and interact with other children from widely varying backgrounds and cultures and take in the extraordinary on a regular basis. In St Lucia, new friends whom we met on the dock in the Rodney Bay Marina gave us our own tour (usually reserved for cruise ship clients) of their tropical garden. In Dominica, a day tour around the island gave us all an intimate insight into the plant, animal and life. The children tasted the M&Ms of the jungle, cocoa beans.

The most precious part of the child's education will be their log:

- It will help with learning such as drawing and labelling maps.
- It will assist them in learning to re-tell their experiences (which initially you will write down).
- It will become home to an eclectic collection of photographs, tickets, postcards, leaves and stickers.
- And it will become a priceless tale of your journey for you, your family and relations. It will also give the children at school some understanding of the new boy / girl's adventures. We wouldn't have abandoned ship without it. Whilst on logs, be aware that cruisers have found the files and course books required for school take up vital space on their boat.

Before 'Play Time', it is important to emphasise, again, that 'team effort and parent support' is essential to the success of cruising children's education.

PLAY TIME

Once you're in port or in harbour, after you've hit the beach, been swimming, snorkelled and been pulled on blow-up bananas, you could hang your offspring in the bosun's chair attached to the boom and swing them out over the water, or hoist them towards the spreaders, about 10 feet up the mast. These aren't activities that would pass health and safety regulations but, clipboard or not, you are in charge of your boat and your family.

WOLSEY HALL, OXFORD

One of the most widely recognised organisations for educating children on cruising yachts is Wolsey Hall, Oxford (wolseyhalloxford.org.uk). If you read the website you will see how it is possible to study for important exams whilst cruising, see 'how-homeschooling-works'. An important element of the courses leading to, for example, IGCSEs, is that the students learn to become 'independent learners'. The students have a tutor for each subject. The student has an initial introduction via Skype during which they learn how the tutor will guide the student through each subject. After that there is an on-line messaging system. They also have a Progress Manager who 'prepares an assignment schedule, monitors the student's progress, and keeps in close touch with both the student and the parents'. Wolsey Hall Oxford 'cannot stress the value of parental support during the courses too highly. This is a team effort'. A wide variety of subjects are offered.

BIRTHDAY IN BLACKBEARD'S BACKYARD

Jack was 5 years old on 7th November and James was 3 eight days later. On Jack's birthday the *Seraphim* crew set off on a treasure hunt with Captain Manley of Beaufort, North Carolina. He and the boys were in full regalia. Armed with detailed and historically researched treasure maps, the boys were led by Manley 40 steps north and 21 south (90 Jack steps) to discover numerous clues such as a noose, an arrow, a mallet, a logbook, and finally a large X in the sand under which they dug for... a chest with treasure.

Darroch and Yewan Wood enjoying the cruising life, here swimming in the Blue Lagoon, Malta

SOCIAL SKILLS

From the age of 5, social skills start becoming important and boat children of this age thrive. The disadvantages

of saying goodbye to children heading in other directions are outweighed by the wide and diverse experiences these children gain. As a palliative, you could arrange to meet in a few months a few thousand miles away. Often, it does actually happen.

By the age of 11 it is time to be thinking about secondary school, team playing and mixing with their peers. Again, what is true on land is just as true aboard. Children should be children, and too much time with adults makes little adults who find mixing it up with the rough and tumble of other children difficult. Sailing on the family boat or in dinghies can continue during the weekends and holidays.

Children on boats become more responsible and self-reliant. There are times when they have to look after themselves because their parents are busy working on the boat. In a storm they will be safe below or harnessed in the cockpit. Being out of the mainstream means that their imagination and alternative thinking will expand. They will be more open to a wider variety of unusual lessons. Although

THE INGRAM FAMILY

Mel Ingram says of the time she and Al spent with their daughters on an Atlantic Circuit:

To be able to share this travelling experience with the Ayla and Molly who were aged 9 and 6 years respectively was a privilege.

I found that initially routine and structure helped acclimatise us all to living in such close proximity and unchartered territory, but this was released and let go of by the end of the journey as we all had found our own coping mechanisms.

The biggest challenge was getting the girls to sit down daily for school lessons

once living in such heat. No matter how creatively these were approached, the

The Ingram family

best results were found when we learnt in bite-sized lessons on the go. I gave up the fight to keep the peace and found that the children motivated one another to learn by being given the space to choose.

I feel the trip required us to let go of expectations and live each day as it evolved, in the moment. At times, it was stressful when inevitable boating jobs arose, with floor boards exposing the bilge, children using up precious space to create dens, oil in buckets and hazards in every direction, heat and frayed tempers. I think we are all more resilient.

THE GIFFORD FAMILY

The Gifford family spent eight years circumnavigating. Behan wrote *Voyaging with Kids*. You can read of their travels on sailingtotem.com. Behan wrote:

We had high-paying jobs, dual income. It was so perfect and white-picket-fence it was almost painful. It makes your teeth hurt. Then in a two-week spell, our eldest daughter was born, and my husband's mother passed away. It was hard to see those milestones of life happening together. My mother-in-law was going to go traveling but she had cancer and literally died within weeks. It forced us to think about our priorities and what we wanted, and when Jamie and I met this was something we were always going to do. We had been telling people we were going to take our children on a boat and sail and we didn't know when we would be coming back, and we got some looks like, 'You're crazy'.

When we left, we felt exhilarated and euphoric. I couldn't believe it. It was something we had worked so long and hard for. It's such a crazy, different way of life from the outside. On one hand, we have given up so much to do this, but we have zero regrets. We barely saw each other before and now our family is very tight. We have had the most wonderful opportunity to experience the world with our kids.

The Gifford family

the internet gives more access than previous boat generations to 'whatever' youth culture, you can still keep them comparatively unspoilt but without turning them into freaks.

The picture is of John and me, with our children, and the Berendson children, Alec and Katie. We sailed in company with the Sergei and Isabelle Berendson from the Caribbean to Virginia, USA. Isabella says of their trip, "I found our trip has unbreakably bonded us as a family."

A typical dinghy ride with friends in St Martin

PETS

Are you going to take your pets with you when you sail away? Dogs can be useful as guard dogs, but they will need walking, so a large dog may not be a good choice. Both cats and dogs can become seasick, in which case they curl up and become sadder and sadder.

A few questions to ponder:

- Will the animal be allowed off the boat in the countries you are visiting?
- Do you have stowage space for bags of dog or cat food and kitty litter?
- If the cat cannot adapt to life at sea, how long will you struggle on with cat sick and wee in the boat?
- On islands where it is tough enough finding good medical attention for humans, will you find a vet?
- How do you feel about the interior of your boat getting ripped up by claws?
- How do you feel about a cat litter tray on your deck? (One extreme cat lover converted one of their two heads into a cat lavatory.)
- How would you feel if they fell overboard and you could not rescue them? (Some boats have a carpet hanging off the transom, so the cat can swim around, and hopefully claw their way up.)
- How wretched will you feel when your cat goes missing?

A distraught cat owner knocking boat to boat is heart wrenching. The good news is that, after days of the desperate owner searching, the cat usually re-appears from a secret nook, or from spending time on other yachts. One ginger Tom in English Harbour, Antigua worked a stay-a-night along the boats berthed at the dockyard. Each boat believed they were the one and only, until each discovered they were merely a one-night stand.

After endless discussion I left my three Burmese cats with my mother before casting off.

IRENKA & WOODY WOOD

For Irenka and Woody their circumnavigation with their three children is starting in the Eastern Mediterranean.

Irenka and Alan 'Woody' Wood met as skippers on a flotilla for Neilson Active Holidays. They lived a carefree life in Greece and Croatia, 'constantly skint, but life was easy-going, fun and wonderfully irresponsible.' When they discovered they were expecting a child they made a vow that they would return to this life with their children. Whilst they prepared to make their dream come true they ran an RYA Centre, Irenka crewed for the RNLI and became the first beach lifeguard coxswain in Brighton. After many 'trials and tribulations' Irenka and Woody and their three children have escaped on a 1997, 53' Amel *Super Maramu*. Presently they are in Greece. Woody declared from his idyllic Grecian anchorage, "We are living proof that selling up and sailing away is not just the preserve of the wealthy retirees, but an achievable goal, even for families with young children. For, sure, it is hard work... We have earnt every rivet, bolt and split pin on our yacht with blood, sweat, tears and sheer determination. Our yacht maybe 20 years old and she may be in need of restoration and constant repair, but she is now our family home, our school, our work place and the key to a lifestyle we promised ourselves all those year ago."

5

TIME TO GO

It's all very well reading the sailing magazines and books and doing endless planning, but there comes a time when you just have to go. It is a testing time on all levels, but keep in mind what Captain Joshua Slocum, the first man to sail around the world on his own, said on his return: 'As for ageing, why, the dial on my life was turned back till my friends all said, "Slocum is young again".'

This chapter looks at choosing and managing your crew, blessing your boat, and adapting to the weather.

CREW

Dame Ellen MacArthur sailed a 22.9-metre trimaran solo around the world in 71 days at the age of 28. For the rest of us mere sailing mortals, a boat that size requires a crew before it leaves the pontoon. Most cruising boats can be handled by two people, but it's better to have a third set of hands. Some couples prefer to rely on themselves, thinking that a third person would be intrusive and hoping that technology such as AIS (Automatic Identification System) and a radar alarm will be sufficient. Others don't feel safe without extra crew. If you are passage making, sailing night after night, a third crew member can be helpful and prevent the fatigue that leads to accidents.

There is no escape at sea, so choose any crew carefully and ask lots of questions. How well can your crew member sail?

Are they great company in the cockpit, as well as reliable in a storm? How well does your best friend work and fit in as a crew member, on land and at sea? Certainly, one Atlantic crossing was marred when the best friend of the husband-skipper, who was a delight ashore, at sea referred to the skipper's wife, an experienced sailor, as 'the cook'.

Can you give orders to them? Will they take orders from you? Many skipper-crew relations founder when the crew ignore the skipper's orders, or 'use their initiative', such as changing the sail plan without consulting the skipper. If possible, and you should really try to make it possible, have a shake-down sail with your crew. Not just a weekend or a week's holiday with day sails, but at least five days at sea. This will open up the cracks. And, if you decide not to take someone, be prepared to sit down and tell them. There is no point in prevaricating or hoping it will get better. All those who have had misgivings about their crews before they leave and have not sorted it out have deep regrets after two weeks at sea.

Do your crew have relevant qualifications? If not, for how many years have they sailed? Can they navigate? Do they have a first aid qualification? Are they willing to go on extra courses? Have they been on a sea survival course? Have they worked with the systems on your boat? You may want a crew member whose knowledge complements yours, such as an engine mechanic or a doctor.

Rob, an ocean-crossing skipper, remarked that one of his best crew was an engineer who was also an excellent cook. Charles, another ocean-crossing skipper, had sailing friends who were an anaesthetist, an engineer and a navigator.

It's unpleasant but true that skippers on superyachts have been known to order their female crew in terms of 'Two blondes, size 8'.

CREW COSTS

Who is paying for the crew's flights? That would be you, for a professional crew. Are you, the skipper, going to repatriate your crew? It seems obvious, but crews should have valid passports and visas for the whole time they are on the boat, for example the passport should be valid on arrival and departure in Gibraltar, and the Canaries and St Lucia.

Who is paying for what ashore? Who is paying for the provisions? Watch out for extra charges that crews incur, for example breakages or – an odd one, admittedly, but expensive – in the dockyard in English

Harbour, where a charge for each crew member per day was due for rubbish collection.

YOUR ROLE

Your role as skipper is more than giving orders as you cast off. If your crew are unpaid, as a good skipper you are obliged to honour the agreements you've made. Once you've arranged for your crew to join you in Gibraltar and they have booked their flights, you have to go to Gibraltar. If you have booked them a few months in advance and you change your plans and ask them to fly to the Canaries, you explain why, and pay the new fares.

Before you take your crew on, establish how long they are going to stay and set a date for them to leave. It is too late when you arrive at your destination. You, as skipper, are legally responsible for them and what they get up to. Regulations are strict concerning crew if they are no longer registered to the boat on which they sailed into a port. An arrival in Antigua turned sour when a crew member claimed that the owners were kicking her off the boat. They were not, they had children a little older than her and felt protective, but one week had been agreed in Gibraltar before the girl joined the boat and they did not wish to be in a hotel for more than a week. The girl found a position elsewhere (looking for a size 8 blonde).

PAPER TRAIL

Get the paper trail correct, or it could become a trial. Make sure that your crew have the necessary documentation to allow them into the country where they are joining the boat. If they have a single ticket into the country, ensure that they have documentation to present to customs officials proving that they are coming to crew on your boat, which is based in, or, in transit at a particular marina. Be conversant with the rules of the particular country or island.

Rudyard Kiplings poem, *The Smugglers Song* is all well by the fireside: 'Them that asks no questions they isn't told a lie, Watch the wall, my darling, while the Gentlemen go by!' But, in 21st century sailing, make sure your documentation is in good order and that the crew know that illegal extras are not allowed.

ACCIDENTS & INSURANCE

Who is liable for crew injuries if they happen on your boat? Are you insured for crew accidents? If you, the skipper, become sick, can your crew cope? It is questionable how many wives could take over sailing from their husband-skippers if they were to become incapacitated.

CREW MANUAL

Before a long passage the skipper must take the crew on a thorough and in-depth tour of the boat, at least twice to ensure that the information sinks in, and stays in. Make sure that each member of crew has read the crew manual that you have prepared. This briefing can be repeated in full or in part if you feel a crew member has not quite grasped all they need to know. Be really sure that everyone understands how to perform their tasks. They could be a hazard to you, the boat and themselves if they are not clear about how to carry out their duties.

Before departure it is also essential (possibly a life-saving necessity) to have a man-overboard drill involving all members of the crew, in which everyone has to take control of the boat and haul a fender out

of the water.

A cruising yacht can quickly become a pressure cooker, so make sure that you have tried and tested your crew. To build on the good understanding engendered by the shake-down cruise, write down what you want from them. The best way to prevent your expectations grating against your crew's misunderstandings is to have a contract or at least a list of expectations, drawn up by mutual consent.

Ports rot ships and men.
Attributed to Horatio Nelson

Do the crew understand that, if they want to go clubbing, they have to be capable of preparing the boat for an Atlantic crossing from 9am to 6pm in the hot sun?

In Tenerife, at nine in the morning, two young stags strutted down the pontoon after a got-lucky night, anticipating collapsing into their bunks to sleep it off. Sue, the skipper, had insisted that whatever they did with whoever on their night out, she wanted them fully functioning at 8am. Irate, she threw them off the boat. Later that evening they were allowed back on (not because they were forgiven, but because they were her son and nephew).

Do your crew realise how hard they have to work both before and after the crossing?

Do emphasise that drugs are not allowed on board. If anyone on your vessel is caught with drugs, your vessel will be impounded, and you could face jail along with the culprit. In certain islands the authorities and drugs dealers are in league, but either way, corrupt or not, you will be the loser.

Cigarette stubs wreck decks. If you are going to allow smoking, establish when and where crew are allowed to smoke. If you are banning smoking, make sure that your crew know. A smoker going cold turkey on a long voyage is not good for morale, even if they make for manic deck scrubbers.

The crew of Seraphim, John and Nicola Rodriguez, with brother and sister Ashley and Emony Nicholls, the author's Canadian cousins, about to set off from Tenerife

WATCHES

Each skipper has their preference: some prefer a long watch such as six hours on, with two crew keeping watch, then six hours off, which means two watches per two crew members per 24-hour period. Alternatively, four hours on and four off is less arduous. Remember, the shorter the watch, the shorter the time to a) get to sleep and b) sleep. An overnight trip is much more tiring than a three or four-day passage. By the third day you are adapting and will find yourself in the groove of the watch system.

A skipper was shocked to discover a crew member had been watching a DVD on watch. Not only did it reduce his focus on regularly watching out for shipping, but it severely affected his ability to see anything when he did look up, as his night vision was shot. Explain exactly what you will accept in terms of behaviour.

If it is a night watch, it is a kindness to wake the next watch up with a cup of tea, or at least have one ready for them in the cockpit. Once the next watch is alert and receptive, give them a full brief on the situation. It is on night watch that the briefing in port comes home to roost. A crew member did not realise that the thing digging in her back was the bilge pump. As she came off a four-hour watch she mentioned it to the skipper, who found the bilge full of water. The situation was saved, but it was a salutary lesson in being doubly sure that your crew are fully acquainted with and understand the boat, inside and out.

DEALING WITH SEASICKNESS

The old saying goes that at first you think you're going to die, and then you wish you had. Over the hundreds of years that humans have set sail, scores of remedies for seasickness have been developed.

Nausea and sickness are caused by the brain's inability to resolve the mixed messages from the eyes, ears and body caused by the changing equilibrium engendered by the movement of the boat. Others attribute seasickness to the forces created by the earth's rotation (Coriolis forces) or disturbance in cerebro-spinal fluid and the cerebellum.

'Mal de mer' can take two forms: either the sufferer becomes pale, feels nauseous, perhaps turns green and vomits; or, more insidiously, they start feeling drowsy and increasingly lethargic. The latter can be dangerous as crew become severely dehydrated and lose concentration. One skipper almost walked off the boat into the ocean because he was hallucinating.

Prevention is better than cure. Try to avoid sailing with a hangover and too full a stomach. Keeping yourself hydrated helps, so drink lots of bottled water. Reading books or watching DVDs can promote seasickness, as can alcohol – beware the sun-downer.

Some say that keeping cool helps, other sufferers want a warm sleeping bag. Obvious but still worth stating, if you can keep away from those being sick it helps, although that's not easy on a yacht. Try to keep calm as, ironically, being anxious about being sick can exacerbate the problem.

Most experts stay up top and look at the horizon or take the helm, it helps to concentrate on the job. When 'riding the waves', the sufferer sits upright and moves with the motion of the boat, rocking backwards and forwards or round in circles.

Another school of seasickness says to lie on the cabin floor or in the saloon in the centre of the boat where the movement is comparatively stable. If you take to your cabin, try to wedge yourself in with duvets and pillows so that your body can relax and not roll around.

Ginger is a favourite remedy, in the form of ginger biscuits, ginger beer or ginger tea. Flat Coca-Cola is also said to help. Among the array of tablets available are:

- Dramamine with active agent dimenhydrinate
- Stugeron with active agent cinnarizine
- Bonine with active agent meclizine hydrochloride
- Marezine with active agent cyclizine

Most sufferers say that if one active agent does not work, another probably will. These are only effective if taken between twenty minutes and half an hour before you leave shore.

Exercise caution if you are on watch and find these cures sleep making. Drinking alcohol with drugs for seasickness has caused drowsiness and double vision, so, as ever, read the information fully.

Start your day the Stugeron way. I took two of these ultimate seasickness pills before I went to bed and woke up floating six inches off the ground. You might be sick, but you wouldn't care.

Sandi Toksvig, Island Race: An Improbable Voyage Round the Coast of Britain

You could also try a sea band, an elastic band that has a stud that applies pressure to the Neiguan acupuncture point, above the wrist joint, which is said to control nausea and vomiting.

LAND SICKNESS (MAL DE DEBARQUEMENT)

After a length of time at sea you can still feel the motion of the boat even when on solid dry land. 'Land sickness' or 'mal de debarquement' is bizarre and usually feels more like giddiness than seasickness. As with the moving boat causing mixed messages to the brain that cause seasickness, so the sudden stillness causes the brain confusion again. While the brain is becoming re-accustomed to land, the giddiness or queasiness could return.

The best cure for land sickness is to sit under a tree.

OTHER PRACTICALITIES

YOUR FLAG OF REGISTRY

It is important to have a flag of registry to fly from the back of the boat. The British flag of registry is the Red Ensign. You can be registered on the Small Ships Register (SSR), which is easy and inexpensive, or the more expensive, and involved, Part 1 Registration. Most cruisers opt for Part 1. Most nations carry their national flags, for example, USA, Spain and the Netherlands.

A British-registered boat sailing in a foreign country is governed by that nation's laws. If you decide to stay beyond the time allowed by the law of the country, you could become subject to the local laws and taxes. You, as the owner, are responsible for finding out about the local regulations and how they are applied. It could be very expensive to have to start paying local taxes or, worse, have your boat impounded for remaining illegally. www.noonsite.com is a good resource.

It is useful also to have the International Certificate of Competence (ICC) in pleasure craft operation, which is recognised by 40 countries. The certificate is translated into nine languages. Some countries do not formally accept the certificate but still want to see it. Some insist on it if using their inland waterways.

BLESSING THE BOAT

There is no specific yacht blessing ceremony because they are tailor-made for each occasion.

A blessing can be based on the blessing of a home in the *Pastoral Prayer*, published by Mowbray, giving it a nautical twist with the addition of Psalm 107:

They that go down to the sea in ships,
That do business in great waters;
These see the works of the Lord,
and his wonder of the deep.
For he commandeth, and raiseth the
stormy wind,
Which lifteth up the waves thereof.
They mount up to the heaven,
They go down again to the depths:
Their soul is melted because of trouble.
. . .
He maketh the storm a calm,
So that the waves thereof are still.

Then they are glad because they be quiet;
So he bringeth them unto their desired
haven.
Psalm 107, Verses 23–30,
King James Bible

St Brendan, the Navigator's prayer is also appropriate. (St Brendan 484-577AD. An Irish Monk from Kerry, ship builder and explorer. It is said his voyage to America probably via Iceland and Greenland, inspired Christopher Columbus.)

Dear Lord

Beyond these shores
And into the unknown

Beyond these shores
This boat may sail

I know this is Your way

And that there will be
A path across this sea.

Dear Lord if I sail beyond
The farthest ocean

Or am afraid of the depths below

I know that wherever I may go
Your love surrounds me

For You have been before
Beyond these shores.

Amen

If you have a friendly vicar, he or she may be willing to take time out from a busy schedule to conduct the blessing. Reverend Michael Turner, who married us and baptised our first son, brought holy water to *Seraphim's* berth in Ocean Village. As ever, 'our' vicar brought his gift of insight, dignity and humour to the official ship's blessing, during which prayers were said and holy water sprinkled around our new home. It was an intimate, profound and moving service, followed by a jolly lunch.

Seraphim, blessed and ready to sail

DE-NAMING

Having very much felt in peril on the sea and mindful of Neptune's wrath, we performed a complex ritual to de-name our second boat. All papers and items relating to the previous name were removed. (Some people go as far as sanding the name off.) Neptune and the gods of the wind were thanked for their favour thus far, and the boat was de-named.

After waiting 12 hours for the old boat to clear, we celebrated by re-naming our new home *Seraphim*. In a blatant effort to curry favour with all the necessary powers that watch over us, expensive champagne was poured over the bow in both ceremonies, saving a few glasses to celebrate the re-naming. Have a look online for suitable forms of words for de-naming ceremonies.

FAREWELL PARTY

With all the preparations for departure, it is wise to arrange a farewell party at least a week before your anticipated departure. By the time your leaving date comes into view you will be increasingly frazzled. The closer the deadline, the faster time moves and the higher the tension. Allow yourself time to enjoy your farewells. Have a cracking send-off, then return to ticking off your lists.

Many long-time cruisers recommend having a party the day before you leave, then be prepared to sail as far as the anchorage next door and have a rest.

WEATHER & WINDS

Weather and tide are non-negotiable. Before you sail away, you have to understand how weather works, how to read weather information and understand how it will affect you. You no longer have work, traffic and the school run. Now, as a cruiser, you are bound by the weather, wind and tides. You can choose to ignore a cold front and get thumped, or you can wait for it to pass. It is best to learn to adapt to the weather, otherwise you will just find yourself continually frustrated. It takes a while, but gradually, if you have allowed for weather and maintenance delays, you can make the most of the waiting time by going on a shore excursion. Every pilot guide and cruising companion for every region will guide the reader on what to expect and when in each area. However, the prevailing wind may not be complying, or the weather may be unseasonal.

As you graduate through the RYA sailing courses, the information on weather, winds and tide becomes more complex and thorough. *The Sailor's Book of the Weather* by Simon Keeling and *Weather at Sea* by David Houghton are a good start as recommended reading.

Remember that time spent in reconnaissance is never wasted. Research what the prevailing winds and currents may be at the time of year you intend being in a particular area. What is the Meltemi? The Mistral? The Tramontana? Which direction do they come from? When? What speed? Where can you hide? And what are the local anomalies?

An El Niño year dramatically changes weather patterns in the Pacific and Atlantic. How will it affect your cruise? Will your winter in the sun be cold and a wash-out? How will the hurricane or cyclone patterns be interrupted?

Once aboard and sailing, you can hear weather forecasts via BBC Radio 4's (92–94 FM or 198 Long Wave) shipping forecast. Further from inland UK waters, there is the BBC World Service, VHF radio transmissions or weather radio (particularly in the USA), or you can download weather forecasts from the internet via mobile or satellite phone, or via Navtex if you have a suitable receiver. There are numerous weather-related websites, including:

- www.metoffice.gov.uk (UK MetOffice)
- www.bbc.co.uk/weather/coast_and_sea/shipping_forecast (BBC)
- www.noaa.gov (US National Oceanographic and Atmospheric Administration)
- www.navcen.uscg.gov (US Coastguard, weather, safety, navigation)
- www.notmar.gc.ca (Canadian Coast Guard)
- www.passageweather.com (Weather Forecasts for Sailors and Adventurers)
- www.weatheronline.co.uk (WeatherOnline Ltd., Meteorological Services)
- www.sxmcyclone.com (Sxm Cyclone, a French site)
- www.bom.gov.au (Australian Government Bureau of Meteorology)

As you sail along different coasts, the radio stations may change, so always check with marinas or in pilot books what the next frequency will be. If you do not speak the local language, ask if and when there is a version in English. (Some people record the transmission and ask for it to be translated.) If you are reading a weather forecast in a foreign language, make sure you know the correct words for weather. Do not fudge this as it could cost you dearly. If you are crossing Biscay, the Atlantic or the Pacific, be clear how you are going to receive your weather information. The Weather page on www.noonsite.com has numerous good suggestions.

WEATHER IN THE PACIFIC

Bob McDavitt the 'weather guru', is agreed to be excellent on weather in the Pacific. He is now in semi-retirement, but, you can contact him through www.metbob.com.

GRIB FILES

GRIB files (from GRIdded Binary) are data files showing the changing direction of the wind and wind strength. Some people like to have the raw information and incorporate it with their own knowledge, others prefer to have it interpreted by forecasters with superior meteorological experience. Use and abuse of GRIB files is an ongoing discussion among long-term cruisers, and one that is unlikely to be resolved. Remember that if you misjudge the information on the GRIB file, you will pay for it with a bad passage.

KEEPING IN TOUCH

Smartphones, (mere) mobiles, tablets and laptops make staying in touch much more simple. Whatever system you use, make sure it has been installed correctly on the boat, well tested on the boat and that you fully understand how to operate it.

Boats crossing the Atlantic can give daily updates via satellite phone or can be fitted with a specialist tracking device from Yellowbrick (www.ybtracking.com). Daily information and messages can be sent with news about everything from halyard and sail disasters to weather, fishing and bread making. Information and emails can be downloaded throughout Europe and the Caribbean. Some ocean sailors call home and have emails read to them. Several cruisers have recommended having a laptop which is only used for navigation and weather. They like to keep it 'clean' without too much memory or applications to clog up space. A dedicated laptop avoids any unregulated downloads.

Communications equipment seems to change with the tide, so keep reading the sailing forums (ask questions) and the sailing magazines which run regular articles with the results of tests for the latest equipment. If using a Sat Phone, I agree with skippers recommending an external antenna fixed permanently on deck which helps resolve connection issues. Of course, whichever stand you stop at during Boat Shows will give you the benefits of their external antenna or sat coms over the next-door stand. Since the first edition of this book, several generations of phones and sat coms have come and gone. At the time of writing, I am reading a message on WhatsApp giving me information about tracking a friend returning from the Caribbean via the Azores, on https://forecast.predictwind.com/tracking/display … right now, 'blue skies, F4, 7knts, 1,200 miles in 9 days', from his pilot house in the Atlantic to my boat in the Solent.

Airline pilots have noted that, since the advent of wi-fi, anchoring patterns have changed, particularly in the Caribbean, as yachts are drawn to the magic circle.

SATELLITE PHONES

It is wise when cruising to carry a satellite phone. The most effective way is to have it wired into the boat. Some cruisers prefer a mobile version, which may not be as clear as the static handset but it can be taken into a liferaft. Satellite phone companies include Iridium and Inmarsat.

FILE COMPRESSION

Companies such as Mailasail in the UK provide services such as an email compression system, which helps reduce satellite or mobile phone bills. There is also a web diary service for cruisers. Go to www.mailasail.com and read through the blogs for a little inspiration. There are plenty of other communication solutions, so shop around for what suits your boat, budget and itinerary.

AMATEUR RADIO (HAM RADIO)

Using a single sideband (SSB) radio used to be a popular means of communicating between boats, particularly in the Caribbean and the Pacific. It was a good way to hear news of other people, as the channels can be listened to by anyone. A lovesick couple on two different boats communicated on a channel known only to themselves at certain times. This remained secret for all of a week before others discovered and listened in avidly.

The 'propagation' area and quality of receiving depend on weather and other atmospheric forces, and the quality of your 'set'. As mobile phone networks become more efficient and economical, the use of SSBs is decreasing in the Caribbean, although SSB fans keep the nets running during the winter season, including the Ocean Cruising Club Net. In the USA schedules can be found on www.nws. noaa.gov/om/marine. Different nets cover different areas.

A licence is required to operate an amateur radio. The foundation exam, for the entry level, is a multiple-choice test. If you want to work at higher powers, there are intermediate and advanced licences. The Radio Society of Great Britain (www. rsgb.org) can provide more information.

SSB radio courses for boats are run by numerous companies, which can be found on the internet, in the back of sailing

John on the radio

magazines or through the RYA. If you are sailing away with a rally, ask the organisers if they offer a course. Most cruisers who have used the SSB to good effect advise becoming thoroughly familiar with the device before you leave.

POST

If you are a member of a yacht club with affiliates, you might ask if you could use their address. In some locations, post offices still offer a poste restante service where they keep your post for a certain time. If possible, near birthdays and Christmas, have a guest fly out with all the goodies, including Christmas pudding and cake.

If you are having your post sent out to you, be very sure that you are going to be there for at least two weeks either side of the due date – and then check again. Delays are inevitable.

BLOGS, FACEBOOK, TWITTER, INSTAGRAM, WHATSAPP ET AL

Setting up and writing a blog keeps everyone informed and can be an outlet for your self-expression. Remember, though, that if you choose to confide in your blog as you may in a personal diary, friends will still be reading your spontaneous mid-Atlantic rant in the cold light of weeks later. Even if you don't update the blog every day, friends and relations really appreciate reading about your adventures. Many have said that they live vicariously through sailing blogs, and it is also an invaluable record of the cruise for you. You can create your own website or use a platform such as www.GetJealous.com, set up for Jason and Fiona Harvey on *Trenelly* when they set off in 2002, which has become a huge success for its creators.

Social media is a great way to communicate quick messages and keep in touch with numerous friends in numerous places. If you don't want to keep an official blog, you can upload messages and albums onto Facebook, Instagram, Twitter, etc. of your travels for all to view. Ways of communicating are constantly changing so these examples reflect where we are at the time of going to press.

SHORE SUPPORT, SURE SUPPORT

Having shore support is essential: a reliable close relation or friend who can be trusted with your post and what is left behind. They should be able to send a FedEx package with a replacement credit card or send a parcel to a collection address. Choose someone who does not become flustered when reading numbers or checking bank accounts, particularly over the phone to you on a bad connection. Shore support would be the person you call if you want your emails read to you: are they willing to do that? (You may want to reconsider why you are receiving emails at this time.)

DROPPING THE LINES

So, it is time to drop the lines, head out to sea and discover more about life aboard: for better – exploring new countries, making new friends among the cruising community, tasting new food in the local markets and experiencing brilliant sunsets pretty much everywhere; and for worse – maintenance and laundry, bad weather and storms. Whether your cruise is a time to explore from place to place and have a great time or a voyage of deeper spiritual understanding, let's sail away.

POSTCARDS FROM THE KEDGE

Peter and Sue Bringloe have spent six seasons in the Caribbean on their Dix 38. They took time out from cruising. They now live between the UK and Caribbean. (See Best of Both Worlds). Sue Bringloe wrote:

Dear Nicola

Here are my favourite anchorages:

- St Annes, Martinique
- Le Borg, Les Saintes
- Admiralty Bay, Bequai
- Hillsborough, Carriacou
- English Harbour, Antigua

Nicola Rodriguez
The Yacht Moonshine
Harbour Town Marina
Cape Canaveral
USA

Best wishes
Sue

6

LIFE ABOARD

The cruising life is not an endless holiday, it is about discovery on all levels – including about yourself. Necessity and flexibility are the twin mothers of invention.

This chapter looks at what you can expect from life on board, ranging from the inevitable maintenance to our favourite recipes, health issues, how to welcome guests and cruising superstitions.

A sign in the Florida Keys, USA

MAINTENANCE

One definition of cruising is fixing boats in exotic places. Most cruisers can chart their voyage from start to finish by where they had to stop to fix a problem or wait for repairs. Each port will be a place to explore the workings of your boat and the new town, in that order, often while in search of a part. The hits keep coming, from the overheating engine in Dartmouth, to boiling batteries in Cameret sur Mer (Brittany, France), to the sail repair in La Coruña (northern Spain), the engine part in the rias (northern Spain) and more repairs in Gibraltar

Our water pump which was repaired after it broke between Gibraltar and Tenerife in the middle of the night

Cruising is fixing boats in exotic places: John working on a winch on Moonshine in Spanish Town, Virgin Gorda, British Virgin Islands

Whether you have crossed the Atlantic or stayed in the Med, you will probably be seeking out mechanics in Antigua or Torrevieja. It is part of cruising and usually the first topic of conversation between cruisers. The tighter the deadline to fix the boat, the higher the tension. By Gibraltar, skippers with the Atlantic crossing on their horizon are strung pretty tight and bursts of blue steam come from engine rooms and cockpits.

Jeanne Socrates, the oldest woman to complete a circumnavigation, solo, unassisted from North America, said when she was first mounting the steep learning curve of sailing solo, that she was assisted in fixing electrical or engine problems, by her knowledge of maths and physics, and that that she would be 'determined' to 'find a way to get it fixed'.

Dee Caffari MBE, like Jeanne Socrates a teacher, changed careers and became the first woman to sail solo, non-stop, around the world against the prevailing winds and currents. Caffari was awarded an MBE in recognition of this achievement.

Now, we're not all solo circumnavigators, but, it is remarkable when the batteries are down, what can be achieved.

A copy of Pat Manley's *Simple Boat Maintenance* could become a very useful on-board reference.

Also, Nigel Calder's *Boatowner's Mechanical and Electrical Manual* and *Marine Diesel Engines*.

You should be prepared to carry a small chandlery on the boat, including parts and

A SINKING FEELING

Freddie and Jacqui Rose crossed the Atlantic on *Shavora*, a Moody 39, arriving after twenty-six days in Guadaloupe. They sailed to Antigua where they discovered water under the floor boards, three times. Each time they went to work. The fourth time, they creatively worked out a method of replacing the seacock with Freddie scuba diving outside and Jacqui working from within, fast. They practised the manoeuvre and succeeded.

Oh, my goodness, we were euphoric! Jumping around the deck, high-fiving each other, running with our t-shirts over our heads in delirium that these 2 novice sailors, who spent most of their lives behind a desk, could actually pull off changing and installing a full through-hull / seacock whilst floating on the water!!! And so our faith in ourselves was restored and we continued on our journey.

You can follow Freddie and Jacqui on Facebook on the Shavora Project.

TROUBLE IN PARADISE

We spent a month in St Maarten working on the boat and recorded the difficulties in a newsletter to friends and family.

Learning to anchor Moonshine was easy in comparison to learning to live 24/7 on her in one place for a month. The vent, the walk-it-off shore was not there. It was a learning curve in pushing through the tensions and reconciling difficulties together. The idyllic, beautiful havens, the stress-less life, the time to write, paint, read, 'do-all-those-things', where were they? Not around Moonshine in Simpson Bay. The Caribbean maintenance regime was the pay-off for our hurried departure. However, it was far cheaper in Dutch St Maarten than with the pirates of Fareham Creek, Hampshire.

We have come across many 'angels', people who help us when we really need it, be it important information or lifts in a car or gifts of equipment. With an urgent need for cooking gas, provisioning and laundry, on one occasion we took a berth for the night, seemingly the last in Nassau (Bahamas). When John tried to negotiate the inflated $50 fee he was told that if he asked again the price would go up. However, the kind deckhand Alex made up for this hard bargaining by offering to drive us about. I am sure if ten years ago I had seen myself delighted to find a good laundry or a McDonald's with wi-fi and a playground, I would have shaken my head in disbelief.

tools. After a year of cruising the spares list changes from expensive sunglasses (which have fallen overboard) to alternators, fan belts, impellers, jubilee clips, oil filters and a water pump. Do not underestimate or throw out the 'use-one-day' box, since time and again, shortly after you throw something out, you will need it. It really is best not to choose the cheap option.

A hippy bus company, Green Tortoise based in San Francisco, California had the motto: 'Arrive inspired, not dog tired.' Sometimes the maintenance will get to you, but a beautiful sunset, a cracking sail or a sublime anchorage will re-inspire you.

COOKS & BOTTLE WASHERS

For those on superyachts and motorboats, cooking on board is very similar to cooking ashore. For those living on a yacht it is more of a challenge, although extremely good food can be prepared on a yacht and not just in harbour.

There were some great meals on our boat, although the anarchist oven did sometimes win. One half of the turkey cooked and not the other? Keep calm. Radio to Daddy to keep the children on the beach. Give the grown-ups another drink. Turn the turkey around and cook the other side.

Rum cake was my currency for thank-yous. One sail on a windy day through Drake's Passage in the British Virgins, the cake went into the oven, the wind got up and we were heeled right over. The cake emerged on a slant, which was at least a talking point.

For a long-term sailor, provisioning a yacht is not just about shopping in a supermarket. It is also about finding a supermarket and transporting your victuals back to the boat, avoiding lettuces falling out of the bag and floating off or sinking. It can take all day. The key is making the best of what you have and being imaginative.

Here is a selection of the best recipes we have come across for life aboard.

Annabelle Ingram and her husband made an eight-year circumnavigation including the Mediterranean, Caribbean, Pacific, Australasia. Here are two recipes from Annabelle.

Fish in a Vermouth and Cream Sauce

We always carry a bottle of dry Martini, which is great with ice with or without tonic. In this recipe people have difficulty placing the flavour, which is delicious.

Ingredients

- Firm fish fillets (works well with salmon)
- Grated rind of lemon or lime
- Butter or olive oil for sautéing
- Dry vermouth
- Fish stock cube
- Chives
- Double cream
- Salt and pepper

Instructions

- Season fish fillets and sprinkle with lemon rind.
- Sprinkle lavishly with vermouth and sauté gently till cooked.
- Add enough vermouth to make a sauce, then a little fish stock and thicken with cream.
- Garnish with chives or spring onions.

Baked Bean Hot Pot with Sausages

Quick and easy, only one pan to wash and tins are a great standby.

Ingredients

- Tin of baked beans (or other tinned beans)
- Sausages or a tin of hot dogs
- Onion, chopped
- Garlic, crushed
- Tin of chopped tomatoes, drained and juice reserved
- Tomato puree
- Herbs
- Dash of red wine
- Salt and pepper

Instructions

- Cut sausages into chunks and partially cook (omit this stage if using hot dogs).
- Fry onion with garlic in olive oil.
- Add all other ingredients and add reserved juice as necessary.
- Simmer gently for about 15 minutes until sausages are cooked through.

This comes from Clive Woodman and Angela Lilienthal on *Cosmic Dancer*, who have sailed extensively through the Baltic, Caribbean, North West Greenland into the Arctic, Canadian and US East and NW coasts. They are presently in Alaska.

Onion Soup
(loosely based on a Jamie Oliver recipe adapted to whatever we have on board at the time)

Our favourite 'no-nonsense' recipe for cooking at sea or in remote places where it is difficult to get fresh produce:

Ingredients
- A selection of whatever mixed onions, shallots and garlic cloves you have on board at the time. The mix of onions is not critical. Leeks can be added to the mix if you have them.
- A knob of butter
- Olive oil
- Stock (any sort will do)
- Sea salt and ground black pepper
- A few slices of stale bread
- Grated cheese (ideally cheddar but any hard cheese will do)
- Worcester sauce
- A few sage leaves (if you can get hold of them but it works without)

Instructions
- Roughly chop all the onions and garlic.
- Melt the butter with 2 lugs of olive oil, the garlic oil and a handful of sage leaves (if available) in a large pan and then added the chopped onions.
- Put a lid on the pan and let the onions sweat for at least 40-50 minutes on the lowest heat possible, stirring occasionally to stop them sticking on the bottom. This is the critical step, the slower you sweat them the more the sweetness and flavour comes out of the onions.

- Take the lid off, turn the heat up, and cook for a further 10-15 minutes to get a bit of colour in the onions.
- Add the stock, season with salt and pepper and simmer for a further 15 minutes.
- Meanwhile toast the stale bread in the oven, add some grated cheese and a splash of Worcester sauce on top of each slice, before melting the cheese on the toast under the grill.
- Serve the soup in bowls with a toasted cheese slice floating on the top of each bowl.

Some of the following recipes are taken, with permission, from the series 'From the Galley', in *Flying Fish*, the Journal of the Ocean Cruising Club, edited by Anne Hammick.

American Cornbread

After cruising on the Chesapeake Bay, along the US Atlantic coast and to all five of the Great Lakes in their previous yacht, Lisa Borre and her husband David Barker embarked on an extended cruise aboard their Tayana 37 cutter *Gyatso*. They sailed to the eastern Caribbean, across the Atlantic to Portugal, into the Mediterranean and most recently around the Black Sea.

Ingredients
- 200g / 7oz cornmeal, coarsely ground
- 50g / 2oz all-purpose (plain) flour
- 2tsp baking powder
- ½tsp baking soda
- ½tsp salt
- 2 or 4tbsp honey or sugar
- 1 or 2 eggs
- 260ml milk or buttermilk
- 2 or 3tbsp melted butter or vegetable oil

Instructions
- Mix all the ingredients together to form a thick batter, adding the oil or butter at the end.
- Pour into greased 9-inch square baking pan or muffin pan with paper baking cups.
- Bake in a hot (400º F / 205º C) oven for 20-25 minutes (square pan) or 10-12 minutes (muffin pan).
- Allow to cool slightly before removing from the pan.
- Serve warm.

For variety, top with grated cheese before or after baking (if adding after, place back in the oven to melt the cheese); add a small can of corn to the batter; substitute sour cream for half the milk.

It's not just cooking to be done regularly – there is also the clothes washing

Boscaiola

Bill and Nancy Salvo left from Marblehead, MA in their C & C 36 *Cascade*. They sailed down the coast of America, through the Bahamas into the Caribbean. They 'rode' with *Cascade* on a Dockwise transport ship to Toulon, France. Since then they have been exploring France, Italy and Croatia by land and sea. Bill says they 'were given this simple, delicious recipe at Lega Navale in Baris, southeast Italy. Boscos means woods in Italian, hence mushrooms...'

Ingredients

- 180g / 6oz tagliatelle
- 400g / 12oz tin artichoke hearts, cut in quarters
- 400g / 12oz tin (or fresh chopped) mushrooms
- 2 or 3 slices prosciutto cotto (cooked ham), cut into small chunks
- 1 large ripe tomato, diced, or about 10 chopped cherry tomatoes if available
- Grated Parmigiano (Parmesan) cheese
- A handful of chopped parsley
- About 30g / 1oz butter
- Salt and pepper to taste

Instructions

- Saute the mushrooms, artichokes, ham and lastly the tomatoes in the butter.
- Cook the tagliatelle, pour the sauce over, and sprinkle on the parmigiano and fresh parsley.

Bethany's Brownies

OCC member, Sarah Smith, aboard *Cape* gave her daughter's recipe for Chocolate Brownies. 'These brownies are the ones that Bethany always used to make for birthdays and special occasions aboard *Cape*.'

Ingredients

- 150g / 5oz sugar
- 50g / 2oz flour
- 20g / 1oz cocoa
- ½tsp salt
- ½tsp baking powder
- 2 eggs, beaten
- 60g / 2oz oil (coconut or olive oil)
- 1tsp vanilla essence
- 80g / 3oz plain / dark chocolate chips
- Splash of milk if needed.

Instructions

- Mix the ingredients well. To give quite a runny batter – add a splash of milk if the mixture seems dry.
- Pour the batter into a greased baking tray.
- Bake in a medium oven (350°F / 175°C, GAS Mk 4) for 20-25 minutes or until a toothpick comes out clean. Don't overcook, as the brownie will continue to cook once out of the oven.
- Allow to cool before cutting into squares.

Slapdash Chicken

Misty and Peter covered 60,000 miles and visited 45 countries on *Tamoure* who, after 25 years, they sold to a younger skipper keen to explore the world.

Ingredients

- Chicken thighs, bone in or out – quantity according to hunger
- 1 onion, cut into smallish wedges (I use red)
- 1 red pepper, cut into squares, not slices
- Selection of potatoes, cut up not too small – quantity according to hunger
- Carrots or any other slow-cooking vegetable if desired, or mushrooms
- 6-8 pitted black olives, if you have them
- 1 lemon, quartered
- A few sprigs of fresh thyme, or a few scatterings of dried thyme
- 75ml / 5tbsp oil
- 90ml / 6tbsp fresh lemon juice (only use bottled juice if you're sure it's not stale)
- 100ml / 6.5tbsp white wine
- Salt and pepper as required

Instructions

- Make slashes in the chicken with a knife – all the better to absorb the flavour.
- Assemble all the ingredients except for the liquids in an ovenproof dish large enough for everything to fit on one level – this is important, as the dish doesn't take much liquid and if packed in layers it will dry out. At this stage there will seem to be far too much but press on. Everything shrinks, and by the time you remove it from the oven you will wish you had added more.
- The volume of liquid suggested is the maximum amount you will need if the chicken pieces are large and there are lots of potatoes. Combine the oil, lemon juice and white wine and pour over – you want all the ingredients to be lying in liquid, but not covered by it. It will not seem to be enough but have faith. The veggies roast, the potatoes come out all crunchy, and the chicken has a nice lemony flavour (remember to remove the quarters). Too much liquid turns it into a stew. Don't overdo the oil (too greasy) or the lemon (too sharp).
- Cook for about an hour (timing isn't crucial) in a medium oven, uncovered. Cover towards the end if it seems to be drying up.
- Enjoy – and there's hardly any washing up!

Boat Cake

This is one to be made ashore and is often given as a gift to a departing sailor.

The Tetleys are based in Truro in the west of England. Maureen baked this cake for her husband, Jem, when he sailed in the AZAB (Azores and Back). Jem was given numerous cakes by friends and relations. On arrival home, he discovered that he had not eaten his wife's cake. Maureen iced it and they had it for Christmas. Maureen says this cake 'keeps for ever – the trouble is, it's usually eaten too fast'. Buy the ingredients, for four cakes. The first will be eaten almost before it comes out of the oven, one can be a gift, leaving two for night watches.

Ingredients (for a 7-inch round tin or 8-inch square tin)
- 500g / 1lb 4oz mixed dried fruit (currants, sultanas, raisins)
- 125g / 5oz glacé cherries
- Rind of 1 orange
- ¼ pint / 150ml sherry / rum / whisky, or to taste
- 175g / 6oz butter or soft margarine
- 175g / 6oz brown sugar
- 50g / 2oz self-raising flour
- 100g / 4oz plain flour
- 2tbsp chopped or flaked almonds
- Pinch of salt
- 1tsp mixed spice
- 1tbsp molasses or black treacle
- 3 large eggs

Instructions
- Chop the raisins and halve the cherries.
- Put all the fruit into a container, pour on the booze and mix well.
- Cover with clingfilm or a lid and leave to soak for at least three days, stirring daily.
- Put butter, sugar, eggs, treacle and chopped almonds into a large bowl and beat well.
- Add the flours and spice and mix thoroughly.
- Stir in the soaked fruits and booze.
- Grease and line the tin with greaseproof or butter paper.
- Spoon the mixture in and level out.
- Cook in a moderate oven for 30 minutes or until set, then reduce heat to very low for 4 to 5 hours (until a skewer comes out cleanly).
- Turn out when cold.

WISH DISHES

I asked cruisers featured in this book about their favourite dishes, perhaps because of taste, place or people, and their most impressive dish, made with the least amount of effort. Here's what they said.

Mike and Devala Robinson who made a nine-year circumnavigation spending seven years in the Pacific.

Venison Medallions with Red Wine Sauce

"We picked up this recipe in New Zealand where they produce excellent venison, courtesy of the animals imported by the colonials. Without predators these deer bred... and bred and now have to be culled. The up-side is a wonderful meat both wild and farmed. This often comes vacuum packed or can be frozen so we usually left NZ with some in our freezer. We're not the best at measuring, so take measures as a guidance."

Ingredients

- 2 venison medallions per person (depending on size of medallions and appetite of diners)
- 1 medium onion (dried onion can be used), finely sliced
- Couple of tablespoons oil
- ½ teaspoon cornflour (optional)
- Generous glass of red wine

Instructions

- Heat oil in frying pan.
- Pat medallions dry on kitchen towel.
- Once oil is hot, add onions and stir fry for couple of minutes until just softening.
- Add and pan fry medallions approx. 3 minutes on either side depending on thickness and how you like your meat cooked – cook for the same time you'd cook a really good quality steak.
- Remove medallions and rest in warm place covered with foil.
- Mix cornflour (if using – gives a thicker sauce) with red wine.
- Add this to the frying pan and stir until thickened or until onions and juices are released.
- Stir in any juices from the resting medallions and pour this sauce over the medallions and serve.

Jonny, an accountant, and Kate, a maths teacher, took a year to sail to Australia from Newcastle upon Tyne on *Newtsville*, their Colvic Countess 38:

Most impressive dish would either be fresh coconut pieces (great snack with beers!) or fresh wahoo curry!

Greg, based in Florida, describes himself as 'a preacher who lives on board *Ocean Ministries*, my 54' ketch between the Chesapeake and the Caribbean':

My cooking is not primitive, but some may say barbaric. Ocean fish in butter and lemon in a pan, just barely cooked, and lentils with hot sauce, garlic and curry so hot it burns...

Al and Mel took their girls Ayla and Molly on an Atlantic Circuit. Mel, says, "Perhaps not most impressive but the most eaten, enjoyed and easily prepared meal":

Thai Chicken Curry

Ingredients
- Chicken breasts cut into chunks – 1 per person
- 1 chopped onion
- 1 sliced red pepper
- Halved handful of green beans (I used sweet potatoes, green beans, carrots at times)
- 2tbs Thai curry paste – red or green
- 2tbs oil
- 1 can coconut milk
- Chopped coriander to serve
- Rice

Instructions
- Heat oil to hot in frying pan, add Thai paste and cook for 1 minute.
- Add veg and fry 1 minute, turn heat down to moderate.
- Add chicken and stir all ingredients to coat and seal.
- Cook for 5 minutes.
- Add milk and turn heat up until simmering point.
- Cook for 5 minutes.
- Turn heat down as rice cooks.
- Serve together with coriander to garnish

Rob Avery is sailing an Atlantic Circuit:
Fish pie made from Dorado caught from the boat sailing across the Atlantic.

Peter and Sue Bringloe have spent many seasons in the Caribbean on their Dix 38. They now live between the UK and Caribbean. They used to be consultants and managers for the pub business:
Chopped cabbage together with Thai red paste, lime juice and anything else that comes to hand! The thing that always seems to impress fellow cruisers when invited over for a drink and substantial nibbles is home-made pizzas. They are not very hard, but they are a bit fiddly to

do. My favourite one is blue cheese and walnut – never fails to impress! Other than that, Thai beef salad is easy, but hard to get the best quality of meat. The next best thing is Thai fishcakes – preferably made with some freshly caught fish.

Peter and Katharine Ingram sailed from New Zealand, Vanuatu, Solomon Islands, Papua New Guinea, Micronesia, the Philippines, Japan, around the North Pacific to Alaska and Canada. From Vancouver they trucked their boat across Canada and sailed back to Europe.
Our easiest luxury meal would have to be tuna, just caught, eaten raw for lunch with

lemon juice and soya sauce. Then cooking the fish in boiling sea water for a minute or two and leaving it covered in the water will then make it last for 3 days, which in the tropics with no fridge is very useful. Our most amusing meal would have to be mashed pumpkin, mashed sweet potatoes and curried red lentils. Although this meal tasted delicious, on the plate it looked like three piles of orange mush. As we were trading for food at the time we only ate the vegetables that were grown on that specific island. On this particular island all the available veg was orange!

David and Nancy and their sons Christopher and Josh are from Texas. They cruised on *Liberty*, exploring in the eastern Caribbean, Bahamas and US east coast.

Favourite would have to be grouper fillets with lobster sauce. As for least amount of effort, that varies. If the grouper lets himself be shot quickly, and the lobster is easy to find, then it's a quick, easy, impressive meal. Basically, one medium to small lobster tail, minced, goes into a couple of cups of béchamel sauce, made with wine, cream, fish stock, or whatever else is handy. Grouper fillets, dusted with Old Bay seasoning, hit a hot pan with half butter, half olive oil, for a quick sear, then get topped with the lobster sauce. Served with rice and a little salad, and wine or rum punch, with a setting sun over the banks, and it's a pretty good meal. When the grouper and / or lobster takes hours and hours of hunting to bring in, then it's still impressive, but with a little more effort. When the grouper is a snapper, or mahi mahi, or even a grunt, well, still pretty good. Barracuda, less good. Then, it's fish tacos.

Ed and Megan Clay's who sailed an extended Atlantic Circuit, from the UK to the Atlantic Islands, the Gambia River, the Cape Verdes, Barbados up through the Caribbean, and up the US Eastern Seaboard, to Nova Scotia, Labrador, to Greenland and home.

Our 'culinary highlight' was snow crab thermidor in Greenland but it took all afternoon and involved several sets of pliers.

In terms of effort versus reward, soda bread on passage and homemade ginger beer in the Caribbean (with suitable amounts of rum) were the winners.

James and Carol Grazebrook sail in Turkish waters in their Beneteau 45. They love fresh honeycomb and freshly baked bread, fruit and local yoghurt for breakfast in their cockpit.

Graham Shaw and Lorraine Zaffiro sailed from Europe to the Pacific on their catamaran, a Fountain Pajot – Athena 38, called *Catacaos*, with their son Lucas.

Gray's favourite dish, chicken royal. Mine is a sweet and sour veg or chicken. The most impressive dish with least amount of effort is tomato and mozzarella pasta, perfect for lunch or dinner in a rough sea, tastes great, and of course lots of carbs, to keep the energy levels up. The stuff is just tipped onto the cooked drained pasta and tossed about for a minute – the mozzarella melts a bit, but not much. It's deeelish!

Malcolm Campbell keeps his Tartan 3000 off City Island, New York. He has sailed the NE USA extensively. His most impressive dish with least amount of effort?

A Heineken.

And as for us? John my husband's favourite, most impressive dish with least amount of work? A dish is based on Bruce

Van Sant's (*Gentleman's Guide to Passages South*) recipe for cooking plantains (large-bananas):

Chop and fry the overripe plantains with crushed garlic, butter, salt and pepper.

BIG-DEAL DINNERS

Thanksgiving? Christmas? You can still do the important meals on a yacht. Perhaps if it is a big celebration you could share the cooking with a friend, who brings the roast potatoes? But beware of too many guests. One cruiser was left washing lettuces for 40 when she drew the short straw for a group Christmas lunch. Others were chatting to friends and missed out on the pounds of potatoes they had prepared.

Remember, dishes can become an elaborate, time-filling indulgence if the boat is not rolling and if you are not too exhausted from sailing. Just because you are on a boat, basic cooking does not change. You can create complex sauces

The author with Christmas dinner, Nassau, Bahamas

and curries or stick to roast and two veg, whatever your preference. If you are shattered or short-handed, boil-in-the-bag dishes are saviours, whether on long or short passages.

VACUUM PACKED

From the supermarket in Porto Colom in Mallorca to the Mediterranean Market on Las Olas in Fort Lauderdale, there are shops that prepare food for yachts in harbour or port. Vacuum-packed meats and dishes are more expensive, but it does mean the treat of posh grub on the boat, with minimum preparation or washing up.

Rather than sitting in a restaurant looking out at your boat, a birthday or anniversary can be celebrated in the beautiful anchorage, where the best view is from your boat looking ashore.

CAKES

For most, making cakes on a boat is about doing it the old-fashioned way, without cake mix, but that makes them all the more special.

Children's birthday cakes can be more of a task, only because small people insist on 'helping'. One mother, who had not stocked up with birthdays in mind when she was in Puerto Rico, was reduced to a panicky monster on a remote Bahamian island where basic ingredients were available, but not the hoopla-and-circus she wanted. If you are somewhere selling Betty Crocker icing, funky candles, cake trays and plastic tiaras, buy them and stow them. And in three months, remember that you've bought them and where you've stored them!

For one birthday my oven struck again, but everyone loved the resulting gooey chocolate brownie. You are on a boat, not in an equipment-filled kitchen. Don't stress.

If you find or make Christmas cake, buy several or make a large cake so that you can save some. It is a good keep-you-going treat, especially with cheese in bad weather.

BARBEQUES

A barbeque suspended over the pushpit is a great way to cook on a boat, especially when the weather is hot. The galley can become a claustrophobic sauna. If the main cooking is carried out in the open, then a salad in the galley becomes a cinch. Some parboil potatoes and sweetcorn, then wrap them in foil and leave them on the barbeque, adding meat (marinated or not) and peppers later.

When cooking kebabs, it's best to be coordinated with ingredients. Cremated mushroom next to half-cooked pork isn't good. If you're marinating, be careful that the coated meat does not catch fire. Meat with honey or marmalade glazes can be swiftly reduced to charred remains.

It is advisable to have a gas barbeque, as charcoal makes a filthy mess over the deck. Also save barbeque days for the anchorage, as marinas do not encourage fires off the back of boats and marina neighbours may be sniffy about smoke. Avoid days when laundry is drying around the boat.

SHOPPING

Sourcing special ingredients can become quite a cuisine quest. Sourcing everyday items can also be a quest, but it's part of the adventure and the lifestyle. When you arrive on a remote island, find out which day the mail boat or the boat with the groceries arrives. And if the boat does not make it, there's no point grumbling – improvise.

In Grand Bahamas three women friends rented a minibus once a week to go shopping. A taxi was too small for their needs and once you get to know the locals, good deals can be done. The minibus driver could go off on a quick job while they were in the supermarket. As old hands they knew that one shop would not do, while three shops might stretch to almost the whole list. This is not an untypical example of shopping while cruising. Cruisers who return from months in the Bahamas indulge in a piled-high trolley or two in the first mall or Publix supermarket they come to on their arrival back in the USA.

It's fun to try the local food. For example, in Spain there are far more types of cheese (like queso Manchega from La Mancha or Cabrales, a blue cheese from the Basque region) and sausages (salchichas or chorizo, a spicy sausage) than you can find 'at home'. Different regions offer different tapas, from prawns in garlic butter (gambas aioli) to Parma ham, fried squid (calamares a la Romana), potatoes in hot sauce (patatas bravas), potato pancake (tortilla de España) and dozens of others.

A shopkeeper in La Coruña, northern Spain, with a wide variety of sausages and beans

Duck in sherry sauce is a variation on the usual tapas fare. If you want paella find a small, family-run restaurant, as too many tourist restaurants microwave yesterday's leftovers and throw on a prawn. Huegos revueltos is scrambled eggs but with all kinds of additions, much more than breakfast. At Easter in Mallorca, Spain they have special lamb pies (panades).

Explore the culinary seas by trying tinned pulpo (octopus) and squid. If you're passing through French territory (either in Europe or in the Caribbean such as Guadaloupe, St Martin or Martinique), cassoulet (a bean stew with chicken, bacon or sausages) is worth stocking up on. Try out some of the other food in tins, such as pâté or confit de canard (duck).

In the West Indies, christophine is a versatile vegetable that can be used in salads or for a potato substitute. At Christmas in the islands you can find sorrel, a red drink from the flowers of the sorrel tree.

Conch is a shell, the meat of which

Tammy (left) who makes delicious guava duff in her bakery Taste of Heaven, Bimini, Bahamas

is removed, beaten hard and long, and fried or stewed. Conch fritters or grouper fingers are a must in the Bahamas. There are also sweet treats. Robin Knox-Johnston on the first non-stop solo circumnavigation described in *A World of My Own* how he often had a currant duff washed down with whisky.

A delicious variation on the theme of a suet pudding is Tammy's guava duff from Taste of Heaven in North Bimini, Bahamas. In Florida and the Keys, try the Key Lime Pie; they have competitions for the best one.

You can also try different drinks. Most Caribbean islands have their own Caribbean-brewed beer, for example in Antigua it's Wadadli, in St Lucia it's Piton and in Grenada Carib, which is widely available on the other islands.

Rum punch is the cocktail throughout the Caribbean. A Painkiller (orange juice, pineapple juice, coconut milk and rum) is the speciality of the British Virgin Islands. Coco Loco (coconut madness) is a cut-off coconut with a vast amount of rum poured into the milk, to be found in Cuba.

In some ports you will discover that you are just in time for a food festival, such as the vendange to celebrate the wine harvest in France. We went to one held in Avignon castle, where various wine growers, resplendent in their gowns and hats, chatted and quaffed. What a result: French ham, wine and cheese, while sitting in a beautiful garden overlooking the Rhône valley. Or the cider festival in Gijon, northwest Spain in late August; or just the daily treat of the banana bread in the bakery in English Harbour, Antigua.

Shopping in the local markets helps you learn the language, especially if you strike up a rapport with a particular stall holder. Culinary explorations are all part of the cruising adventure.

CRÊPE EXPECTATIONS

In August, we had just set off and were waiting for a part in Camaret sur Mer in Brittany. We wrote in our blog:

We continue to eat like kings... langoustine, moules, frites and mayonnaise. A £4 sortie to the top fish shop provided supper of 2 mega chunks of monkfish (which I cooked in lemon and the fish shop's beurre blanc) and 1kg of crevettes (marinated in rosé and then garlic buttered).

With crêperies at every turn (we both love Le Bretonne – hot apple with calvados-flambéed crêpe – heaven), croissants and tarte tatin which flake at your feet, and the fromage honestly creeps up from behind, not to mention the cider and wine... it hasn't been too bad waiting for the alternator.

STOCKING UP

To stock your galley lockers, think of your cupboards at home – tea, coffee, sugar, marmalade, jams, chutney, spices, herbs, mustard, ketchup, soy sauce, mayonnaise, oils, vinegar, stock cubes, Marmite – then transfer that onto your boat, trying to avoid glass. Although not environmentally sound, it is best to buy oil or Marmite in plastic bottles rather than glass. Broken glass anywhere is a danger, but on a sailing boat it is particularly bad news. Also avoid tins with bottoms that can rust, such as treacle or Old Bay seasoning.

Even if the passage starts as a short hop, it could turn into a long haul if the weather and your shipmates are up for it. This is when galley contingencies pay off. Try to have the basics for breakfast, lunch and a simple supper on board, such as butter, cheese, bacon, ham, muesli, porridge or cereal, or eggs, dried milk, longlife milk, flour (for pancakes) and either bread or bread-making ingredients. (The lesser of two weevils, joke aside, keep your flour in an airtight container.)

Dried fruit (apricots, apple, mango) is a good alternative to the sugar highs and lows of chocolate, but too many apricots

Fruit stall in Santa Catalina Market, Palma, Mallorca

can cause severe indigestion and diarrhoea.

When you've been shopping, wash all the fruit. Leave cardboard boxes in the supermarket, as they can provide breeding grounds for uglies and insects.

In bad weather, cooking is reduced to first-gear basics. It's an idea to keep at least two days of meals from tins in an accessible locker. If you are feeling ill, or the boat is rolling in the dark, a ready supply of tins and a bag of pasta or noodles are a blessing. This is when tins such as baked beans, lentils, sweetcorn, soups and custard that can be opened and swiftly heated come into their own. Keep your bad-weather locker well stocked. By the time you discover you have not re-stocked, it will be too late. In rolling conditions, the pressure cooker will become your one-pot-saves-gas best friend.

Coca-Cola and Lucozade can help the crew on night watches. (For the real

Washing fruit which we had purchased before bringing it onboard

caffeine junkies Red Bull is an answer, not forgetting that you have to get to sleep after a four-hour watch.) Find out from your crew what they would like in their tuck boxes. Mars bars, energy bars, flapjacks or chocolate biscuits are favourites, while others prefer cheese and crackers. Very few go for the healthy option of nuts and fruit. If you are away from shops with several overnights, have a very good hiding place for the tuck-box goodies. Be very clear with the crew that you know how many bars of everything you have, and that you count them all out and you count them all in, even if you don't.

PROVISIONING FOR BLUE-WATER SAILING

Provisioning for a long passage is intimidating the first time. If you anticipate the crossing taking 25 days, allow for at least 30. Even when you are sure the boat is full, it will open up new stowage potential.

When starting to plan for a long voyage, take a breath and begin with the easy items, such as breakfast cereals, ingredients for bread making and dried milk – lots of dried milk – and bottled water. Keep a detailed list of what is in which locker in a notebook and keep it up to date.

For how many are you catering? How generous do you want to be with portions? What are they having for breakfast? Are you having a special breakfast on Sunday or 'Halfway day'? Pancakes are not easy in ocean swells. Also, depending on the screw motion of the waves, working the grill can be a gymnastic feat.

Draw up your menu, with or without consultation and input, depending on who is going to cook. If you attempt a democratic kitchen, be careful; it's best to have a head chef and cooks. As 'head chef', instil in your crew that you wish the galley and all cooking equipment to be thoroughly cleaned and put away in the correct position at the end of each cook's session. While elegantly laying down the law, be clear that everyone understands your definition of washing up, and thoroughly cleaned, and put away. Establish whether the cook of the day is willing to wash up, and if not that they come to an arrangement with another cook, or yourself. One crew played highly competitive card games for who washed up. Incidentally, if you're using a bucket to wash up, beware of throwing out the cutlery forgotten at the bottom of the bucket.

Lunch can be sandwiches, cheese, coleslaw or soup. Be flexible, quite often the late-night watch has just woken up and is still having breakfast at official lunch time. For the evening meal, start with your easiest 10 suppers. After that, look up recipes in a book, or fill in with other people's favourites. Take the pressure off yourself: you can be planning this for weeks, months or even years.

Once you have prepared your breakfast, lunch, snack, tea, supper and night-watch snack menus for 30 days, start shopping weeks or even months in advance. As the time to depart approaches and a 'cook' comes up with a menu they would like to make, send them off to buy the extra ingredients, and agree where you will stow them so there is no confusion with ingredients for other menus. As the crossing goes on, crews tend to graze

Fresh rations for a trans-Atlantic passage

John washing up using a lobster net in Red Shanks anchorage, George Town, Exumas, Bahamas

through the lockers or fridge, which can lead to shortages of vital stocks.

When provisioning for a crew, clarify who likes what – and how much. One crew member shocked the owner by demanding four large sandwiches at lunchtime, not realising that cruising across the Atlantic he would be using far less energy than he did on land. (Obviously, racing crews eat more). One cook had to be restrained when a crew member who had claimed to be vegetarian, and insisted on vegetarian meals across the Atlantic, chewed down on a thick, red steak at the arrival dinner.

GALLEY TIPS

One-pot cooking is your best solution aboard, whether pressure cooker or casserole. Cottage pie, lasagne, shepherd's pie, chicken with rice and sweetcorn or peas ('sorta risotto'), stew and thick onion soup are simple, hearty meals for sailing. (Some people say that curries and chilli con carne can make them feel queasy.)

Bully beef is a favourite sandwich filler on passage, and it can also kick up a mince dish if you are short of meat. Nursery foods such as fish-finger sandwiches or sausages or chicken drumsticks can be left to cook and are good cockpit snacks. Tinned tuna is versatile but be careful of tuna mayonnaise sandwiches on rough days. Atlantic cook Lisa Avery recommends homemade tortillas, fresh fish and tomato salsa.

If you are heading into the Pacific be aware that fish and meat can be in short supply, so stock up on quality tins. Remember that spam is spam is spam, however you try to camouflage it.

Fresh bread is a real morale booster.

John playing cards with the crew for who does the washing up

YOU CAN'T MAKE AN OMELETTE WITHOUT CRACKING EGGS

An ocean-going yacht saved two Frenchmen and took them on board. The admiral – as most wives are known – takes up the tale:

The incident with the eggs occurred the day after we rescued our Frenchmen. We were going to cook a breakfast and the younger of the two said: "I am chef de cuisine, I would like to make the breakfast." I wanted them to feel at home, so I handed over our eggs and bacon. He cooked the eggs and bacon French-style in our very large skillet, together, and using 11 eggs of our 14 eggs that we had planned would last the 2 of us the next 10 days. I didn't have the heart to say anything, just watched helplessly, but it did taste very good! Portion control came into serious effect for the rest of the trip. Coffee, in particular, had to be rationed towards the end!

You can make bread the traditional way or use a one-pack mix, complete with yeast. Long-life, par-baked bread is a quick and easy alternative, though bulkier. One skipper described the first attempts at bread making as, "It's bread but not as you know it." By Antigua, they were all experts.

Your beautifully planned menus may literally hit the deck if you are using flat plates. Many cruisers use 'dog bowls', bowls with high sides, which prevent the dish-du-jour going overboard, or at least overbowl. You may also be more successful with one-implement eating with such devices as 'Sporks' (made by Light My Fire and others), a spoon and a fork with a serrated edge, all in one.

Try to keep all foods close to the stowage surface. The last thing you want to be doing is pulling up berths in search of lost tins on passage. Be realistic. Whatever you have at the back of your cupboards at home (sardines? frankfurters?) you'll have taking up space at the back of your lockers. If you're heading away from shops selling alcohol, stock up, with enough for yourselves, and enough to take to a party or two.

If you're leaving one country and entering another, be clear about the restrictions on what is allowed into that country. If you have just been on a major provisioning trip, it's a frustrating waste to throw food or drink away or have it 'confiscated', a trick in Cuba and a few Pacific islands.

SHELF LIFE

Cabbages and carrots are good for two weeks at sea; after that carrots begin to shrivel. Potatoes last around three weeks, whereas pumpkins can survive for months if they are not cut open.

To use up cabbages and carrots, coleslaw is easy to prepare and a staple for lunch with sandwiches. You can always brighten it up with soy sauce, wasabi, mustard, pumpkin seeds, nuts, currants and raisins. Onions and garlic are good for several weeks and help pep up most dishes. Carrots are good in stews, as are aubergines and courgettes, although they start to fade after ten days.

Eggs last at least a month and the consensus is to turn them once every two days to prolong their life.

Be prepared to have no refrigeration because there is not enough power or because the water temperature is heating up and the fridge, which is fine in temperate climates, cannot cope in the tropics. Time and again on ocean crossings, boats anticipating five-star cuisine have power failures, leaving them with barely enough for running lights (night lights) let alone a fridge or freezer. Weeping cooks have thrown weeks of frozen meals overboard.

GAS & GIMBLE

The oven will swing on a gimble, making cooking liquids safe. It's quite mesmerising watching a large pot of soup rocking with the waves, almost but not quite spilling, time and again. Even so, it's wiser not to fill the pot too high. Check that your gimble is in full working order and secure when loaded with heavy pans. Also, if you do lock it off in harbour, make sure that the lock is firm.

With all this cooking, continually keep a watch on your gas supplies. Cooking pasta is quicker than rice or potatoes, so uses up less gas. Using a pressure cooker also helps to preserve fuel.

Gas is not always easy to locate near a marina; obtaining it can sometimes mean renting a car or an expensive taxi ride to the docks or out of town.

TOO MANY COOKS

Martin Thomas, a member of the Ocean Cruising Club describes some culinary adventures in the club's journal, *Flying Fish*:

Two sailors I know well... had put to into La Coruña on their way south because they had lost the tin opener. Those days are over for most crews – food has now become an important aspect of any voyage. Ashore we can eat so well these days, and with such choice, that at sea we expect similar and a good skipper must attend carefully to the victuals. Good food, hot food and, if available, fresh food served regularly will raise morale. On long ocean passages, especially when the weather is fine and the going is good, mealtimes become the high spots of the day and we look forward to them. Nowadays yachtsmen are also much more imaginative in the preparation of food at sea. The fridge and the freezer have helped... Maybe we all just expect to eat better and are prepared to make an effort.

I recently crossed the Atlantic in *Charm of Rhu* with two friends. One was a restaurateur. He was incredulous to find no spices, fine herbs or garlic crusher aboard, and delayed our departure while he stomped off to the shops. My other shipmate baked bread most days and insisted on properly filtered coffee – wonderful aromas which were completely unknown on our little bilge-keeler in Wales. Once we were underway and into the ocean swell I prepared the first evening meal, not corned beef and cold baked beans but not much better. I was soon relieved of my culinary duties and reduced to washing up. Instead we had stuffed chicken breasts, exotic casseroles, elaborate sauces on pasta or meat and, of course, onion and garlic with everything. Not a baked bean, cold or otherwise, passed our lips. Some of the tins I had hoarded aboard are still in the locker and well-travelled. Anyone for a second-hand meat pie, in perfect condition despite 7,000 miles at sea?

My shipmates have raised the role of cooking at sea from a necessary chore to a joy, one reason why the trip was such a success. I have learned new skills, put my tin-opener away and reduced my intake of corned beef and beans... but I still get stuck with washing up.

WATER

If you think you can use seawater to cook with, think again. It is far, far more saline than any water you would use for cooking. A little sea (from the open ocean) water with boat water will go a long, long way.

Water is your most essential provision. Yes, you're loaded to the gunwales, but water is essential, so have bottled water, and plenty of it, in addition to what's in your tanks. Separate tanks are a good idea, in case one is punctured or contaminated. Plus, a manual pump should the electric one fail. The ultimate is to have a watermaker. Emony Nicholls, one of our crew who has taken canoe expeditions into remote locations in Canada, reminded us that our pee should be 'clear and copious'. If you start seeing stars, it is definitely time to drink more. Use tape or a marker pen to identify water bottles for each crew member so that they can monitor their intake.

Most crews arrive in the Caribbean with weeks of water and food left over, and that is how it should be. One crew were shocked to discover that the water from the tanks on the boat was undrinkable, and they had just enough bottled water to reach Antigua.

BOOKS FOR COOKS

Two reference books that will help are *The Atlantic Crossing Guide*, edited by Jane Russell, and Lin Pardey's *The Care and Feeding of Sailing Crew*.

Lin Pardey's book is 30 years old but still apt, although her preference for an ice box is a little spartan for most. She includes numerous recipes, ideas for ingenious devices and advice from thousands of miles at sea. Cookbooks take up room, so be ruthless with your choices. If you're taking a Mary Berry cookbook, for example, just take one.

HEALTH

There are various health issues that you need to be aware of aboard, and precautions you can take in each case.

MOSQUITOES

Fly screens across hatches and washboards will help prevent flies and mosquitoes. In areas with malaria, mosquito nets hung over beds are necessary (children love picking off the mosquitoes in the morning). The worst times for mozzies are the two hours around sun down and sun up. Smoking coils, citronella candles and various oils such as lemongrass, eucalyptus, cinnamon, castor, rosemary, cedar, peppermint, clove or geranium can discourage them. Some people wear citronella-impregnated ankle bracelets. The debate on the side effects of DEET continues, but it is potent in repelling mosquitoes, either in spray, cream, band or wipe form.

FLIES

Flies spread disease. In the tropics, covering food or putting it in the fridge or lockers is important.

Do clean work surfaces, again and again. Spray or sticky fly paper (which children find fascinating) is ugly and slightly disgusting, but effective.

CIGUATERA

This is not an infestation or an insect but a toxin. Fish consume toxin-producing dinoflagellates found on coral and seaweeds. Via the food chain ciguatera can reach snapper, mackerel, parrot fish and barracuda. In humans, the symptoms include vomiting, abdominal pain and diarrhoea. Tingling of the extremities can be followed by paralysis and even death. Seek local advice before fishing around reefs. Fish caught mid-ocean are safe.

COCKROACHES

Boric acid mixed with condensed milk or sugar, then left in cupboards or corners, is said to kill cockroaches. Others swear by crushed bay leaves.

Cockroaches come aboard as stowaways in corrugated cardboard or fruit and vegetables. If you can leave all the cardboard packing at the supermarket and wash fruit before it comes aboard, that can help stop an infestation.

JELLYFISH

From the Caribbean to the Chesapeake, these can really spoil your day. Antihistamine should be applied fast. The Portuguese Man of War is considered to give the most vicious sting. The Pacific, if you reach it, has some even nastier offerings.

RATS

Most cruisers use cut-off plastic bottles or a bucket with a hole in the bottom to prevent rats climbing up the mooring lines. If you do not have children or animals on board, poison or traps may be necessary in areas of high rodent infestation.

SANDFLIES

Sandflies are also known as no-see-ums – you don't see them, but you sure feel their bite. If you are out on a barbeque on the beach at night, be careful that you are not bitten by wearing protective clothes and using a rug or chair to sit on. Insect repellent containing DEET and lemon eucalyptus oil can deter them.

SNAKES & SPIDERS

Be careful when bringing boxes on board, particularly in the tropics. Seek local knowledge and take necessary precautions on land. Most snakes in the Caribbean were eaten by the Mongeese introduced to sugar-producing islands to eat them since they were biting the slaves. In Martinique the Fer de Lance is poisonous but it is highly unlikely you will come across one.

KEEP FIT!

Whilst cruising there are all kinds of temptations – food, drinks, all sorts. Cruisers will caution that it is important to remain fit. After long passages, or even a heavy night, go for a swim, hike or bicycle ride. Shopping via bicycle or roller blading with a back pack keeps the fitness levels up. One of my best yoga classes was on Pigeon Beach, Antigua. I found the local teacher by an advertisement on a notice board, similarly my classes in Grand Bahama.

I found walking an easy way to exercise and explore the local area. My quests for post offices to send wedding thank-you letters became family folk lore. These mini expos morphed into sending 'bounty' or birthday post cards. They invariably led to meeting locals and discovering an unexpected delight. As you will have seen from the 'what to take' lists, cruisers take tennis rackets, some even golf clubs, and diving gear.

GUESTS

Fish and visitors smell after three days.
Poor Richard's Almanac, 1736

'Beat to quarters' was the cry which went up ordering the beating of the drum which summoned the crew to action stations before a battle.

I hope your time with your guests will be a joy, but, best to be ready. When you are expecting guests, before they leave home suggest that they don't bring the smart luggage: a small, beaten-up rucksack or small holdall is best. Keep reiterating 'small'. Also, mention the obligatory gifts for their hosts (you), such as your favourite scent, tea, chocolate, curry paste. If there is any entertaining post for you, that is welcome too. Guests of friends who fly out with laptop batteries or spare parts such as a vital water pump before an Atlantic crossing are awarded bonus points. Also remind guests that British newspapers are a treat from home, so they shouldn't leave them on the plane.

Rendez-vous with your guests in a place that is convenient to you. Many dangerous passages have been undertaken in order to meet visitors. Most seasoned cruisers insist on guests coming to the boat rather than the boat plugging through foul weather. As thrilling as they are, meetings at airports are time and money consuming. In the Caribbean it is usually a long and expensive taxi ride from anchorages to the airport. At 6 miles an hour it takes much longer by yacht than by bus or train or taxi, and a hire car can be an advantage for a few days.

A short, simple tutorial on hatches, knots and switches, lights, VHF radio and the lavatory will make guests feel almost at home. The power required for a hair dryer or an iron is prohibitive on most yachts. A lesson in water consumption is equally wise. One long shower and luxurious hair wash and that's the tanks empty. And, dodgy segue or not, while on consumption, let's mention consummation. One skipper complained about the noises coming from the cabin of his guest and his new girlfriend. Keep it down, while, keeping it up.

Make clear the pros and cons of accommodating your friends' dreams. Explain that changing plans and leaving now means an easy sail to drop them off. Four days in this secluded paradise means a rough sail into the wind before they can leave.

A yacht becomes incrementally more claustrophobic the higher the number of people on board, and that doubles if resentments begin to bubble. Excursions ashore are the ideal way to decompress.

If you cannot afford to stay in a marina, make it clear that the guests will be dinghying in and out, and that you are not a dinghy taxi service at 4am. Cruisers in Ibiza became extremely irritated by their guests' nocturnal VHF radio calls for the dinghy.

If your friends want to go to pricey tourist bars, remind them that they are over your price, and go elsewhere. Being your friends, they should have already offered to take you out to a slap-up dinner anyway.

When our front-cabin-fevered chum in an elaborate display of polite excuses confessed that he would rather spend $200 a night on a hotel room than face another drench-and-bail exercise in our tippy dinghy, we suggested that he foot the bill for dockage. Win-win.

Ed and Megan, who sailed an extended Atlantic Circuit, write, 'We had friends and family on board for 30% of the time. We were careful to stress beforehand, particularly to non-sailors, that while they could book flights early we wouldn't know where we would be from day to day. So they should be prepared to change plans, wait, travel to find us, or enjoy a holiday exploring by land without us.'

SUPERSTITIONS

It is easy to see how sailing superstitions arose in the days when mariners thought that you could sail off the edge of the flat world and vessels were at the mercy of huge winds or acres of calm in unchartered seas. Even now, a raging storm puts the fear of whatever is their god into a crew. For some folk, superstitions are real, and a black cat really can bring good luck; for others they are a sad misconception. So, believe them or not, here are some maritime superstitions to muse on:

- Sailors often wear a charm of one of the patron saints of mariners, travellers and the sea: St Elmo, St Nicholas and St Christopher.
- Neptune, the ruler of the seas, must be revered and assuaged at all times. Ocean-racing Ellen MacArthur sacrificed half a pack of her precious ginger biscuits to the god. When crossing the line, or sailing across the Equator for the first time, homage is made to Neptune. The sins of the uninitiated, the pollywogs, are read out by the shellbacks, those

Crossing the Equator

that it's just because the skipper and crew are tired at the end of the week. I know that all three times we have set off on a Friday, the boat, the weather and one of us have had problems. The story goes that sometime in the nineteenth century, the Royal Navy tried to dispel the superstition by naming a ship HMS Friday. Her keel was laid on a Friday, she was launched on a Friday and she set sail on her maiden voyage on a Friday; in some versions, she was under the command of Captain James Friday. She is supposed to have disappeared and never been heard of again.

- Three other days with biblical roots for the really superstitious are the First Monday in April, said to be the birthday of Cain and the day on which he killed his brother Abel; the second Monday in August, believed to be the day that Sodom and Gomorrah were destroyed; and 31st December, the anniversary of the day on which Judas Iscariot hanged himself.

who have done it before. All forms of initiation are carried out, from shaving foam to dunking in green goo.

- The superstition that it is bad luck to have women on board still persists among some fishermen but has long been lost to the waves in other sea-going vessels. The tradition may have roots in the belief that women did not have the physical and mental stamina for life aboard a ship at sea, or that they distracted the sailors from their work. Ironically, sailors believed that if they saw a naked woman it brought good luck or calmed the sea, hence the figureheads on the bows whose naked breasts were said to shame the waves.

- One superstition that most long-term cruisers and rallies adhere to is never to leave on a Friday, said to be because the crucifixion took place on that day and the source of the well-known saying, 'A Friday's sail, always fail'. Others claim

- Well into the twentieth century sailors believed that wearing the caul of a newborn child (usually in a locket) was meant to prevent the wearer from drowning.

- In Patrick O'Brian's *Aubrey* and *Maturin* books, the crew, even the captain himself, are known to whistle for wind. It is believed that if there is no wind, then whistling will bring the wind; although if a gale is blowing, whistling will increase the wind. Some say that whistling at all is bad luck, and certainly bad form on another boat. There is a variation on whistling, which is that scratching the backstay brings winds. Another wind-blown superstition decrees that a sailor should throw the head of an old broom overboard in the direction from which they want the wind to blow.

- Green Bananas. In the 1700s, the speed of ships sailing with green bananas from the Caribbean to the US east coast meant that sailors hoping to catch fish en route failed. Another theory suggests that ethylene given off by the rotting bananas was trapped below decks, poisoning the slaves in the hold. The most likely reason was spiders with a lethal bite, the Brazilian wandering spider, hid within the bunches of bananas.
- Dolphins at sea are a good omen. Petrels are said to be a good omen. The albatross is said to carry the souls of sailors lost at sea, hence shooting an albatross (as per Coleridges's *Ancient Mariner*) is very bad luck.
- A Jonah is someone who brings bad luck on a ship. Again, in Patrick O'Brian's novel *Far Side of the World*, Midshipman Hollom is ostracised because he is perceived as a Jonah. The name comes from the biblical character who was commanded by God to save Nineveh. Instead, he caught a boat from Jaffa. God, angry at his disobedience, sent a great storm. The sailors discovered that Jonah was the cause of the storm and threw him overboard. A whale sent by God swallowed Jonah. After three days and three nights in the belly of the whale, Jonah was spewed out on the shore, from where he hastened to Nineveh.
- In South East Asia and China, boats will cut across your bow so that any bad luck that is following them will transfer to your boat. And while we're on Chinese superstitions, uneven chopsticks mean you are going to miss a boat, plane or train.
- The appearance of St Elmo's Fire is said to be a heaven-sent warning of an approaching storm, or that the worst of a storm has passed. However, if it appears around the head or body of a man, it is a bad omen and it is said that the man will be dead within 24 hours.
- Supposedly, hearing church bells at sea was a sign that there would be death within 24 hours. (The ship's bell did not count.) Likewise, some people believe that a ringing wine glass predicts a shipwreck or the death of a sailor.
- A priest with his black robes which could be interpreted as funereal, is considered an ill omen, as is a black travelling bag.
- Flowers carried aboard are considered an ill omen, as they are thought, particularly by submariners, to be destined to form a wreath.
- If a sailor died on a voyage, it was unlucky to wear his clothes. However, once the ship reached port the shadow cast by the dead man lifted, and the clothes were up for grabs.
- A ship is launched with a bottle of champagne smashed across the bow. If the bottle does not break, it is said to bring bad luck on the boat. At re-naming ceremonies, a whole bottle of good champagne is poured into the water. The deities of the old boat are allowed to depart.
- A second bottle of good champagne may be shared between the boat, the owners and the crew. But avoid cheap fizz, which could anger the gods.
- An ugly tradition, now no more, is the belief that blood on the keel of a warship brought success. Slaves were lashed to the keel blocks and, as the galley sped down the slipway into the Mediterranean, the slaves were crushed, and their blood spattered over the hull and keel. Norse sailors forced prisoners of war into the same service on their longships.
- Other superstitions include not saying the word 'pig' and that losing a bucket or mop overboard brings bad fortune.

7

DECIDING WHICH WAY TO GO

This chapter looks at some of the options facing sailors looking for cruises starting in northern Europe. Most long-term cruisers head south for the sun, especially if they're intent on an Atlantic crossing. However, the Baltic is a possible summer cruise for those who prefer to stay in northern Europe.

THE BALTIC

The Baltic Sea is surrounded by Denmark, Sweden, Finland, Russia, Estonia, Latvia, Poland and Germany.

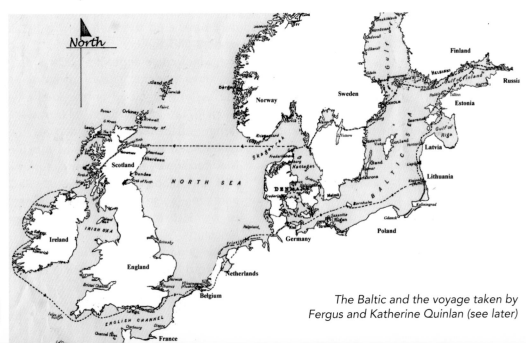

The Baltic and the voyage taken by Fergus and Katherine Quinlan (see later)

Most cruisers who really want to explore the Baltic approach the region as a series of summer cruises leaving the boat over the winter. Five summers is a good starter. The sailing season in the Baltic lasts between May and September. The schools are on holiday during June and July when it can be extremely busy. Wintering in the Baltic can be expensive so be prepared to do your homework.

En route to the Baltic in Leeuwaden

Nigel Wollen, who was Commodore of the Royal Cruising Club, and is the editor of the RCC Pilotage Foundation's *The Baltic Sea and Approaches* which includes chapters by experts on the different regions such as Poland and Germany, Russia, and the Baltic States. Nigel writes:

We sailed our boat Wish Hound (a Bowman 40) up to Denmark and cruised Denmark that summer. We laid up in a yard near Copenhagen. The next year we sailed round the southern end of Sweden (visiting Bornholm and Christianso on the way) and up the east coast of Sweden as far as the Stockholm archipelago, before heading on to the Aland Islands and Finland as far as Helsinki (returning to a yard near Stockholm for the winter). The following year we sailed across to Estonia and cruised most of its coast as far as Tallin before crossing to Finland, Aland Islands and back to Stockholm. Then we had a year off as

we were moving house! Last year took us to the Aland Islands and then the Swedish High Coast. This year we have crossed Sweden via the Gota Canal and cruised the West Coast of Sweden and then the Oslo fjord and part of the south coast of Norway, where we have left the boat for the winter.

Winter berthing is readily available in most of the countries but needs to be booked well in advance. Much of the Baltic freezes, and so you have to decide whether to go into a shed (quite expensive) or 'winterise' the boat very thoroughly.

It all gets very busy during the holidays (roughly from the end of the first week in July until early August), but everything closes down very quickly after mid-August. Mid May and June are lovely, as is late August and September. I have not sailed later than September but believe it's very good but dark comes early!

I would recommend anyone going to the Baltic to join the Cruising Association. They have a really excellent Baltic Section, and publish a number of good guides to each of the Baltic countries, as well as a guide to all the laying up options and organising specialist seminars. They welcome new members.

Nigel Wollen's Introduction to the RCC Pilotage Foundation's *The Baltic Sea and Approaches* includes the following:

Why Go To The Baltic?

The attractions of the Baltic to the cruising yachtsman are very varied, and really include something for everyone.

- *Although subject to the normal vagaries, the summer weather is governed by continental weather patterns and is generally far warmer than one might expect in those latitudes.*
- *The days are long during the main season, and there is little need for*

night sailing. For the Scandinavians, the season starts late (on or around mid-summer on 24th June), and the harbours are less crowded in the earlier and later parts of the season. The holiday season ends by mid-August, but it is perfectly possible to continue cruising well into September or even later.

- There is no tide, so no need to crawl out of one's bunk in the early hours. There are, however, some currents, which may be used to good effect. These are generally wind driven.
- There are hundreds of anchorages, and a huge variety of harbours with well-developed facilities. The latter tend to become busy during the holiday season, but it is not difficult to find a quiet anchorage.
- In the sheltered waters of the archipelagos there is relatively flat water and very little swell, with short distances between anchorages. This makes it ideal for sailing with young children or less experienced crew.
- All the Baltic countries have a rich and eventful history, which is evidenced by the number of great castles and churches as well as beautiful historic towns and cities which provide plenty to do if the weather turns nasty.
- There are plenty of places to leave a yacht, or to lay up for the winter, but early booking is strongly advised.

Skagen, meeting of the Kattegat and Skagerrak

In addition to reading Nigel Wollen's excellent Baltic pilotage guide, you can read his account in the RCC *Roving Commissions 58*, 'High Coast Summer', along with Hugh Stewart's 'A Sailor's Smorgasbord'. Similarly, the Strobel's accounts (over four *Roving Commissions*) of sailing in the Lofoten islands in NW Norway 'To Lofoten the Long Way' will give a good insight.

The eastern Baltic along the coast of Russia, Estonia, Latvia and Lithuania includes cities such as St Petersburg, where you can see the Summer Palace and Hermitage Museum. Along the coast is Riga (the capital of Latvia and known as the Venice of the North) and Tallinn (the medieval capital of Estonia).

Other books on the Baltic are listed in the appendix. As ever Lonely Planet and Baedeker can be useful. In this region, also, keep an eye out for the guidebooks for cruise ships such as the *Travellers Guide – Baltic Cruising*, it can give some good ideas for shore-based outings.

Fergus Quinlan in Russian waters

A ONE-SEASON TOUR OF THE BALTIC

An example of a one-season tour is that made by *Pylades*. Fergus and Katherine Quinlan completed a three-year circumnavigation, before setting off on a swift one season, 109 days, 3800 miles, on *Pylades*, a 12 metre, van de Stadt designed, cutter. (You can read their account in the Ocean Cruising Club, *Flying Fish 17/1*.) From Galway Bay, Ireland they sailed to Plymouth and Poole on the south coast of England, to Dunkirk, Belgium, Netherlands, through the 60-mile Kiel Canal, a 'short cut' into the Baltic, onto Ronne, Klaipeda in Lithuania, Lativa, port Pirita for Tallin in Estonia, St Petersburg in Russia, across to Finland, and Sweden's Aland Islands, and through the Gota Canal. From Gotenburg, they crossed the Kattegat to Skaden, Denmark from where they headed home via Inverness, Scotland, and the Caledonian Canal, a 'shortcut' across northern Scotland, and south from Oban to Ireland.

Fergus provided the following reason for their trip:

The Riddle of the Sands by Erskin Childers, which I had read as a child, developed a fascination of the waters around the Frisian Islands. The smuggling of 1,500 rifles and munitions for the rebellion in Ireland from east of the English Channel by his sailing yacht The Asgard, the Bolshevik revolution of 1917 and its echoes in history. These events provided a rich historical background, which combined with a desire to sail in the Baltic, the Kattegat, the Skagerrak, the North Sea and the wild waters of Scotland and Irelands west coast. Where else could one spend a more fulfilling three months?

UK TO THE MEDITERRANEAN

There are three main routes to the Mediterranean:

- Cross the English Channel and coastal hop all the way, following the edge of the Bay of Biscay and then south. (RCC Pilotage Foundation's *Atlantic France* by Nick Chavasse is the book for this.)
- Sail from the west of England, straight across Biscay to northern Spain and south. Most UK cruisers leave from ports such as Dartmouth, Plymouth and Falmouth, heading southwest across Biscay, maybe to La Coruña in northern Spain.
- Cross the Channel, step the mast and motor down the French canals.

We will look at the last of these three options first.

UK TO THE MEDITERRANEAN VIA THE FRENCH CANALS

If the coastal Atlantic does not appeal and if your boat is under a 1.5 metre (5 feet) draft, then the French canals are an option, from Le Havre in the north to Port St Louis, near Marseille. After crossing the Channel to Le Havre, de-mast and truck the mast south; some prefer to carry the mast on an A-frame on the boat but, depending on the length of your boat and the length of the mast, this can mean an overhang that can be a challenge when negotiating the locks.

It is possible to approach France from the Netherlands or Germany. There are three routes through France to the south:

- The Canal du Garonne and Canal du Midi,

The routes south from the UK

the shallow option entering from Biscay.

- From the north, from Le Havre to Paris, south on the Route Bourbonnais via the Loire and the Rhône.
- From the north, Le Havre to Paris, east towards Germany along the Marne–Saône via the Champagne region and the Rhône.

Before you leave there are certain things you need to consider:

- You should have already passed your CEVNI (Code de Voies de Navigation Interieure).
- You cannot have enough fenders along the side of your boat.
- Do not set off on your chosen route until you have ascertained the water levels. Late in the season boats in the south have been literally landlocked, forced to return north or wait until the canals refill months later.
- Allow at least eight weeks for your southbound journey.

The French canals

From Le Havre follow the tides to Rouen and buy a cruising permit. The Cruising Association (CA) publishes a useful pilot guide, *Cruising the Inland Waterways of France and Belgium*. The Navicarte / Fluviacarte pilot books (www.frenchwaterways.com) are also essential, providing charts and pilotage information. As ever, a road map and guidebooks make the trip more interesting.

Motoring into Paris on your own boat is a spectacular experience, passing the Eiffel Tower, the Louvre and Notre Dame, bridge after bridge. You can berth in the centre of the city in the Port de Plaisance (marina) in the Bastille, Port de L'Arsenal.

Travelling from Paris south on your chosen route (Marne–Saône or Bourbonnais) is a landlocked motor through fine dining, breath-taking scenery and scrumptious treats in local shops. For blue-water sailors it is a bizarre experience, closer to an overland journey, but is definitely worth considering as a gentle alternative to the Atlantic coast route.

Tying up to the bank on the French canals

UK TO FRANCE TO SPAIN TO PORTUGAL TO GIBRALTAR – MAY TO OCTOBER

Do not mess with the Bay of Biscay. The continental shelf extends into the sea so, from many thousands of metres deep, the Atlantic Ocean shelves and becomes comparatively shallow. If a gale blows up it will be much worse in Biscay, the worst storms in Europe are reputedly found here. If you cannot make it across in the prime months, May to June, then build in extra, extra time to your schedule to allow for weather windows and more weather windows.

There are many variables to be considered when deciding when to depart, and no right answer. A delivery passage from Falmouth to La Coruña can be sailed in five days, but that's seeing it in a blur, it achieves the miles but not the experience. If you want to sail down to Gibraltar with time to explore and time to wait for weather and for the inevitable repairs, allow at least 12 weeks from the UK to Gibraltar. You may want to indulge yourselves in Brittany and sail across Biscay from there or sail straight from Dartmouth to Spain. If you can leave in June, you will have a leisurely trip. (For those leaving from the Scandinavian countries, June is pretty much the deadline.) Most people, particularly those with families, leave in mid-July.

By late August you should have crossed Biscay. Allow at least ten days of waiting for weather. Yachts pushed for time push the boundaries. Where is the seamanship in being beaten up by a force 7? Here may be an appropriate place to remind ourselves that there are many old sailors, and many bold sailors, but not many old and bold sailors.

You must do your homework before leaving the UK. Thoroughly read Jimmy Cornell's *World Cruising Routes* concerning the times to cross Biscay. For guides to routes and ports, also see *The Shell Channel Pilot*, Tom Cunliffe; *Atlantic Spain and Portugal*, Henry Buchanan; *Atlantic Islands*, Anne Hammick and Hilary Keatinge; *South Biscay*, Steve Pickard. (If you are cruising down the coast of France, as above, read Nick Chavasse's *Atlantic France*.)

If you know you are crossing the Atlantic you should also be familiar with these books as you fit out your boat and sow the seeds of a good cruise: *The Atlantic Crossing Guide*, Jane Russell; *The Atlantic Sailor's Handbook*, Alastair Buchan.

RALLIES TO NORTHERN SPAIN OR PORTUGAL

The World Cruising Club run ARC 'Rally Portugal', which departs in late Spring from Plymouth, southwest England, crosses the Bay of Biscay to Bayona (Spain), visiting several Spanish and Portuguese ports, and ends in Lagos in the Algarve, southern Portugal. (www.worldcrusing.com, www.facebook.com/arcrally)

Rallies provide cruising camaraderie but, more importantly at this stage of the journey, they impose a deadline for setting off. (Rally deadlines are not always a good option, and this will be discussed in Chapter 8.)

Once across Biscay, the Spanish and Portuguese coasts are your playground before Gibraltar and the five-day sail to the Canaries.

The cruise from Galicia in northern Spain to Gibraltar can take six weeks, and could easily take six months. Cruisers can spend weeks 'gunk holing', exploring inlets and bays in the rias of Galicia, northwest Spain.

Or a coastal hop from the UK to Gibraltar can be a cruise in itself. If crossing an ocean is not for you, then this route down to the Mediterranean is an ideal way to explore the west coasts of France, Spain and Portugal, before heading east towards Croatia, Greece and Turkey.

Cruisers with limited time and the Caribbean aforethought often head south fast, missing some 'delight-full' European discoveries. The inside of the Bay of Biscay is longer, but nevertheless offers charms such as the Île de Ré, Île-d'Aix, beaches of La Rochelle, Bordeaux and cities such as Biarritz, Bilboa (slightly inland), Santander and Gijón.

FALSE START

The first time we set off to cross Biscay we were hyped up and full of hope until the gear lever snapped, and the wind died, leaving us floating towards the vicious rocks of the Raz de Sein. Time passed, the rocks were closing in. We started waving orange flares on the bow at an approaching French fishing boat. But the *Tor Pen* (a pox on them) sped past us. Thankfully, the wind got up and we sailed home (again) disheartened to Cameret, where a crazy adolescent in a Zodiac towed us in at speed, intent on rafting us up to the smartest, most gleaming yacht (Halberg)... the adolescent's Zodiac virtually under *Moonshine*... the tow rope wrapping around his propeller... thankfully, the gods had had enough sport that day... the owners leapt from a nearby boat and we slid in... the potential crunch avoided. Not a scratch.

A new gear lever and confidence renewed, we were ready to sail away, or at least make a short hop or two around Brittany.

We waited ten days for weather, gently meandering down the coast of Normandy. That's most people's ideal holiday. Finally the weather for the three-day crossing was benign, and we set off from Bénodet, Normandy, crossing a millpond in early September, arriving in Gijón in time for the Cider Festival, an introduction to Galician cooking that is utterly mouth-watering and takes seafood to a new place.

Source: *Moonshine* blog, August 2002

SIGHTSEEING IN SPAIN

Expecting the unexpected is par for the course in cruising, so be prepared to hire a car or jump on a train while waiting for weather. For some tourist sites you plan, others are a bonus.

Santiago de la Compostela is a popular tourist spot and site of pilgrimage. You can catch a train or coach from La Coruña or further down the coast from Vigo or Bayona.

The Islas de Bayona give a taste of the Caribbean in Europe.

Chipiona is a seaside town where you can berth and catch a bus to Seville for a couple of days if you do not want to traverse the 55 miles up the River Guadalquivir to the city.

In Jerez you are in Spanish sherry country. You will be closing in on Gibraltar and time may be short, but do not forget that Cadiz is across the bay from Chipiona and should not be missed.

Land was created to provide a place for boats to visit.

Brooks Atkinson

POSTCARDS FROM THE KEDGE

Graham Shaw and Lorraine Zaffiro from the Channel Islands have been sailing on their Catamaran *Catacaos* with their son Luca since departing on New Year's Eve. Lucas was 23 months when they set off from the Canaries to cross the Atlantic. They were in the Pacific at the time of writing.

Dear Nicola

These are Graham's top favourite anchorages.
(Lorraine's come later ...)

- Dinan, Brittany (technically not an anchorage, but my fave stopping place)
- Gustavia, St. Barts
- Bay of Virgins, Fatu Hiva, Marquesas
- Bras d'Or Lakes, Cape Breton Island, Nova Scotia
- Les Saintes

Best wishes
Graham & Lorraine

Nicola Rodriguez
The Yacht Moonshine
Browns Marina
Bimini
Bahamas

THE MEDITERRANEAN

MARINAS IN THE MED

Most marinas in the Mediterranean are set up for stern-to or bow-to berthing, sometimes with an anchor laid out to hold the boat off the dock. This is when a passarelle (metal gangplank), or the cheap version, a wooden gangplank, comes into use.

Anchoring stern-to is second nature to the locals and full of potential hazards for the uninitiated – cross-winds can blow you into the next-door boat or your anchor used to hold the boat in place can get tangled with other anchors or

Bow-to in Alcudia, Mallorca, Spain

debris in the marina.

Marinas often have a 'slime line', a mooring line that spends most of its time in marina water. One end is tied to the dock and at the other end is a chain weighted to the marina sea floor. Once you are tied to the dock (bow or stern), the marinero (dockhand) passes you the slime line, which you pull up along the boat. It becomes heavy and really gooey. At the 'back' of the boat (be it the bow or the stern), you cleat it off. This keeps the boat straight. It is easier than an anchor but can cause confusion if the marinero has mixed the lines along the pontoon, resulting in boats being held at an angle and making the exit tricky, as the departing boat straightens up while the others remain slanted.

It's all good practice for when you sail into narrow anchorages surrounded by rock walls, such as Calas Covas in Menorca, where you tie onto a rock. The spare anchor with line (rope) or chain is then lowered to a strong person in the dinghy. Once the boat is pulled straight or into the best 'parking position', the strong person throws (hurls with a shout) the anchor into place. Experienced yachtsmen in their own boats encourage other cruisers to 'park' or moor beside them, leaving those more likely to bump and grind, charter boats, on the outside.

This operation is carried out under the eye of amused local boats. You know you are their entertainment, and you know they're giving you marks out of ten. At weekends in the summer it's pretty much guaranteed that just where you plan to drop your anchor, a small weekender drops his first.

Calas Covas: one yacht tied to a rock, the other rafted on

THE COASTS & ISLANDS OF THE MEDITERRANEAN

The Mediterranean has been compared to a soup bowl slopping about. Gales in the Gulf of Lion (south of France) cause swells hundreds of miles away in the Balearics and so on, around and around. The main exits from this inland sea are the comparatively narrow Straits of Gibraltar in the west, between Gibraltar and Morocco, and the Sea of Marmara and the Bosphorus, linking the Aegean and the Black Sea. At the far eastern end are the Suez Canal and the Red Sea.

The cruising areas in the Mediterranean – the Balearics, Corsica, Sardinia, Italy, Croatia, the Adriatic Sea, Greece and Turkey – are geographically small compared with the Pacific, but the number of must-sees per kilometre is higher than the Caribbean and Pacific.

It can take at least 10 years to explore the East and West Mediterranean; it could take a season, May to September, 'just' to explore Croatia. Another summer cruise would take in three islands, Sardinia, Corsica and Elba, or the Maddalena Islands and Sardinia.

Once in the Mediterranean you can choose to explore east along the French coast to Italy and Croatia. Greece and Turkey are many cruisers' favourites, because they are not only beautiful cruising grounds, but the locals are genuinely welcoming, and it is much cheaper than the western Mediterranean. May and June are the best months to cruise in Greece and Turkey, before it becomes too hot – 90° at 9pm is not unknown.

Chart of the Mediterranean

THE WESTERN MEDITERRANEAN

From the mouth of the Rhône, near Marseilles, you could go west towards Spain and Gibraltar, and even across the Atlantic, with a view to taking in Europe from the western Mediterranean (Turkey and Greece) en route home. Or you could sail south to the Balearics.

OUR BALEARIC ADVENTURE

We spent three years on and off sailing around the islands, as we reported at the time in *Blue Water Sailing*.

Some of the most amazing sailing and beautiful anchorages in Europe are to be found in the Balearic Islands in the Mediterranean off southeast Spain. Although sometimes challenging, the sailing around Mallorca, Ibiza, Menorca and Formentera can be heavenly. The islands offer a wide variety of topography and on-shore diversions. There's the sophistication of Palma, Mallorca's capital, ancient culture, tourist beaches, traditional Spanish fiestas and superb cuisine. May and September are the best months to cruise, particularly early September when most of the holiday makers have left, the water is warm, and the winter gales have not yet set in. A useful pilotage / cruising guide to have on board is *Islas Baleares*, produced by the Royal Cruising Club Pilotage Foundation, available from www.imray.com.

As with all sailing, weather plays an essential role, but it is key within the Balearics. Beware of the localised systems around each island, as they interact with the systems around the Balearics as a whole and the Mediterranean.

In our first two years of cruising aboard our Moody 38, *Seraphim*, we were often pounded by changeable weather. By the third year, we had learnt to wait and change plans constantly to accommodate the 'go'. John, my husband and skipper, used at least four sources for weather. An excellent resource is Frank Singleton's Weather and Sailing Pages, which can be found at www.weather.mailasail.com/Franks-Weather/Home.

Anchorages in the Balearics can be idyllic but are sometimes affected by swells from storms up to 300 miles away, particularly in the Gulf of Lion near southern France. Often, we were toasting an anchorage when a rolling swell began, resulting in an uncomfortable night. Entering the Bays of Alcudia and Pollensa has the extra spin of sea planes practising dousing forest fires.

For a truly peaceful and sheltered anchorage, Cabrera is a beautiful island in a nature reserve 20 miles south of Mallorca. If you visit one place in the Balearics, make it this. Before setting out for Cabrera, do secure a permit via a marina. Our Cabrera permit allowed us two specific, dated days. A romantic fourteenth-century castle rises out of the rocky hills at the entrance to the large anchorage. Cabrera is renowned for the protected sea grass or Posidonia oceanica meadows, so most of the anchorages are mooring fields.

The anchorage off the island of Cabrera, Balearics, Spain

I feel when the buoys go down the magic disappears, but here it remains special. The sea grass is known for its oxygenating properties, and swimming above it felt strangely energising. Our stay was too short. From Cabrera the small but popular Cala Pi anchorage on the Mallorcan coast beckons, or it is a day's sail to Palma.

Mallorca

Sailing across the Bay of Palma past the cathedral is the ultimate introduction to Palma, a cosmopolitan city with numerous sites of interest. Considered by most the yachting capital of the Mediterranean, the marine facilities and chandleries are eclectic and numerous, as are crew agencies and charter companies. Within the grounds of the Real Club Náutico is the highly efficient Audax boatyard, where *Seraphim* was hauled out several times.

Anchoring in Palma is discouraged. I suggest a berth at the Real Club Náutico, Club de Mar or Pier 46. (There are others such as the Port Authority, Marina Port de Mallorca and, at a push, along the Paseo Maritimo.) If these are full or too expensive, there is an anchorage west around the Bay of Palma, outside Puerto Portals Marina. From here it is a 15-minute bus ride into Palma. The sea life attraction, Marine Land, overlooks the Portals anchorage. One night we were woken by a rising swell and amused by the barking of the seals.

Around the western side of the bay are lovely Portal Vells and Cala Fornells; unfortunately, their proximity to Palma means a crush, particularly at lunch time. Sail on telling stories of mythical beasts as you pass Dragonera Island and head to Andratx, a little of the French Riviera in Spain. This upmarket town is filled with

Punta de sa Foradada, Mallorca, Spain

real-estate agents, restaurants and a large supermarket. It is a popular departure port for Ibiza.

Further along Mallorca's west coast is the intriguing Punta de sa Foradada, a large, almost circular hole in a huge rock. In the 1870s, when the Archduke of Austria was buying large chunks of the west coast, he remarked, "The whole estate cost me as much as the value of the hole in sa Foradada."

Mallorca's most spectacular coastline is from Deià north to Cap de Formentor. The poet Robert Graves put Deià on the map with his home there. The imposing Tramontana mountain range reaches down to the coast. Whereas the southeast coast has numerous safe havens, the north

Cala de la Calobra, Mallorca, Spain

Weather permitting, spend a night here watching the late-afternoon sun in the gorge, then sit on the pebbled beach for sunset.

Rounding the magnificent Cap de Formentor with the lighthouse soaring above, where even in good weather the waters can be feisty, introduces the delights of Pollensa, Alcudia and Coll Baix, with its strangely 'corrugated' cliff.

Seraphim was berthed in Alcudia at the Alcudiamar Marina for two years. The boatyard behind the marina is helpful. Alcudiamar has good chandleries and the best yacht facilities outside Palma, including a very large travel lift. Port Alcudia is a family tourist resort. Anchoring outside the marina is good and sheltered, but in parts the sea grass is thick and setting anchor is occasionally a problem. Epic provisioning is easy in the street of Mariners, near the dinghy dock. Provisioned and fixed? Weather permitting, jump off to Menorca.

Alternatively, head down the east coast of Mallorca, taking in breath-taking anchorages such as Cala Magraner, Cala Mitjana, Cala Mondrago and Porto Cristo, with its famous caves where the public quay is half the price of the Club Náutico. Cala D'Or is useful for supermarkets. The tourist beach is packed, but a five-minute dinghy ride to the entrance of Cala D'Or reveals a far superior beach used by the locals.

Continuing on, Porto Colom is a large, protected harbour with a wide variety of restaurants. One of our most entertaining evenings was watching all the local boats, dressed up, parading to celebrate the Virgin del Carmen on 16th July.

has only Soller. If conditions become ugly quickly, which they can, it's a hazardous run for shelter. Sudden strong winds such as the Tremontara or mistral turn this coast into a treacherous lee shore.

The Port of Soller anchorage is well protected and surrounded by hills that constantly change with the light. Just sit and drink it in. A tram runs from the port through orange and lemon groves to the inland town of Soller, connecting with a train that clatters through the mountains to Palma, an hour of picturesque moments.

Just up the coast is Cala de la Calobra, a spectacular bay that opens into a deep gorge cut by the Torrent de Pareis.

Menorca
Menorca's east and north coasts offer up some of the most magnificent landscapes

in the Balearics, especially in the glorious evening light.

Fornells is a mile-long natural harbour in the north. It has been described as 'an outpost of St Tropez'. The port may be where the beautiful people go, but the various anchorages are certainly where to go for beauty. If you're hiring a car try finding Cavalleria, a remote promontory near a lighthouse where people build little stone towers.

The port of Mahon on the south east of Menorca has another long harbour with numerous anchorages and facilities for yachts. The first anchorage on the right is one of our favourites, below La Mola, the huge fortress complex of Isabel II, a secure anchorage run to by all in bad weather. Closer to the main town the continually changing views, particularly magical at night, and the convenience to the dinghy dock made the mooring buoys near Cala Llonga and Isla Pinto our preferred choices.

Mahon's quaint streets are full of history. In August the famous rearing black horses perform in festivals throughout Menorca, culminating in the craziest fiesta in Mahon.

One in a series of classic yacht races comes to Mahon at the end of August. We were thrilled by the classic yachts competing in the third stage of the 2nd Panerai Classic Yachts Races – awesome stuff when these ladies' sails unfurl.

On the south coast of Menorca, Calas Coves is surrounded by ancient caves, which are now blocked off to prevent modern-day habitation. As with Cala Mitjana in Mallorca, it can become tightly packed with no swinging room. Drop the anchor and back down against it, then either swim or dinghy to a rock and tie off securely. Occasionally you will find a post or ring set into the rock.

Nearby are postcard favourites Macarella beach and Son Saura, with its huge semi-circular beach. On the west coast of Menorca is Ciutadella, one of the most picturesque towns in Spain. In 1558 it was decimated by pirates. It is now besieged by tourists in high summer, but in September returns to its tranquil self.

Ibiza

Andratx on Mallorca's west coast is a good port from which to sail to Portinaix in north Ibiza, a safe natural harbour. If weather bound here, the local buses make the one-hour trip to Ibiza Old Town. Or hire a car to see the hippy market, vineyards and folkloric dancing. If you're inclined, Ibiza is famous / infamous for nightclubbing.

South along the west coast, San Antonio is a down-market tourist town, but a useful anchorage and provisioning stop. The west coast provides an entrancing backdrop for the sail south to the most popular location in the Balearics, the island of Formentera.

Formentera and Espalmador's waters are similar to the Caribbean. Sadly, buoys have turned the sanctuary of Espalmador into a car park, but it is possible to escape by anchoring around Formentera, for example southeast Playa Mitjorn or west Playa Tramontana. We moved up and down the east-coast beaches between the main town of Savina and the islet of Espalmador, depending on the weather.

Back in southern Ibiza we dropped the hook in Cala Roig, where red cliffs dominate the anchorage. (Don't tell too many people, it's special.) The next-door anchorage is pretty Cala Yonda and nearby Ibiza Old Town, where anchoring is not permitted. Go to Santa Eulalia on the southeast coast to victual before crossing back to Mallorca.

WEST TOWARDS THE FRANCO-SPANISH BORDER

As another route from France, from the mouth of the Rhône (near Marseille), if you head west to the Franco-Spanish border you curve around southwest France, the Languedoc-Roussillon region, which includes the Camargue (home of white horses and feral mosquitoes). Agde is a tacky tourist resort, but a good port in a storm if the Gulf of Lion begins to blow up, which it can. From there sail to Collioure, which is an enchanting anchorage en route to northeast Spain and the spectacular Bay of Roses.

COLLIOURE

After weeks landlocked in the French canals, we rejoiced at the opportunity to unfurl *Seraphim*'s sails and take flight. The invigorating sail ended in a Matisse painting, on the Franco-Spanish border. Artists have vied for decades for the best angle of Collioure harbour and we were in the centre, whichever way we looked was gorgeous. Often there is a dent in the view, not here. We dropped the hook beneath a thirteenth-century castle, built by a King of Aragon with the hills of Provence as the backdrop. My skipper felt that he stepped back in time as he secured our dinghy to a ring on the mediaeval wall.

For us in September the town was busy but not packed. The mistral drove Van Gogh mad, but this skittish wind was taking a break, leaving us an Indian summer.

It was a delight to wander around the narrow, cobbled streets squeezed to bursting with artist galleries, intriguing shops and regional vintners. Although the eclectic restaurants, particularly in the evening, were tempting, we ate on board, enthralled by the harbour at night.

From Collioure, the home of Fauvism (cousin of Impressionism), we headed south across the border along the unexpectedly magnificent Costa Brava to Port Lligat, where our coast of art concluded with Surrealism in the anchorage below Salvadore Dali's summer residence.

Source: Blue Water Sailing

Collioure, France

WEST ALONG THE SPANISH COAST

From Cadaques, a national park and Dali's summer home, the beaches, inlets and cliffs of the Bay of Roses are charming. Puerto L'Escala is another concrete so-what, but a useful stop. If you want to city hop there are Barcelona, Tarragona and Valencia (where the America's Cup was held in 2007 and 2010). Denia has a large marina near the quaint town where some cruisers winter. It's a good port to arrive or leave for the Balearics. Campello, near Alicante, is where Spanish families holiday. Rather than spending out on berthing in Alicante, head to this sweet spot.

Torrevieja is a tourist centre but is a useful place to carry out maintenance using the chandleries and ironmongers, who are used to odd requests from cruisers. The May Fair is a truly Spanish affair with tapas, horsemen and flamenco, so do try to include it in your itinerary.

The May Fair in Torrevieja, southern Spain

Cabo de Gata, the 'corner' from east to southern Spain, is a dangerous area. On land there is a national park, while the seabed is littered with wrecks. It is the Costa de Morte (death). At Costa Blanca around the southern coast, you leave Spain and enter holiday Spain, from Alicante to Malaga and Marbella.

This region of Spain is Andalusia, where they take their religious ceremonies seriously. Easter is celebrated in style, with full Easter Week (Semana Santa) processions.

Semana Santa, Cartagena, southern Spain

Almeria is another Andalusian town that celebrates the traditions in style. In the old town there is a fort high above the city with an excellent view. Try to take a berth in Cartagena for the week. Perhaps use it as a base to explore Granada, for which it is definitely worth hiring a car. The thirteenth- and fourteenth-century palaces within the Alhambra were my favourites in mainland Spain. Many of the merchants' houses have been turned into intriguing hotels, with odd-shaped rooms on different levels, with no one room the same.

About 15 miles along the coast westwards is Puerto de Almerimar, an artificial yacht harbour in a development that provides winter accommodation for scores of cruising boats. I agree with those who have wintered in interesting cities that, even though the prices are competitive, and the facilities are good for this area, it is a concrete so-what at least a bus ride from anywhere worth being. Compared to the magnificent cliffs in the northeast, the southern coastline is rather dull, particularly with the acres of polytunnels hot-housing fruit.

Marbella old town is a fun stop if you can find a berth. The marinas from here west are good, although Puerto Banus, a hot spot for the rich who live on the Costa del Sol, is expensive, so it's perhaps best to stay in Duquesa, Estepona or Sotogrande. Buses run up and down the coast regularly. Next stop Gibraltar.

Estepona, southern Spain

Pilot guides to the southern Spain include *Mediterranean Spain*: from the RCC Pilotage Foundation. Paul Theroux's, *The Pillars of Hercules* starts on the Pillars of Hercules overlooking the Straits and continues on a 'Grand Tour of the Mediterranean'.

GIBRALTAR

Take care if you're approaching Gibraltar from Sotogrande in the fog. Tankers are anchored near Europa Point, in your path, and can be disconcerting.

The British Ministry of Defence owned much of the island of Gibraltar – as they say, control the Rock and you control the Mediterranean. In recent years there has been a great deal of redevelopment. In October yachts converge on the Rock for the facilities, provisioning and final checks before sailing to the Canaries.

The Gibraltarians are loyal to the UK, although most have Andalusian roots. They speak a mix of Spanish and English. The Treaty of Utrecht in 1713 gave the British sovereignty over the island and in one way or another the Spanish have tried to regain it ever since. In 2002 a referendum asked the people of Gibraltar if they wished to remain British. An 87% turnout gave a 98% answer 'Yes'.

Sacarellos is a tea house in Irish Town, dating back centuries so, once you have organised your last-minute Mark & Spencer tins, jams and cheese scones in Main Street, drop down a few streets for an epic piece of cake. Gibraltar is duty free.

For fresh produce – vegetables, cheese and meat – check out the market near the Casements. The large Safeways is used to cruisers filling up but remember that the Spanish supermarkets across the border are cheaper, so consider buying there. During all the preparations, spare a few hours for the Rock Tour, including the

Fresh produce market in the Casements, Gibraltar

Barbary apes, the Pillars of Hercules and St Michael's Cave.

La Linea, the town across the Gibraltar border, used to have a bad reputation but it is improving and has Alcaidesa, a new marina. The town provides good supermarkets for provisioning and entertaining bars.

There is a t-shirt available from a charter company in Gibraltar showing that the sailor has sailed between two continents, Europe and Africa. Colin Thomas's *The Straits Sailing Handbook* is considered the authority on this stretch of water. From Gibraltar across the Straits of Gibraltar to Ceuta, which, although on mainland Morocco, is still technically part of Spain, takes about five hours. Smir is another comparatively easy Moroccan port to sail to, but whereas Ceuta is in the middle of a town, Smir is a modern marina seemingly in the middle of nowhere, certainly a five-mile taxi ride from anywhere.

The Straits of Gibraltar, the 'Gateway to the Mediterranean', are busy with shipping traffic, an estimated 30,000 ships a year, and a vigilant watch should be kept. As Colin Thomas says, 'Both the Rock itself and the geography of the Straits have a substantial influence upon our local weather.' The winds are changeable, the tides are strong. Where the Mediterranean Sea meets the Atlantic it looks as if the sea boils. The Atlantic tide is forced through a funnel 8 miles wide at the narrowest point between Europe and Africa.

Miles Kendall, in 'Sail to Africa' from *Ultimate Sailing Adventures*, recommends:

A night crossing can be easiest because navigation lights are harder to confuse than modern hull shapes, which are so various that it's impossible to tell the bows from the stern of many craft... There are few places where a day's sail takes you to a different continent and a different millennium, but Gibraltar is one of them.

FROM THE RHÔNE DELTA EAST TOWARDS ITALY

Heading east towards Italy from the Rhône delta takes the sailor past Provence and into the most beautiful, most expensive and most crowded waters in Europe, particularly in July and August: the Côte D'Azur and the Riviera. Parisians describe August as the white diary month because everyone leaves the city to go on holiday, and most of them seem to be on a boat in the south.

CORSICA OR L'ÎLE DE BEAUTÉ

Corsica is a French island, but it is not France. As with the mountains on the west coast of Mallorca, Corsica's mountainous coasts are an awesome sight, although they can be treacherous and should be approached with caution.

Boats from France make for the northern town of Calvi. During the summer months superyachts unload the smart set on this mostly unsophisticated island. Like most of the eastern Mediterranean, the island is full of nautical history. From 500 BC Phoenicians, Greeks and Romans used the safe harbour of Calvi, where a massive citadel was built in the thirteenth century.

Corsica was thrown up in a volcanic eruption. It is the most mountainous island in Europe ¬ two-thirds is made up of mountains. Having been awed and amazed by Corsica's coastline, venture inland to discover the dramatic scenery of the interior. A railway runs from Bastia in the northeast to Ajaccio, Napoleon Bonaparte's birthplace, in the southwest.

The huge bay of Porto Vecchio has numerous anchorages and good shelter for boats arriving from Menorca, Italy, or Sardinia.

Bonifacio is on the southern tip of Corsica, 6.8 miles from the northern tip of Sardinia across the Strait of Bonifacio. In *Ultimate Sailing Adventures*, Miles Kendall writes of the approach to Bonifacio:

A strong nerve and plenty of faith in your navigation is needed to approach Bonifacio. You know where it should be but all you can see are limestone cliffs that tower 70 metres above. With compass in one hand – and the fingers of your other hand firmly crossed – you sail towards this solid, imposing edifice. You know that you must be close because on the edge of the cliffs are the houses and fortifications of the ancient town.

Suddenly you see a fishing boat come around the headland – they must know how to find the way in. The breeze is rising and it's time to get out of the Strait of Bonifacio whose funnelling winds and scattered rocks and islands have claimed

hundreds of sailors' lives. The fishing boat has vanished. It was there one second and gone the next. You sail towards the point where it disappeared, and you suddenly see an opening in the cliff face and the entrance to the breath-taking and historic harbour that once sheltered Odysseus.

Most people remember Corsica for spectacular scenery rather than impressive cuisine. For good food and wine, it might be advisable to sail south to the Balearics, or to Italy.

A pilot guide for Corsica is *Mediterranean France and Corsica Pilot*, by Rod Heikell, and a recommended book is Dorothy Carrington's *Granite Island: Portrait of Corsica*.

SARDINIA

As the Corsicans are French with a difference, so the Sardinians are Italian with a difference. In the northeast, the Maddalena Archipelago and its islands provide a collection of tiny bays, rocky coves and beaches. This is a national park and marine reserve where holding tanks should be in operation. Check the latest rules on diving and fishing with the tourist office. Deadman's Reef Passage on Budelli is worth an anchor. (If you're heading north, the nearby island of Lavezzi in Corsican waters is worth a stop.)

In July and August yachts are tossed around by the wakes of powerboats speeding around Costa Smeralda. The mayhem starts as you round Capo Ferro and is centred on Porto Cervo. The Costa Smeralda Yacht Club hosts superyacht regattas and races.

In the south, Cagliari is a busy commercial port. It is a useful stop if not particularly beautiful.

Look at *Corsica and North Sardinia,*

John Marchment, from the RCC Pilotage Foundation.

WESTERN ITALY

East from the French Riviera is Italy and the Ligurian coast, including Genoa, birthplace of Christopher Colombus. Shipping companies use Genoa as their European destination. To the east, the Gulf of Genova is the Riviera de Levanta, the Italian Riviera. Whilst heading south down towards La Spezia, along the dramatic Ligurian coast taking in Porto Fino, the Cinque Terre, don't forget Santa Margherita Ligure, a rather overlooked gem. Livorno (Porto Turistica) and Pisa on the Arno river (Marina di Pisa), are good ports from which to explore. The train system in Italy is efficient. Catch a train to visit inland Florence and Siena.

Pilot guides include *Italian Waters Pilot*, by Rod Heikell.

The Tuscan archipelago includes the islands of Elba, Capraia and Montecristo. In the summer this area is crowded as yachts use the islands as stops en route to and from Corsica and Italy.

A summer cruise could include sailing from the Balearics to Sardinia to Corsica and across to Livorno and making an inland Italian excursion from there.

Fiumicino and Citavecchia are coastal ports from where you can travel to Rome. If you missed Tuscany, you could leave the boat here and head to Tuscany and Umbria by train or hire car.

Between Fiumicino and Naples, you could explore the Pontine islands, then the islands of Ischia and Capri off Naples. Cruisers have reported that if you rise very early in the morning you can have the famous Blue Grotto (Grotta Azzura) to yourself.

There are yacht harbours around the Bay of Naples, but you must book early for a visitor's berth. Pompeii (Marina di Stabia), Salnero (Marina d'Artechi), Vibo Valentia (Marina Stella de Sud) are good bases from which to visit Naples, Herculaneum and Pompeii.

The Tyrrhenian Sea lies between Sardinia and Italy, extending as far as the top of the boot of Italy and the north coast of Sicily, including Palermo. As you sail south there is the island of Stromboli with its active volcanos, worth a day's stop. From Scilly you can drop down to Tunisia, or further east to Malta, Greece and Turkey.

THE ADRIATIC SEA

The Adriatic Sea is surrounded by Italy, Slovenia, Croatia, BH Montenegro and Albania. To the south is the Ionian Sea. Pilot guides include *Adriatic Pilot*, by Trevor and Diana Thompson.

CROATIA

From the Istria region in the north, bordering Italy, south to Dalmatia, Croatia has become a popular cruising destination.

Dubrovnik, the mediaeval city and a UNESCO World Heritage Site, is a must visit, as are Korcula, said to be Marco Polo's birthplace, and Split. Another mediaeval city overlooking the Adriatic Sea is Hvar, a yachting centre that is increasingly attracting superyachts drawn from French and Italian waters to spend a summer cruising up and down the coast between Split and Dubrovnik.

Superyacht skipper Mark's favourites are Mljet, near the monastery at Polace, or one of the little inlets of the Pakleni Islands,

Dubrovnik (www.marinas.com)

west of Hvar.

Most cruisers in recent years have been following Lonely Planet's advice, 'Get in before the crowds return.'

Suggested reads to illuminate the complex history of the Balkan area are a travel book written in 1941 by Rebecca West, *Black Lamb and Grey Falcon*, and Robert Kaplan's *Balkan Ghosts*.

EASTERN ITALY

The east coast of Italy is not as popular as the west. However, it is worth the flog up the coast to sail into Venice. Just think of sailing up the Lido to the city of canals. There are marinas such as Marina Santelena and, if you go very early in the morning, you can dinghy up the Grand Canal. Or you could anchor off Poveglia island, just outside Venice, and catch the vaporetto (water bus).

After Venice try Grado, where you can moor in the middle of the town, and take a bus to Aquileia, which has a Paleo-Christian church with an entire floor of mosaics.

THE EASTERN MEDITERRANEAN

THE SEVEN WONDERS OF THE ANCIENT WORLD

A charter holiday or flotilla does not a long-term cruiser make, but if you want a taste, the Dalmatian coast, Greece and Turkey are full of charter companies. By the time they have cruised Greece and Turkey some cruisers complain about being 'ruined out', just as in the Far East they are 'templed out'.

If you are into lists, here is where you can tick off three of the ancient wonders of the world, with an eye to two more:

- The Temple of Artemis (ruin) in Ephesus. Setur Marina in Kusadasi is about 18 kilometres away.
- The site of the Mausoleum of Halicarnassus is beside the holiday resort of Bodrum.
- Colossus of Rhodes – the island (on the tip of Turkey) remains, but not the statue.

For two other wonders – the Lighthouse of Alexandria and the Pyramid of Giza – see the information on rallies below. (The Hanging Gardens of Babylon are in Iraq. Technically you have to go on a Baltic voyage to find the restored Statue of Zeus in the Hermitage in St Petersburg, Russia.)

GREECE & TURKEY

Those who really want to explore the Greek and Turkish waters take at least three seasons. Ten years is not uncommon. An example of the distances, in an area many will know, from Istanbul along the south coast to Antalya will take two weeks, and that does not take time for the Black Sea Coast or exploring east towards the Syria border.

The Wood family motoring through the Corinth Canal

To the west of Greece lies the Ionian Sea. At a push, you could include the Corinth Canal and Athens when you're exploring the west coast of Greece.

The Aegean lies between Greece and Turkey. The Dodecanese, from the Greek, are made up of 12 islands and the best known of these is Rhodes in the south, others include Kos and Patmos. These islands provide centuries of history per centimetre. Samos, Agathonisi, Arki, Lipso and Leros are small islands that give a relaxed cruise with easy distances, and are recommended as having 'pretty harbours, good anchorages and fine tavernas.' Pythagorion, the main port of Samos, is named after Greek mathematician Pythagoras. Many cruisers' favourite island is Symi, (Panometi Bay). Pedi in the NE corner of Symi is Tanya Leech's favourite. Whilst sailing around Symi she fell in love with cruising and with her husband Graham.

Bodrum and Leros airports are useful for guests. Cruisers report that Gulluk Marina is only ten minutes from Bodrum so good for meeting guests who no doubt will be drawn to the islands.

The Meltemi is the wind that blows down the Aegean in the summer, sometimes with great force and for days on end. There are numerous well-protected anchorages on the Turkish coast between Cesme and Kusadasi. Sailing in Greece and Turkey can be challenging. Many cruisers have stories of being pinned by strong winds while tied up to harbour walls because the marinas are full.

The northern Aegean Sea is quieter than the south, and you can find an anchorage to yourself. Mithymna on Lesbos with its mediaeval village and Genoese castle is spectacular. South of Kusadasi in high summer it becomes busy.

In the Dardanelles, Australian and New Zealand cruisers in particular stop at Canakkale, the town from which to visit the battlefields of Gallipoli. Anzac Day, 25th April, honours those in the Australian and New Zealand Army Corp (ANZAC) and those who have served and died in military campaigns since. Troy in the south of the Dardanelles is another of the many sites mentioned by Homer in this area.

Istanbul contains dozens of attractions such as the Blue Mosque, the sixth-century Hagia Sophia, Topkapi Palace with the Iznik tiling in the Harem, the Florence Nightingale Museum (by arrangement with the Turkish Army), plus, of course, Turkish baths.

The Bosporus is a busy waterway with a strong current. If its hustle and bustle are not for you, the Atakoy Marina is a bus ride from the main city. One cruiser arranged to celebrate a birthday in two continents by having lunch on the west bank, in Europe, and dinner on the east bank, in Asia, on either side of the Bosporus.

From west to east, pilot guides include

Knidos in Turkey

Ionian, Rod Heikell; West Aegean Cruising Companion, Robert Buttress; Greek Waters Pilot, Rod and Lucinda Heikell; East Aegean, Rod Heikell. In addition to these, cruisers have recommended www.sunflowerbooks.co.uk who publish three guides to the Turkish Coast, from Anatalya to Kas, Kas to Dalyan and Marmaris to Bodrum. Also, the magazine, Cornucopia, 'for connoisseurs of Turkey' (www.cornucopia.net).

Spices in Turkey

POSTCARDS FROM THE KEDGE

David and Susie have cruised extensively in the Caribbean. Now with several seasons in the Greek and Turkish waters under their keel, their advice is: 'Free anchoring is often in relatively deep water, commonly with a line ashore to a tree or rock.'

Dear Nicola

Our top 'must-see, must-dos' are:
- Istanbul from Atakoy Marina
- Cappadocia (3- or 4-day trip from anywhere in Turkey)
- Pergamon from Ayvalik Marina
- Athens from Kea Marina
- Corinth Canal

Our favourite anchorages in this region are:
- Thessalona (aka St Georges Bay, Symi) – stupendous, all-time favourite
- Kekova Roads, Turkey – walk over the isthmus to ancient Aperlae
- Moudros Bay, Limnos – peace, glorious peace!
- Sounion Bay – under the temple of Poseidon on Cape Sounion, south of Athens
- Keci Buku, Hisaronu Korfezi – just a lovely bay and local village

Nicola Rodriguez
The Yacht Moonshine
Studland Bay
Poole
UK

Best wishes
David & Susie

Their top 5 town anchorages are:
- Symi
- Mithymna, Lesbob
- Pythagorion, Samos
- Bozborun, Turkey
- Erdek, Sea of Marmara

FAR EASTERN MEDITERRANEAN

In *Ultimate Sailing Adventures*, Miles Kendall voices the concern of many cruisers in the eastern Mediterranean:

The Mediterranean is an idyllic cruising ground, but many sailors limit their exploration to its northern shore. More adventurous yachtsmen and women may want to sail the eastern and southern coasts but are put off by political uncertainty, flag safety issues or problems with bureaucracy.

The situation in the Middle East is never predictable. If you wish to explore this area it would be advisable to enquire about the Eastern Mediterranean Yacht Rally (EMYR) and keep an eye on information from Noonsite.

The itinerary changes depending on the situation.

BLACK SEA

A very long and, in places, hazardous inland route is from Rotterdam via the Rhine and Main waterways of Germany through the Rhine–Main–Danube Canal (RMD or Europa Canal), into the Danube and through eastern Europe via Budapest, coming out in the Danube delta in the Black Sea. Alternatively, enter at Le Havre and follow the Seine via Paris to the German waterways. This route is a way across Europe, but it is not recommended.

From the Sea of Marmara passing through Istanbul on the Bosphorus, north to the Black Sea, is a more established route.

The RCC Pilotage Foundation produce a pilot guide on *The Black Sea* by David Read Barker and Lisa Borre.

WINTERING IN SOUTHERN EUROPE

If you decide to winter in the Mediterranean, do not underestimate the severity of the winter storms. It is advisable to organise your winter berth in the summer. Prized winter ports include Seville, Barcelona, Palma in Mallorca and Fiumicino near Rome. Marmaris in Turkey is also a popular place with good marine facilities and social life, alternatively Kemer is smaller and quieter. Gibraltar is compact and quirky, and there are still numerous cruisers after the crowds have headed across the Atlantic. Don't forget you have Spain across the border!

Wintering in southern Europe is not a hot option – it is cool, even cold in January – so fix your heating in advance. You will need winter clothes

ROUTES TO THE CANARIES

Gibraltar to the Canaries is the most popular route. Another is from Portugal or southern Spain to Funchal or Porto Santo, Madeira, then on to the Canaries. Remember, in October this comparatively small island is crowded with other West Indies-bound boats.

Some cruisers fast track to Gibraltar and across to Marrakech, Morocco to see the Atlas Mountains, then onwards to the Canaries.

The RCC's *Cruising Guide to the Canary Islands* is by Oliver Solanas Heinrichs and Mike Westlin.

Life is short. The world is wide. I want to make some memories.

From Mamma Mia Here We Go Again, filmed in Vis, Croatia doubling for Kalokairi, Greece

WINTERING IN PALMA

Wintering in the Real Club Náutico, in the heart of Palma de Mallorca, was very special. Palma is an eclectic mix of old Spanish culture and highly sophisticated European city. The historic centre and first-class shopping were within ten minutes' walk. The Christmas decorations in the old town were magical. On Christmas Day we sat in the cockpit in shirt sleeves enjoying a bright blue sky. The New Year's Eve fireworks were a 360°, 30-minute spectacular. And on 6th December, the Three Kings sailed through the harbour past our pontoon en route to parade through the city.

Winter in the Real Club Nautico, Palma de Mallorca, Balearics

WEST AFRICA

If you are considering sailing down the coast of West Africa (e.g. Senegla, The Gambia, Guinea-Bissau), look up Steve Jones' *Cruising Guide to West Africa* for the RCC Pilotage Foundation.

POSTCARDS FROM THE KEDGE

Ed and Megan Clay included Greenland in their extended Atlantic Circuit which also took in the Gambia River in West Africa.

Dear Nicola

Our 5 favourite anchorages are:

- Selvagem Grande – between Madeira and the Canary Islands. The holding is bare rock and atrocious but the feeling of being on an isolated island in the middle of the Atlantic is hard to beat. You need permission to anchor in advance (by email) as it is a nature reserve.
- Bird Island, River Gambia – hippos snorting by the boat at sunset.
- Getting off the beaten track in the Caribbean – find a likely looking spot on the chart, that isn't in the main pilot books and be happy to beat to windward for a few miles and you can have a perfect sand beach to yourself. I'm not going to tell you ours as it will spoil the fun.
- Woods Island, Newfoundland – provided excellent shelter after a squally arrival in Newfoundland. Though the house on the shore that had blown over suggested it isn't always so calm.
- Appamiut, West Greenland – excellent shelter and holding and a short scramble up the hill gives superb views of the mountains and glaciers.

Nicola Rodriguez
The Yacht Moonshine
Real Club Nautico
Palma De Mallorca
Spain

Best wishes
Ed & Megan

8
BLUE-WATER SAILING

Blue-water or ocean sailing is the true aim of most of those who sail away.

Once the initial fear of sailing for hundreds of miles away from land out into an ocean subsides, tranquillity descends. By the third week most people want to just keep going.

The night sky over the Atlantic is truly breath-taking. One sailor described how he came on watch with his book and took a moment to look around. Four hours later, the book was still closed, and he was still enraptured.

Crews occupy themselves by fishing, reading, playing cards or craft work such as knitting and beading. As the days pass and the Zen permeates, the pastimes become more prosaic. Most boats have a once-a-week party planned before departure, so there are costumes or masks or props to be prepared for that.

The days literally roll past: from watch to watch, breakfast to lunch to dinner, and on through the night watch.

Boats within radio range of each other have a morning and evening radio net, in which there is a comparison of positions, weather and conditions – and most importantly the size of fish most recently caught.

THE 'KNOWN UNKNOWN'

The go-to guide for crossing the Atlantic is not surprisingly, *The Atlantic Crossing Guide* by Jane Russell. In the 7th Edition, Jane writes of her first Atlantic Crossing:

Despite all the advice and preparation, as we cast off I remember feeling that I was embarking on a personal journey into the unknown. I'm sure it's true of everyone who first sets out to cross an ocean, which is why it still remains a challenge and why the rewards are many and varied, and sometimes unexpected. Living under a light-polluted sky I had no idea how completely out of touch I was with the rhythms of the moon and stars. To be alone on night watch in the middle of the Atlantic and see the full-night sky laid out above me from horizon to horizon, with the occasional shooting star triggering a flash of pure joy, is an experience burned into my soul. So too the incredible intensity of phosphorescence as a display team of dolphins surfed and raced along in the ocean swell. I remember a frequent feeling of surprise – there were so many 'firsts' and there was much to learn about the ocean and about the places and people I encountered.

SET SAIL FOR ADVENTURE
SAILS UNFURLED

Sailing guru, Tom Cunliffe, (www.tomcunliffe.com) in his book, *Topsail and Battleaxe: A Voyage in the Wake of the Vikings*, writes about the point of view of a 'typical, tenth-century Icelander' compared with a 'present-day Westerner. He knew the size of the Atlantic Ocean – not in miles, but in days or weeks – and he knew how small he was by comparison. He had personally confronted elemental forces that could snuff him out at a stroke and he understood that, however great his machismo, he continued to exist in an immense cosmos, only by courtesy of nature and his own fate.'

Before you do set sail, ensure that you have all that you need to ensure your health and safety on the ocean. Be sure that your crew are physically and mentally fit and that they have good-quality foul-weather gear. If they take medicines, do they have sufficient? Perhaps everyone is nervous about setting off, but is anyone too stressed? Do your crew gel together? You don't want tantrums or rows that have been brewing on shore to erupt suddenly 10 days out, with many more days to go.

As with all sailing, the golden rule is 'Keep the water out and the people in.' As mentioned in Chapter 5, it is important to have at least one man-overboard drill with the whole crew, even when time is short and preparations many. When you have given the crew a thorough tour of the boat, remember that what is obvious to you is not to new crew members.

In the second edition of *The Pacific Crossing Guide*, Dr Nicholas JH Davies writes:

I remember a retired couple voyaging from Vancouver to Panama, their first significant cruise. When well off the Pacific coast of Mexcio, a large sea knocked the husband off the deck of their 44-foot ketch while he was taking an evening star-sight. The wife had to come to terms with the fact that she was unable to retrieve him. I met her just after she had brought their yacht, by herself, 250 miles into Puntarenas, Costa Rica. Even the most unexpected and severe challenges may be overcome with resourceful determination.

This is not the place for sad stories but be sure you can haul in heavy members of crew.

When stowing items, particularly tins and batteries, make sure that they are securely stowed. These heavy items become lethal missiles as they fly across the saloon because a locker has not been properly locked. It is important to keep the interior of the boat as tidy as possible, so that crew stumbling around in bad weather and / or at night do not trip over sleeping bags or rucksack chords.

LIVING THE DREAM
From *Moonshine's* log, November:

Solent veterans with Blue Ensigns and other coastal folks with decades more experience had poured out advice with the gin and tonics. They were still gathering dust in the posh clubhouses. Here we were in the Atlantic, encircled by empty horizons and awesome night skies. Despite the steep learning curves (waves) of our rock 'n' roll, shake-down cruise from the UK to Gibraltar, we still felt like children who had just taken the stabilisers off our bicycles. Here we were flying along without holding the handlebars. Here we were surfing down the Atlantic rollers. Here we were.

IF AT FIRST…

Freddie and Jacqui Rose are a great example of 'if at first…'. They set off on their adventure on *Shavora*, a Moody 39, fully equipped and seemingly ready. Two days out of Southampton they hit turbulent conditions off Portland Bill, a tricky headland. They returned to their home port severely rattled and deflated. However, the next year they set off again, and sailed to Guadaloupe. It was not the end of their troubles, but now they have established themselves in Carriacou, in the Grenadines.

A YEAR AROUND THE WORLD

The planner and map on the next few pages focus on the west-about route (with the prevailing winds) around the world via the Red Sea.

For those choosing to sail around the tip of South Africa, it would have been argued that they face the tougher challenge, but most people currently agree that the pirate situation in the Indian Ocean is a greater risk than rounding the Cape of Good Hope.

The information here is not meant as a definitive guide but as an indication of popular routes and timings. There are other sources, such as Jimmy Cornell's excellent *World Cruising Handbook*, and www.Noonsite.com, to help with the finer details. *Ocean Passages and Landfalls* by Rod Heikell and Andy O'Grady is a publication aimed at cruisers crossing oceans. See also Jason Trautz's information on Noonsite, 'Crossing the Indian Ocean Guide'.

We start our tour of seasonal sailing around the world in November, when the Atlantic fleet are heading off west from the Canaries.

SHIPPING ACROSS THE ATLANTIC

There are two shipping methods, either float-on-float-off or lift-on-lift-off, usually referred to as flo-flo and lo-lo. In 'float on' the yacht is motored into a semi-submersible ship such as those used by Dockwise. Once the cargo is loaded, the yachts are chocked off by divers and secured. The ship is dried, sails and then reverses the operation on arrival. In lift-on-lift-off, the yachts are craned on and secured as deck cargo.

On the Dockwise transporter, *Super Servant 4*, depending on the number and size of vessels, owners or crew are allowed to stay aboard their own boats for the journey; they are then known as riders. There are between 12 and 14 riders, some of whom are engineers or deck hands who maintain the boat systems. Meals are usually taken with the Dockwise crew. One couple worked through the tins that would have sustained them if they had sailed themselves.

RALLIES

The World Cruising Club organises numerous rallies from the previously mentioned Rally Portugal (from Plymouth to Portugal from where you can sail down to the Canaries and join the Atlantic Rally for Cruises) to the Atlantic Rally for Cruises, the ARC, which sails from Las Palmas in the Canaries to Rodney Bay, St Lucia in the West Indies. There are additional options such as stopping at the Cape Verdes or sailing to St Vincent. This Rally has been run for more than 20 years and regularly attracts more than 200 boats.

Rallye des Iles du Soleil (Islands of the Sun), (www.rallye-ilesdusoleil.com), is a

DECEMBER – MAY
CARIBBEAN
Whether heading to the western Caribbean to transit the Panama Canal or enjoying a Caribbean cruise before heading north to the USA or south out of the hurricane belt, or heading back to Europe, this is the time to have fun in the Caribbean

FEBRUARY – MARCH
EASTERN CARIBBEAN
Most yachts arrive in mid-February and transit the Panama Canal in early March

JUNE – OCTOBER
ATLANTIC – WEST TO EAST
Boats crossing from the USA and Caribbean should have arrived in Europe (eg Falmouth or Gibraltar) by the beginning of July

APRIL – JUNE
ATLANTIC – WEST TO EAST, eg USA (Beaufort)
to US Virgins to Azores and Europe
Those heading to Europe should be en route in May before the hurricane season starts officially in June

JUNE – NOVEMBER
CARIBBEAN
Hurricane season

MARCH – APRIL
CARIBBEAN
By April you should be heading out of the hurricane belt or finalising your hurricane season arrangements

LATE NOVEMBER – JANUARY
Canary Islands to the Caribbean
Atlantic crossing

MARQUESAS, PACIFIC
It is best to arrive in the Marquesas before the end of April. May, June and July can be spent in French Polynesia

PACIFIC
In March boats take in the Galapagos Islands, then sail the stretch of 3,000 miles to the Marquesas

SEPTEMBER
If in French Polynesia, now is the time to consider where to spend the cyclone season. Tonga? New Zealand? Australia? Those not remaining in the cyclone area make the passage to New Zealand or Australia. Cyclone season starts 1st November and ends 30th April

ARCTIC OCEAN

GREENLAND

USA

Aleutian Islands

CANADA

Vancouver

Toronto

New York

UNITED STATES OF AMERICA

Los Angeles

Beaufort

Bermuda

MEXICO

The Bahamas

Hawaiian Islands

US Virgin Is.
Antigua

Caribbean Sea

Barbados
Trinidad

Panama

VENEZUELA

Galapagos Islands

ECUADOR

Marquesas Islands

FRENCH POLYNESIA

PERU

BRAZIL

Recife
Salvador

Rio de Janeiro

Tonga

Valparaiso

SOUTH PACIFIC OCEAN

CHILE

ARGENTINA

SOUTH ATLANTIC OCEAN

NORTH ATLANTIC OCEAN

BRITISH ISLES

Falmouth

FR

PORTUGAL SP.

Azores

Gibraltar

Canary Islands

MOROCCO

ALG

Cape Verde Islands

Cape Horn

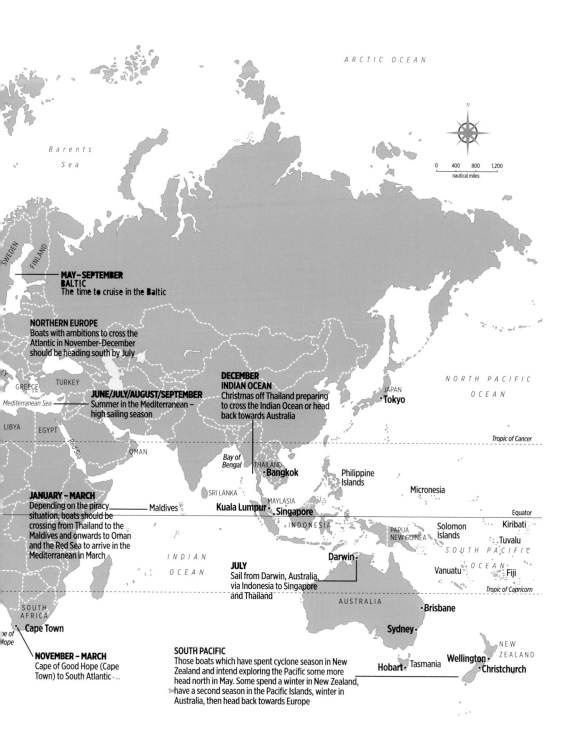

ARCTIC OCEAN

N

0   400   800   1,200
nautical miles

B a r e n t s
S e a

SWEDEN
FINLAND

MAY–SEPTEMBER
BALTIC
The time to cruise in the Baltic

NORTHERN EUROPE
Boats with ambitions to cross the
Atlantic in November-December
should be heading south by July

GREECE
TURKEY

Mediterranean Sea

JUNE/JULY/AUGUST/SEPTEMBER
Summer in the Mediterranean –
high sailing season

DECEMBER
INDIAN OCEAN
Christmas off Thailand preparing
to cross the Indian Ocean or head
back towards Australia

NORTH PACIFIC
OCEAN

JAPAN
•Tokyo

LIBYA   EGYPT

Red Sea

OMAN

Tropic of Cancer

Bay of
Bengal   THAILAND
•Bangkok

Philippine
Islands

Micronesia

SRI LANKA

JANUARY – MARCH
Depending on the piracy
situation, boats should be
crossing from Thailand to the
Maldives and onwards to Oman
and the Red Sea to arrive in the
Mediterranean in March

Maldives

Kuala Lumpur

MAYLASIA
•Singapore

INDONESIA

PAPUA
NEW GUINEA

Solomon
Islands

Kiribati

Equator

Tuvalu

INDIAN
OCEAN

JULY
Sail from Darwin, Australia,
via Indonesia to Singapore
and Thailand

Darwin•

SOUTH PACIFIC
OCEAN

Vanuatu

Fiji

Tropic of Capricorn

AUSTRALIA

SOUTH
AFRICA
•Cape Town

e of
ope

NOVEMBER – MARCH
Cape of Good Hope (Cape
Town) to South Atlantic

SOUTH PACIFIC
Those boats which have spent cyclone season in New
Zealand and intend exploring the Pacific some more
head north in May. Some spend a winter in New Zealand,
have a second season in the Pacific Islands, winter in
Australia, then head back towards Europe

•Brisbane

Sydney•

Hobart• Tasmania

Wellington•

NEW
ZEALAND

•Christchurch

	Atlantic	Caribbean	Pacific	Indian Ocean	Europe
Nov	Atlantic East to West: Atlantic crossing west from the Canaries.	Hurricane season.	1st Nov: Cyclone season officially starts. Most boats are in safe harbours in Australia or New Zealand.	Christmas off Thailand, preparing to cross the Indian Ocean.	
Dec		Time to enjoy the Caribbean.			
Jan				If risking pirates in mid Indian Ocean, cross from Thailand to Maldives & onwards to Oman and Red Sea, to arrive in Med in March. Some leave on southern Indian Ocean route in late Jan.	
Feb		Western Caribbean: Most yachts arrive in mid-February and transit the Panama Canal in early March.	Take in Galapagos Islands, then sail the 3,000 miles to the Marquesas.		
Mar					
Apr	Atlantic West to East: For example, USA (Beaufort) to the Azores and Europe. Those heading to Europe should be en route in May before the hurricane season starts officially in June.	Time to head out of the hurricane belt or organise your stay.	Southwest Pacific: Head north to the Pacific islands.		
May			Spend in French Polynesia.		
Jun				'Southern' Indian Ocean: Sail from Darwin (AUS) via Indonesia to Singapore, Thailand, Sri Lanka, Rodrigues, Mauritius, Mozambique, South Africa	Boats with ambitions to cross the Atlantic in November / December should be setting sail in June / July.
Jul					
Aug		Hurricane season.	Decide where to spend the cyclone season.		
Sep				South Indian Ocean Route World ARC Sail from Darwin to Malaysia	
Oct				Cocos (Keeling) to Mauritius, Reunion, South Africa arriving in November.	Boats should be arriving in Gibraltar or Canaries.

WHY WE PIGGYBACKED ACROSS THE ATLANTIC

We did not want to sail the Atlantic with children aged 2 and 4. What could we do? The first option was for John to sail *Seraphim* with a crew of friends and for me to fly with the boys. That idea was a 'no': we went as a family or not at all. The second 'no' was for a hired crew to take her. In addition to the cost of £8,000, it was too much wear and tear on the boat, and us, while she was crossing. Yacht transportation on a ship was the next option. Until that point we had dismissed this as prohibitive and only for superyachts.

We researched the costs and weighed up the pros and cons: for example, how much would it cost to stay in the Real Club Náutico de Palma for another winter? How much would another summer season in the Mediterranean cost versus the costs of living in the Caribbean? Yacht transportation became feasible. The Caribbean was cheaper, because we would not need to stay in marinas. In these circumstances, whether high or low season, we could justify the cost of transporting *Seraphim* rather than staying in Europe in expensive marinas for another year.   Source: Yachting World

Seraphim afloat in the Dockwise transporter

French rally organised by Grand Pavois which sails from La Palma (in the Canaries) to Marie Gallant (Guadaloupe).

It costs money to join a rally and the participants are expected to keep to a schedule. Most rally-ers appreciate the support of the organisers taking the weight of the administration such as customs and immigration, marina berths, and a team to welcome the boats on their arrival in each port. The team are on hand if problems arise. The friendships made are enduring. There are many advantages of sailing on a rally, particularly when blue-water sailing,

but I would time and again remind rally-ers that if the deadline does not suit you, do not leave.

Rally detractors, with time, say 16 months is too fast to circumnavigate, and, they are constantly arriving in a crowd. The 'independents' express the desire to make their own way, explore in their own time without a schedule. If they run into problems, they know they can rely on themselves or fellow cruisers. They would prefer to spend the money having more time away.

Most cruisers, whether on a rally or

sailing independently, keep blogs, (www.getjealous.com, www.sailblogs.com, http://blog.mailasail.com/). This will give you an 'in' on numerous other posts on Instagram, Facebook, etc. These give a useful view of the different experiences of sailing with a rally or independently. Some cannot afford a world rally, others wish to choose their sailing companions. Reports from independent cruisers sailing all over the world can be read in the OCC (www.oceancruisingclub.org) magazine *Flying Fish* and The Royal Cruising Club (www.rcc.

org.uk) journal *Roving Commissions*, both available online.

Once you have reached Australia you may like to look up the Rally organised by www.downunderrally.com of which more when we get to Australasia.

An alternative is the Clipper Round the World Race (www.clipperroundtheworld.com), where individuals can buy a place on a leg of this amateur round the world race, for example from the UK to Brazil, or, if they have the time and the money, around the whole world.

AROUND THE WORLD ON A RALLY

If you are considering a circumnavigation, the World ARC Rally supports cruisers who want to venture from St Lucia through the Panama Canal, across the Pacific, to Australia, the Far East and back via South Africa to the Caribbean in 16 months covering 26,000 miles. Participants receive a book with the how-to of sailing around the world with the Rally. The organisers provide safety advice as well as support ashore and a daily reporting network at sea.

It is also possible to take part in the half world rally, choosing to leave the rally in French Polynesia (before Australia) and explore the Pacific. The rest of the rally continues to Australia, and on to the Cape of Good Hope, South Africa and back to St Lucia for April, 16 months later. These boats could then explore the Caribbean or head home with another ARC rally leaving from the BVIs in early May, following the usual route via Bermuda and the Azores.

OUR RALLY EXPERIENCE

This is an account of our experience of sailing the Atlantic with a rally.

Ten participating yachts ensured that we all got to know one another. If not a family, we became a close-knit community that ranged, this year, from 19 years old to over 60. The cohesion within the rally could be gauged by the speed and variations of the latest jape or prank, usually sparked off by the young or young-at-heart at play. In our mid to late 30s, like three other couples, we were the 'in-betweeners'. Despite the bijou nature of the rally, it was diverse: an Oyster 66, a Mystic 60, a Contessa 55, a Nijad 50, two

Marlos, a Dix 38, our Westerly Corsair and the Contest 32 that led the Rally across the pond. The home-built Whisper, 9 feet wide and 42 feet long, was in every way a law unto herself. The owners of the Oyster and the Contest were Blue Water Rally veterans, having been on the Trade Winds Rally and Biscay Triangle, respectively.

In addition to the directors' counsel, we found the instant access to a pool of generous knowledge extremely useful. Although we still made friends and received wisdom from the Atlantic veterans on the dockside, being part of a rally made it easier, be it impertinent questions or comparative notes on such perennials as weather and crew. Certainly, in Tenerife when we asked Tony Diment for his take on a thorny crew issue, his advice was excellent.

The organisers often repeated the mantra, that this was not a race. Indeed, predictably, gentle competition drifted through our fleet, but no one was selling their soul and that of their crew for shiny trophies. Perhaps a side deal with the dogs of hell for an extra knot was contemplated, but none was made. A rally fuelled with race fever and start-line crashes was a far cry from the adrenaline-fuelled, bon-voyage-to-all send-off at Europa Point, Gibraltar.

In Tenerife, before the Atlantic crossing, it was decided that, since the larger boats would find it difficult to turn back if help was required, the three smaller yachts (a Contessa 32, our 37 Westerly Corsair and a 38-foot Dix) would leave five days before the larger yachts.

The crossing briefing was held on the morning of Sunday 10th November, with anticipated departure for the small boats on Wednesday, since the exact weather at that time was 'tba'. We three did leave in fine weather on Wednesday 13th November. It was unfortunate that an unexpected and barely forecast storm that had been scuffing its heels in Africa clocked 180 degrees, kicked out into the Atlantic, and into us, half a day out. A sunny afternoon blew up into three awful days of gales during which, although we could bemoan our situation over the VHF to the other two (*Fidgets Five* and *Odyssey*), we were still alone and, on *Moonshine*, feeling very vulnerable. The winds grew and grew until we were being pounded by 55-knot gusts, and 25-feet seas. At one point two of us were disabled by seasickness and the others prostrate with exhaustion.

We reefed our wing and wing rig right down but were still surfing wildly at 11 knots. John insisted that we went below to the tumble dryer interior of the boat. He crept under the spray hood and prayed that the hydrovane self-steering would hold our course and, if nothing else, keep the massive winds behind us. Below we heard the proverbial screech of wind through the rigging. The hydrovane held. *Moonshine* flew towards the Cape Verde, we were too frightened to take down our sails until the winds died. The larger rally boats were storm bound and could only SSB radio us weather reports and support.

We have experienced rough weather on our three blue-water 'offs'. On the Biscay Triangle we set off from Torbay in a force 6, which swiftly grew to an 8; ditto through the Straits of Gibraltar. On our Westerly Corsair, a heavy, safe guardian through big seas, we have learnt that Rally D-day or not, if the weather is not with us, we'll wait. The Blue Water Rally directors were always clear that individual boats could choose to wait if they wished. Easy choice if it's blowing a hooley in the marina. But if it's a glorious day, the camaraderie has built up, the starting 'launch' is standing by, then it is a sticky decision for a skipper to remain tied to the dock watching the others take flight. If it's a race you go, weather or not.

The initial nightmare storm abated. It was then that we all admitted to our intense fear during the maelstrom. Although it was a difficult crossing, we were no longer sailing in the teeth of storm force 10 winds. Every day at 10am we 'attended' the radio net, during which we gave our positions and weather. This was passed on to the Blue Water Rally for the website, which kept our landlubber friends and relations informed of our progress. A sense of calm pervaded the net when two airline pilots administered it: bring on the locusts and plagues, Peter and Malcolm are in control. I'm biased, but John tended to inject a certain maverick charm to his proceedings. Once the serious business was completed it was a time for catch-up around the fleet and, of course, tips on lures for Challenge Fish, an informal competition, as boys are wont to do. I'm sure groupies would gather around the SSB radio for certain of our net controllers.

Our best day's run was 159 miles employing the poor man's twin-head sail rig. This was achieved by poling the genoa out to starboard, hanking the storm jib onto the emergency inner forestay and using the boom as its pole. Sadly, we only got wise to this on day ten of our 24-day crossing. For the first nine days we flogged the main as we sailed

Being Hemingway: John (Rodriguez) and Ashley Nicholls fishing mid Atlantic

wing and wing. In the second week we also invented a new form of pump for washing up and salt water showers, 'saline control', by jury rigging a bilge pump to pump the ocean directly into the cockpit. A spin was added to washing up with card sharking for who would pump (top job) or wash and dry. The task was pepped up by talking for 'Just a Minute' on subjects such as (not surprisingly) 'Washing up at sea' and 'Sea monsters'.

We were advised to make land fall in Antigua in daylight, which we all did, remarkably intact, although of course there were the inevitable blown sails, exploding blocks, generator problems and lost fishing tackle. We had discovered the New World, or so we felt. Other yachts, winning their rally a priority, flew past Cade's Reef, through Friar's Shoal, often after dark, and had the yachting equivalent of springs hanging out on the 'finish line'. Peter Seymour, who had guided every yacht into Jolly Harbour, took each skipper on a full recce of the marinas and anchorages in which their yacht could moor over Christmas. He then arranged the prized stern-to moorings at English Harbour dockyard.

My mother flew out to celebrate our joint birthdays. Peter helped to ensure that she was delivered smoothly through the chaos ensuing after three jumbos landed almost simultaneously in a small airport. It is that bit of 'sugar and stir' that is typical of the Blue Water Rally.

Source: Blue Water Sailing

From 1998-2011 The Blue Water Rallies organised rallies across Biscay, the Atlantic and around the world, assisting hundreds of sailors to live their dreams.

So, you have crossed the Atlantic, been welcomed by your friends and felt your wobbly legs walk on land for the first time in weeks. Now it is time to indulge in the Caribbean.

9

CRUISING THE CARIBBEAN

Hurricane season is June to November, so a Caribbean season lasts from December to May.

Don't forget that the Caribbean encompasses the West Indies around to Mexico and Colombia in the east, so cruisers can spend six or seven seasons in the Caribbean and still not see it all. In one season you can acquire a good taste, however.

From the outpost of Barbados, we will work north through the West Indies and around to the eastern Caribbean, Mexico and Belize, exploring the highlights. It will need to be a whistle-stop tour, but there are plenty of sources for more detailed information, many mentioned in this chapter.

The book *Morgan Freeman and Friends: Caribbean Cooking for a Cause* was written to help the people of Grenada after Hurricane Ivan. It combines movie stars talking about their favourite islands and Caribbean dishes. Of the many souvenir books, I think it best captures the 'flavour' of the Caribbean.

John Rodriguez on his own island (Green Cay, British Virgin Islands)

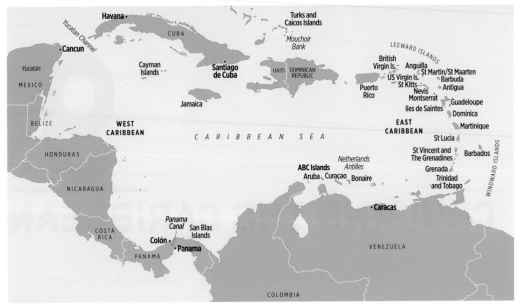

Chart of the Caribbean

POSTCARDS FROM THE KEDGE

Graham and Lorraine Zaffiro from the Channel Islands have been sailing on their Fountaine Pajot catamaran, with their son Lucas, since departing on New Year's Eve. Lucas was 23 months when they sailed from the Canaries across the Atlantic. They are presently in the Pacific. Lorraine writes:

Dear Nicola

So far, my top anchorages are:

- Tobago Cays for all the turtles
- Grenada Prickly Bay – I love this place, it is just one big happy family, they have a net, great bars, good food, easy access to town, beaches, I can see how people stop here and never go any further
- BVI – Just beautiful place, beautiful beaches almost paradise, great snorkelling
- St Barts Gustavia because it is like no other place in the world
- Mustique rolly but the place is worth it, it is what I envisaged the Caribbean to be like

Best wishes
Graham & Lorraine

Nicola Rodriguez
The Yacht Moonshine
The Bay
Gibraltar

CARIBBEAN WEATHER

The National Hurricane Centre and NOAA (National Oceanic and Atmospheric Association), www.nhc.noaa.gov, provide information on the Caribbean and South West Atlantic in sectors, for example 18N to 15N, 80W to 85W. Three other sites worth checking are Weather Forecasts for Sailors and Adventurers: www.passageweather.com; Weather Online UK (providing current weather and worldwide weather forecasts): www.weatheronline.co.uk; and French site www.sxmcyclone.com. (www.caribwx.com, the Caribbean Weather Centre, has ceased operating.) Weather guru and wit, the late David Jones, who once ran the Caribbean Weather Centre net in his inimitable style, did not appreciate cruisers asking about weather for a cruise from St Martin to St Barts, about a four-hour sail. His reply in a crisp British accent was: "Look outside."

WINDWARD AND LEEWARD ISLANDS

The south eastern Caribbean is divided into the Windward Islands, the southern curve of the Caribbean chain, Martinique, St Lucia, the Grenadines and Grenada; and the Leeward Islands, the northern curve of the chain, the main islands of which are Dominica, Guadeloupe, Antigua and St Martin (St Maarten).

The British named the islands because ships sailing to the West Indies came to the Windward Islands first and then to the Leeward Islands – those further around the chain, in the lee or downwind.

Chart of the West Indies

The anchorages open to the Atlantic (the east) are usually untenable; the Caribbean Sea (west of the islands) offers sheltered anchorages. There are exceptions, such as the area around Green Island, Antigua, which is protected from the ocean rollers.

Boats crossing the Atlantic usually head for St Lucia or slightly northwest to Antigua. From St Lucia, the Grenadines, which include Bequia and the Tobago Cays, are an easy sail. From Antigua it is also an easy sail south to Guadeloupe and the Îles des Saintes. Going northwards takes you to St Barts, St Martin and the Virgin Islands. It is difficult to recommend different islands because they offer such a diverse range of discoveries. In addition to the usual Caribbean delights, the French islands such as Guadeloupe, Îles des Saintes, St Martin and Martinique offer French cuisine and excellent provisioning.

Whilst exploring, do check in and out of Customs and Immigration correctly. It is important to clear when you are leaving the island if you have a 24-hour window. The officials can be pedantic.

The most useful guides to the Windward and Leeward Islands are written by Chris Doyle, a veteran Caribbean sailor, available from www.cruisingguides.com.

BARBADOS

The most easterly of the Caribbean islands is usually the first point of call for boats crossing the Atlantic on their own from the

---

POSTCARDS FROM THE KEDGE

Anchorages in Barbados

Martin Smith was born in Barbados. After studying Ship Science in the UK, he sailed the ARC in 1986. He worked for the RNLI (Royal National Lifeboat Institution) in Portsmouth, UK, and in 1994 sailed the Atlantic again, to Barbados, after which he worked as crew in the Caribbean, USA and UK. In 1996 Martin returned to Barbados, where he is a marine surveyor and keen yachtsman.

Dear Nicola

Here are my top anchorages in Barbados:

- I suppose Carlisle Bay is the most well known, and it is usually the most sheltered if the wind is north of east, but there is still often a swell on the beach if landing in a dinghy, and although there is a jetty owned by the boatyard I think they want a daily landing fee for yachties using it.
- It is possible to anchor off the Port St Charles breakwater – our boat is moored there – but it can often be rather rolly there.
- Sailing in Barbados, one can go for a potter along the west coast up and down, or do as we did a couple of weeks ago and 'tag along' on the Mount Gay Round Barbados race. But there are no anchorages on the east coast very suitable for yachts. And no other islands within a short day sail range.

Nicola Rodriguez
The Yacht Moonshine
79ᵗʰ Street Yacht Basin
New York
USA

Best wishes
Martin

Canaries or Cape Verde Islands. Boats come into the ports of entry at Port St Charles in the north or the capital, Bridgetown, in the south. The ARC (Atlantic Rally for Cruisers) at one time sailed to Barbados; however, it moved to St Lucia.

Sailing eastwards from the islands into the prevailing wind is not recommended. Bahamian sailors are used to the challenging seas, but Barbados is not a really cruiser-friendly island. For boats under 150 feet there are no marinas and the two official anchorages, Port St Charles and Bridgetown, are open to swell. A saving grace is the turtles that swim through the anchorages: it is possible almost to touch them from a dinghy.

Barbados is a gem and different geographically and topographically from the rest of the Caribbean. It is set apart from the other islands and this is reflected in how the Barbadians perceive themselves, slightly superior to the rest of the Caribbean.

Taxis can take cruisers on a tour of the island. It is worth negotiating with the taxis at the rank in Bridgetown, near the Houses of Parliament.

The Barbados Wildlife Reserve is a quirky one, worth a visit if just for the huge boa constrictor in the cage of elegant 'lace' wrought iron. Other creatures such as iguanas live with rabbits in ornate cages too. Monkeys and tortoises roam freely. One viewed the aviary from above.

Among other tourist musts are Harrison's Cave, a spectacular underground network of awe-inspiring, cathedral-size caves through which we were trundled in a large rolling train, Disney-style. A day waiting for weather was filled with a trip to the Orchid Garden full of exquisite blooms, even if some had been destroyed by a monkey attack.

BRIDGETOWN

Bridgetown is the capital of Barbados and offers supermarkets, department stores and markets for those who have just crossed the Atlantic.

It feels like Britain might have done in the 1950s. For cruisers it is interesting to note that five minutes from the dinghy tie-up, in Broad Street, there is a good Woolworths (which still survives, having split from the now closed British chain in the 1980s) and, at the top of the street, a health food shop.

There are several department stores and numerous duty-free shops selling the usual electronics, sparklies, scent and make-up.

Barbados is the best place for cruisers to pick up Visas for the USA. Most cruisers organised their interviews with the US Embassy via the internet while in Rodney Bay Marina, St Lucia. Wealthier cruisers fly to Barbados and stay in hotels, guesstimating how long it will take and hoping for a quick turnaround.

THE GRENADINES

There are over 600 islands in the Grenadines, some of which are more island-cum-rocks, for example Catholic, Petit Rameau, Petit Bateau, Jamesby and Baradal.

This section describes a few of the larger islands. From one sublime anchorage to another, the easterly winds give cracking sails. Admittedly, it's 'blowing old boots', but still on the best side of exhilarating, which is why the islands are a draw for cruisers and charterers.

While in Bequia, Mustique or Grenada, it is advisable to cash up, as the cash machine facilities in most of the Grenadines are unreliable. Provisioning is pretty basic here too.

BEQUIA

Bequia's special magic charms cruisers. Admiralty Bay, off the 'capital', Port Elizabeth, is utterly heavenly. Port Elizabeth itself has one main street and two or three blocks. Look out for the 'gingerbread' work around the edges of the roofs.

The Old Hegg Turtle Sanctuary is an inspiring visit, a taxi ride from Port Elizabeth.

Bequia has a vote on the Whaling Commission, for which it is courted with medical facilities and expertise. Bequia is allowed to catch four humpbacks a year. Although whales rarely pass the island these days, if they do, the islanders are obliged to hunt in the traditional way, in open sailing boats with harpoons. In Port Elizabeth you'll find a whaling museum, whale jaws at the entrance of a bar, and scrimshaw and grisly postcards on sale.

Before you leave the island, look out for the Moonhole community, whose homes are built out of the rock of the promontory. They are a rather fascinating sight and are something different.

MUSTIQUE

Mustique used to be British Princess Margaret's retreat, and is up-market and exclusive. The charge imposed on yachts per day puts some cruisers off. Charges aside, it is one of the most beautiful islands and, like Bequia, retains a touch of magic.

Basil's is the bar on most people's list, although some yacht folk have commented that those who own property on the island or are staying in the expensive rentals have been unwelcoming to cruisers.

SOUTHERN GRENADINES & THE TOBAGO CAYS

Allow time to snorkel and sit and be entranced by the changing light of the Grenadines. Chatham Bay on Union Island,

the famous Saltwhistle Bay on Mayreau and the Tobago Cays are heavenly, even if they know it. Clifton on Union Island is the main 'town', where you can anchor off. Most people prefer to stay in Chatham Bay and walk across the island.

The world has discovered the Grenadines and part of Saltwhistle Bay is now taken up by a resort. In the last few years mooring balls have been laid in the Tobago Cays, which is now a marine park.

'Boat boys' motor out to offer beer, lobster, fruit and bread. They will all have a story of where Johnny Depp anchored his boat during the filming of Pirates of the Caribbean. (His island, incidentally, was Little Hall's Pond Cay in the Bahamas.)

Palm Island is now a private resort, but it is possible to anchor off and enjoy the view, which you can see in advance on www.palmislandresortgrenadines.com.

Among the other islands are Petit St Vincent and Carnouan. Petite Martinique and Carriacou are counted as Grenada Grenadines. Other island-cum-rocks are Mushroom and White.

GRENADA, THE ISLAND OF SPICE

St George's anchorage in the lagoon is a short dinghy ride to the Carenage Harbour. The old town of St George's has a market, tourist shops and some good restaurants overlooking the wharf. Mahogany carvings and spices (particularly nutmeg) are for sale in shops, stalls and from vendors on Grand Anse Beach, near St George's. If a cruise ship is in, gently tell the vendors that you are a cruiser, not from the cruise ship, and they will probably not bother you again or, even better, might offer you a cheaper price.

Tours of the island take travellers to the mountainous area of the Grand Etang

Grenada as described by Kitiara Pascoe in her account of her Atlantic Circuit: In Bed with the Atlantic, available in Fernhurst Books' Making Waves series

Forest Reserve and a waterfall, usually the Annandale Falls. The more energetic can hike to the Concord or Mt Carmel falls or, slightly more of a stretch, the Seven Sisters waterfall.

For divers, Grenada offers some of the best and most interesting diving in the Caribbean, including 15 wrecks and, near St George's, the intriguing Jason de Caires Taylor Underwater Sculpture Park.

Four bays in a row – Prickly Bay, Mount Hartman Bay, Hog Island and then Clarkes Court Bay – attract cruisers particularly towards hurricane season, when they gather before leaving their boats on the hard in Prickly Bay or St David's. These are breath-taking anchorages with a social hub, a pretty good mix.

TRINIDAD

Chaguaramas is the main yachting centre in Trinidad and used to be a popular place for the hurricane season. Over the last ten years it has become increasingly violent, for example there have been stabbings and thefts on the buses from the capital, Port of Spain, down to Chaguaramas. There are cruiser-safe areas. Be cautious and do not go to remote beaches with bad reputations, as some have done and regretted it.

If you do choose to spend time in Trinidad there are many places to visit, for example the bird sanctuary at the Caroni Swamp, where at sunset you can see hundreds of Scarlet Ibis nesting. There is also the Asa Wright Nature Centre.

Carnival (Mardi Gras) is celebrated in February or March, depending on the date of Easter, and from March to July Leatherback Turtles can be seen nesting in Matura and Grand Riviere.

ST VINCENT

The author and many other yachts have not stopped at St Vincent because of the reports of boardings and aggression towards visiting yachts from 'boat boys'. It is an eight-hour sail from St Lucia to Bequia. Many would prefer a long sail to security issues such as outboards or dinghies being stolen. For one boat, whilst the owners were asleep, when the thieves could not force the locks, they stole the flips flops hidden in the dinghy. The next morning the owners discovered their night time visitors.

The author sails past St Vincent, but didn't stop

If you are considering spending time in St Vincent check the latest on www.noonsite. com: they recommend being 'vigilant'. The St Vincent Coastguard have recently been given a 33-foot 'coastguard vessel' by the USA and two RIBs from the Japanese. Some cruisers have not been put off and report the hike up La Soufriere is a highlight of the Caribbean.

ST LUCIA

The Atlantic Rally for Cruisers arrives in Rodney Bay in the north of St Lucia. As the ARC boats sail in, the bay becomes busier and busier. ARC parties blare out and locals appear looking for work cleaning the boats. Friends and relations fill up the nearby hotels.

International flights from the UK and USA fly regularly to St Lucia. The small airport near Castries should not be mistaken for Hewanorra International in the south, at least an hour and a half on St Lucia's basic roads from Rodney Bay in the north.

The Pitons are the famous landmark of this volcanic island. Cruisers heading south to the Grenadines stop in Marigot Bay, which is charming but often full during peak ARC season, or off Soufrière, below the Pitons.

Many cruisers say that Vieux Fort on the southern tip is their favourite anchorage of the island. Perhaps after the bustle of the tourist centres and the ARC, it has a more secluded and local flavour.

An island tour to the volcanic spring and mud pools should be on the agenda. Take the advice of local cruisers: some tours are good, some are a shambles.

The provisioning in Castries town is poor in comparison to Martinique, the next island north. However, it is better than on St Vincent and the Grenadines to the south.

Adrian with the drum he makes and with which he sang Happy Birthday to the author in Rodney Bay, St Lucia

WORTH THE RISK?

Peter and Sue Bringloe have spent six seasons in the Caribbean on their Dix 38. They now live between the Caribbean and the UK. Sue writes of her visit to St Vincent:

For the last few years we have, like many cruisers, avoided mainland St Vincent and just passed right on to Bequia, 11 miles to its south. Every time we managed to persuade ourselves that we were indeed missing out on one of the Caribbean gems, someone would recount yet another bad tale.

Oddly, it was after a boarding and thorough ransacking of Odyssey in St Lucia that we made the decision this year to take the risk and go visit. Perhaps it was the naïve view that surely, we could not be so unlucky twice in one season, or maybe we realised that most of our possessions had already been taken so we had less to lose.

Our first stop was the more touristy Young Island Cut, on the south of the island and close to the capital, Kingstown. We were met by the cheerful Rasta going by the name of Jamo (although we later learnt that his real name was Kenneth Williams!). Jamo helps you onto a mooring, will taxi you to the shore and arrange for taxi tours of the island, all for a price of course. One thing you have to get used to in St Vincent is that your hand is often in your pocket and, if you are of a sensitive and kind disposition, you are easy prey for the many jewellery and fruit sellers that will surround your boat on your arrival. Young Island Cut is well placed for tours of the island and also for visiting Kingstown, only a short bus ride away.

Kingstown was a pleasant surprise, with more sophistication than you might expect. Politics is everywhere, as the islanders try to find their way out of poverty and the large number of schools shows a true commitment to the mantra 'Education, education, education'. The people are generally friendly and leave you alone to go about your business, unless you require any help, when they are quite likely to go out of their way to be of assistance.

A pleasant few hours can be spent at the botanical gardens, a good walk up the hill or a quick bus ride, where Sinclair will, for a small consideration, give a very engaging tour. You will see a tree called the Mickey Mouse bush, smell freshly crushed nutmegs and gather bright red jumbie beans that can be made into bracelets for your grandchildren.

Coming back into town, make sure to stop at the Catholic church with its courtyard and pleasant, welcoming atmosphere, before heading back into the hurly-burly of downtown Kingstown. By this time lunch is probably beckoning and Veejays restaurant, near the port, is a popular local meeting place offering simple, good-value food in clean, bright surroundings.

Of the numerous island tours on offer, we chose the Vermont Nature Trail that promised a hike into the rainforest. Our guide, Elroy, was a softly-spoken local farmer who imparted his huge reservoir of knowledge in a steady, gentle flow, without pride or bias. He showed us how to appreciate the forest and taught us about the history and politics of the island during the two-hour trail.

The second anchorage we visited on St Vincent was Wallilabou (of Pirates of the Caribbean fame), where the local boys have organised the stern-to mooring of the boats into a slick operation. Once you have placed your trust in one of these guys it is just a matter of dropping your anchor (in 30 metres of water) and backing up until they ask for your stern line, which they quickly take and tie somewhere ashore, leaving you to worry about what knot they have used and whether your anchor is actually doing any good. Everything usually works out fine, though, and you have little time to worry as you are quickly surrounded with boats selling all sorts of goods and services. Ashore the local businesses have utilised various parts of the film set, and you become convinced that Johnny Depp or Keira Knightley is going to come and join you for a drink. The deep bay of Wallilabou is truly beautiful, with the hills the most stunning shades of green. A waterfall hike just a few minutes up the road is worth the trip and the snorkelling around the north edge of the bay is scenic and full of life.

All in all, our visit to St Vincent was a success and we felt that we had made some friends and learnt a few ropes to ease our next visit, as there has to be a next time.

MARTINIQUE

In the north of Martinique is a spectacular anchorage, St Pierre. On 8th May 1902, Mount Pelée, which had been rumbling for months, exploded, destroying the Paris of the Caribbean and its 26,000 inhabitants.

The theatre is one of the remaining ruins of the prosperous town. Tours reveal grim details, such as that the only person to survive was a criminal imprisoned in the jail, which saved him from the molten lava. Just as W B Yeats asks us to 'tread softly for you tread on my dreams', I found the town rebuilt over the old one strange and discomforting, sensing that I was walking over the graves of the comparatively recently incinerated. I found it preferable to take in the changing vistas of St Pierre and Mount Pelée from the anchorage.

DOMINICA

Dominica, in the Leeward Islands, does not have many beaches and relies on eco-tourism. Think hiking through rainforests, waterfalls, a boiling lake and all remarkably unspoilt by tourism. It is more intriguing because it has not been too developed.

There is a hot spring near the Trafalgar Falls that you have to indulge in, in as small a group as possible. (If you take yourself to a tranquil place when you meditate, this is it.) Send the others off to hike the waterfall. Try to avoid the waterfalls when cruise ship tours are there.

In the ten square blocks of 'downtown' Roseau, the capital, there are some charming wooden houses with gingerbread trim and aged stone buildings where there is also a tourist market, several supermarkets and restaurants. One day the waterfront is an empty pavement, the next day a souvenir village. You can wander along the instant stalls that appear, as ever, when a cruise ship docks.

In the north of the island is Prince Rupert Bay, which is near Portsmouth, the second largest town. 'Boat boys' can be difficult on occasion. If you find one you like, stick with him and the others will go away. Go for a walk ashore and find the supermarket selling eggs in plastic bags.

The American Ross University, offering degrees in Medicine, is based nearby. On one evening, hundreds of graduating students descended to celebrate graduation at the Blue Bay Restaurant, which has a dock on the bay, where dinghies from the anchorage can tie up.

MARIN, MARTINIQUE, WEST INDIES

"Shall I send three strong men?" A French-accented man on a dive launch replied to my wild gesticulations for help.

I was 4½ months pregnant, reluctantly grinding on a winch. My husband John had just crushed his thumb and was now hanging onto 120 feet of anchor chain with a 45lb CQR swinging from the bow in 400 feet of water. We were literally between a rock and a hard place: Diamond Rock and the cliffs of southern Martinique, West Indies. The answer was "Yes."

The three strong men dived into the 4-foot swell and swam over. They were fit and muscle bound, perfect to haul up the chain, hand over hand. On the rolling bow, counting off the metres in French, they heaved. At 20 metres, they rested. Heckling erupted from those seated in the dive launch. I motored us away from Diamond Rock and stopped when the chain gang wrestled a 45lb anchor and 120 feet (40 metres) of 10mm chain from the depths. Cheers came from the dive boat as the anchor emerged. Almost without taking breath, they shook rust-covered hands with John, and dived off the bow to swim back to their launch. We motored to nearby Marin, where a new windlass was fitted to replace the one that had just failed.

Our second arrival was plane sailing with Air France. *Seraphim*, our Moody 38, sailed on a Dockwise transporter ship from Palma, Mallorca. Martinique is central in the Caribbean chain and Marin, in the south, is an excellent place to carry out work on your boat.

Marin is a useful anchorage where the holding is good and the services excellent. With a choice of chandleries most needs are catered for, although in the case of our windlass, the right type and price was not available in Marin.

3 strong men haul up the chain while an injured John looks on

Sea Services in the capital Fort-de-France took up the strain. There are marine services and skilled labour of all kinds, from refrigeration to rigging, woodwork to carbon fibre. For example, in our experience, the new anchor windlass was fitted by Plastik Services, anti-fouling was carried out by Carenantilles, new cockpit cushions and repairing the dinghy cover by Voile Assistance and a new anti-UV strip by Voilerie Caraibes. Getting to know the place is made easy, as with all the Caribbean islands, with Chris Doyle's *Sailor's Guide to the Windward Islands*.

Marin has dinghy docks at Carenantilles (the shipyard), the local market, the marina and Leader Price, a large, reasonably-priced supermarket. The other supermarket nearby, Champion, provides better quality. Either the new mall (next to McDonald's) or the shabbier old town can provide most things, from towels, DVDs and shoes to a post office and banks. Near Fort-de-France, a 45-minute, €5 TC (taxi collectif) or hire car trip away, is a large Carrefour and Lafayette shopping mall. Once fully provisioned, loaded with new kit and broke, sail around the bay to St Anne's, a beautiful anchorage off a quaint Caribbean town and pretty beach. Locals spend weekends there.

Marin's long-term cruisers congregate on the south side of the bay, an anchorage further from the services but rather charming, with egrets nesting in the mangroves and a little river down which we took the children on dinghy safaris to see crabs running up mangrove roots.

Our favourite restaurant was Ti Toques. However, the hub of the marina is the Mango Bay, which provides good pizzas and internet with typically French service. At the other end of the scale, long-term cruisers and shipyard workers hang out in Bichik, which is a shack beside the fuel dock providing beer, laundry, internet, book swap and car hire. After being stung for £56 for an epic load to be laundered, we felt extremely smug when at 8am on Sunday morning we secured five DIY washing machines at inexpensive Lav@ mat and went for breakfast and a shop in Champion.

If you are considering chartering, Sunsail and several other small charter companies are based in Marin. It is worth remembering that flying with Air France can be cheaper, even with the flight from, for example, Southampton to Paris, because Martinique is an internal French flight.

While we waited for the Dockwise transporter to arrive and for the anti-fouling to be completed, we stayed in the Residence

John, Jack and James on a dinghy safari in the mangroves in Marin, Martinique

des Iles self-catering apartments, with a pool and a view over the bay.

Between December and January, we returned to Marin from next-door island St Lucia and from Barbados in the southeast. Just before we headed north at the end of January there was a regatta, a fast-paced and high-energy morning with competing crews racing around the bay. Ashore there is music and dancing, with spectators following their teams through binoculars, or just toasting them with the local rum, again and again.

Source: Cruising Notes, Practical Boat Owner

Regatta in January in the Bay or Marin, Martinique

A TOUR TO REMEMBER

Of the many, many tours we took up and down various islands, the Bahamas and the USA, the most fascinating and entertaining was with Seacat, who is based in the capital of Dominica, Roseau. Take up a mooring ball near the dinghy dock and discuss a tour of the island with him. Whether it is a five-hour hike to the boiling lake or an island tour in his bus, his enthusiasm, knowledge and wide-ranging introductions to locals with whom he is friends will be a treat of a day. Seacat's real name is Octavius, meaning eight, which led to octopus, otherwise known as a sea-cat. As with most communications from boats in the Caribbean, call him up on the VHF.

Seacat introduced us to freshly cut sugar cane with a squeeze of freshly picked lime, a real taste sensation, and the M&Ms of the jungle, cocoa beans. Later we met locals who were descended from the first Indians living on the island, who gave us chocolate from the garden. As we sped along, Seacat would see something beside the road, stop and show us.

Seacat, an outstanding guide to Dominica, West Indies

The Indian River is the main tourist attraction here because it featured in scenes from *Pirates of the Caribbean: Dead Man's Chest*, the second film. This is very expensive to visit and has been described as disappointing.

ÎLES DES SAINTES

These are an enchanting collection of islands with a French twist. Allow time and budget here just to sit on the boat and read a book, swim, snorkel, dive and dine finely in the evenings. Or snorkel, indulge in a long lunch and doze.

For a small set of islands there is a large concentration of excellent restaurants.

Find an anchorage for a day or two or three around Terre D'en Haut, where some folk's favourite is Pain de Sucre, which looks like a 200-foot, sugar-loaf rock. The other islands to anchor around are Ilet Cabrit and Terre D'en Bas.

GUADELOUPE

Shaped like a butterfly, this French island is an excellent stop for divers and good provisioning.

It is possible to sail through the middle via a canal and lifting bridge on Rivière Salée. The butterfly wings are called Basse Terre, with two mountains, and Grand Terre, without.

Divers should check out the Jacques Cousteau Underwater Reserve, www.cip-guadeloupe.com.

If you're sailing south from Antigua, Deshaies is the first stop in the north of the island. It is a quaint fishing village with some outstanding restaurants. If you are in Deshaies for a day, go ashore to the botanical garden.

MONTSERRAT

Montserrat is an island with an active volcano. Although the last major explosion was in 1995, it remains active. Some cruisers prefer to catch the (expensive) ferry from Antigua to explore the island. There are anchorages within the restricted zones in the north of the island from where you can organise tours. Some who have been complained that their decks were covered in ash and cleaning them was difficult. The Montserrat Volcano Observatory (www.mvo.ms) monitors activity.

ANTIGUA

Antigua is a major yachting hub in the Caribbean. The main yachting centres are Falmouth Harbour and English Harbour in the south and Jolly Harbour in the west.

As with most Caribbean islands, the top guide to anchorages etc. is Chris Doyle's *The Cruising Guide to the Southern Leeward Islands.*

December sees the Charter Yacht Show take place in Falmouth Harbour Marina. Christmas in next-door English Harbour is one of our sailing highlights, when jolly cruisers with fizz in plastic cups celebrate Atlantic crossings and Christmas.

On 23rd February 2009 the first RORC Caribbean 600 Race set sail from Antigua. Maxis, superyachts, multihulls and much in between competed over 605 nautical miles

north to Barbuda and St Martin, south to Guadeloupe and back again. It is now an annual event.

Within English Harbour is Nelson's Dockyard, where our naval hero careened his ships. It is also the home, in early April, of the Antigua Classics Regatta (www.antiguaclassics.com), which is followed by Antigua Sailing Week (www.sailingweek.com). We preferred the elegance of the Classics but partied hard during Sailing Week.

At the entrance to English Harbour, Freeman's Bay is one of the most beautiful anchorages in the world and is one of our top anchorages. Galleon Beach beside the bay is a favourite. We tied our dinghy to the dock of The Inn at English Harbour and walked on to the beach. Antigua claims one beach for every day of the year. Dickenson Bay in the northwest is impressive, a long stretch of white sand with numerous restaurants and tourist shops.

Between Falmouth Harbour and English Dockyard most marine services and varieties of restaurants are covered. These include A & F Sails (www.afsails.com), where owner Franklin and his team have repaired our Atlantic-worn sails and made our bimini; we highly recommend him. The Antigua Slipway provides haul-out and summer hurricane storage facilities. Its upstairs chandlery is good.

Antiguahistory.net provides information on Nelson's Dockyard. The Dockyard Museum is worth a quick visit, the shop has good souvenirs. Whilst buying 'bounty' look out for pictures by Gilly Gobinet, who we think captures Antigua better than anyone (www.originalcaribbeanart.com). The Dockyard Bakery is a must stop for breakfast and banana bread. One year my mother and I celebrated our joint birthdays at the historic Admiral's Inn.

English Harbour, Antigua, West Indies

POSTCARDS FROM THE KEDGE

Andrew Blatter has sailed extensively, including a 'round-the-world' trip, and 6 Trans-Atlantic crossings. Andrew then lived with his wife and children on a 37ft yacht anchored up and down the Caribbean, while he put together the first Superyacht Services Guide (www.superyachtservicesguide.com).

Dear Nicola

My favourite anchorages in the Caribbean are:

- English Harbour, Antigua
- Port de Gustavia, St Barths
- Prickly Bay, Grenada
- Port Elizabeth, Bequia
- Britiannia Bay, Mustique

Nicola Rodriguez
The Yacht Moonshine
Benodet
North West France

Best wishes
Andrew

Within the Falmouth Harbour complex there are crew agencies, books and clothes shops. Upstairs, Antigua Yacht Club offers excellent cuisine. Downstairs the crews hang out in the café and the Skulduggery Bar, which provides intoxicating coffee martinis. Jane Midson at Jane's Yacht Services, English Harbour, (www.janesyachtservices.com) is a company providing yacht services: I can recommend her. During a trip back to the UK we left the boat in the good care of the Catamaran Marina.

Jolly Harbour Marina (www.jolly-harbour-marina.com) is another storage site for yachts during hurricane season. Friends Peter and Sue Bringloe on *Odyssey* and John and Sue Bradney on *Exuma* found it a good facility. Some cruisers rent villas in Jolly Harbour to recover from their Atlantic crossing or during haul-outs. Also, for recuperation the palm-fringed beach just outside the Jolly Harbour complex is gorgeous. While berthed in Jolly we would lunch at the BBR sports bar and use the swimming pool. Peter's is a popular restaurant, as is the Dogwatch. Jolly's many boat services include a large Budget Marine chandlery, electronics, electrics, painting, refrigeration and varnishing.

Provisioning in Antigua is not cheap. If you are going north I would wait for St Martin, which offers French and Dutch supermarkets. If you're heading south, Guadeloupe and Martinique await. In Jolly Harbour the large Epicurean supermarket is eclectic and includes numerous British specialities. There is another Epicurean in the Woods Mall, outside the capital, St John's, which also has a useful Radio Shack. Cruise ships dock in St John's, where Heritage and Redcliffe Quays offer all kinds of Caribbean souvenirs.

Antigua is a good place to meet visitors. British Airways, Virgin and Continental fly in regularly. Yacht charter companies include Nicholson Yacht Charters and Services, Horizon Yacht Charters and Sunsail.

Car hire can be expensive. The local buses run to St John's. If you want them to stop, just call 'bus stop'. It's a great way to meet the locals. When travelling from Jolly Harbour across the island to English Harbour, change at St John's. My 80-year-old mother and I were jammed into a bus full of singing and laughing, dusty Rastafarians who had just finished work building a new casino.

Diving is well catered for in English, Falmouth and Jolly Harbours. For horse riders there is Springhill Riding Club (www.antiguaequestrian.com), where the rides can include beaches, tracks and fields. Lessons in dressage and jumping are available. There are several hikes around the English Harbour area, including both hard and easy trails up to Shirley Heights or the less strenuous walk to Fort Berkeley. For more of a stretch, hike over to Pigeon Beach, which has a children's play area.

A highlight of any week in Antigua is the Sunday Night 'jump up' barbecue on Shirley Heights, overlooking English Harbour and beyond. The steel band gets folks jumping and the reggae ramps it up. The faster the rhythm, the stronger the rum. I seem to recall a mass skinny dip

The jump up at Shirley Heights, Antigua: the faster the rhythm, the stronger the rum

fuelled by Shirley Heights high spirits.

If you want to escape, Five Islands anchorage outside Jolly Harbour is charming. Alternatively, head northeast to the anchorages around Green Island and Nonsuch Bay. (Perhaps splash out on a meal at Harmony Hall?) Further around the north of the island is the more remote Great Bird Island.

BARBUDA

North from Antigua is neighbouring island Barbuda, one of the most undeveloped islands and considered one of the highlights in the chain, with miles of powder beaches and an outstanding Frigate Bird Sanctuary (www.antigua-barbuda.org).

Barbuda, like St Kitts and Nevis to the west, is slightly off the track wind wise. That and the challenging anchoring put some cruisers off. The only town is Codrington, named after the family who owned the island.

SABA, SINT EUSTATIUS, ST KITTS & NEVIS

Saba and Sint Eustatius (known to the locals as Statia) are Dutch. St Kitts and Nevis are British.

These islands of mountains and rainforests are often visited when coming south, because of their position. It is a beat (into the wind) to reach them when heading north. The lack of good harbours

BEST OF BOTH WORLDS

Sue and Peter Bringloe sailed extensively in Europe, the Caribbean and America on an Odyssey, Dix 38. They have crossed the Atlantic three times. (Once with us!) After two years as full-time cruisers they took time out.

They still wanted to cruise, hoping for 'the best of both worlds', however, with elderly parents and grandchildren spending time 'here and there' was a good compromise. After five years away from full-time cruising, they bought a Beneteau 50, *Santosa*, (meaning, 'deep contentment / at ease when all is going crazy'). During the hurricane season they leave *Santosa* in a marina in Marin, Martinique with gardinage (guards) who look after the boat.

Whilst the Bringloes are away, the gardinage run all the systems and send updates. If a hurricane threatens, the gardinage ensure the boat's safety as much as possible. Sue says, 'You have to think outside the box for insurance, but it is possible.' Sue and Peter's plan is

five months in the Caribbean, and seven months at home, near Chichester, south of England. Sue writes:

There are many ways to enjoy the Caribbean cruising life – you don't have to take on the big Atlantic voyage... it's not all about baking bread at 4am in the morning mid Atlantic... It is possible to have some interesting sailing experiences, some a bit too interesting... hops up and down the islands without having to kit a boat out to nth degree. Daily radio nets help to give a sense that you are part of the sailing and local community. For me, being able to continue with my love of teaching yoga whilst away, gives me that sense of independence and focus. It's easy to connect with other like-minded people via the radio nets and sailing facebook groups, enabling one to drop into a different life fairly quickly. You can pop out in November, pick up, and return home in mid-March/April ready to enjoy a British summer!

also makes them less attractive than neighbouring Antigua and St Martin.

In St Kitts, Basseterre, the main town, provides eclectic souvenir shopping and a taxi to the edge of town will take you to supermarkets. It is said that the Circus, a roundabout surrounded by stone colonial buildings with a clock tower, was based on Piccadilly Circus in London. Just as in Antigua you can hike to the remains of British rule, so in St Kitts you can tour Brimstone Hill, a massive fort.

ANGUILLA

Anguilla is a morning sail from St Martin and another island of exclusive, up-market villas and hotels. The interior is scrubby and rather monotonous in comparison to the other exclusive island nearby, St Barts. The beaches are its main attraction.

There is a charge for entry, and a daily rate for yachts, which can seem expensive. If the wind is in the right direction it is worth a visit. Road Bay is the best port of entry for yachts.

SAINT BARTHÉLEMY

Saint Barthélemy (known as St Barts) is a small island with two main anchorages, Gustavia and Anse de Colombier. The others are weather dependent and tricky, for example there can be a problem with low-flying planes.

St Barts was French, then Swedish – hence the capital Gustavia, after the Swedish King Gustav III – then French again.

The capital is full of up-market shops, chic boutiques, delicatessens and restaurants. The anchorage in the harbour is usually full. If you do get a mooring, hang on to it. Superyachts pay super prices to take a stern-to berth along the quay. The anchorages outside Gustavia, mostly open

to the west, can be rolly.

Anse de Colombier, an anchorage in the north, is a charm. It is part of the St Barts Marine Reserve. Yachts are encouraged to take mooring balls. Anse de Colombier is a place in which to soak in the view of the sublime beach in changing light, like St Pierre in Martinique and Soller in Mallorca. A rather bizarre structure sits incongruously on the point. I agree with Caribbean writer Chris Doyle that it looks like the top of the Eiffel Tower.

Motoryachts often speed across from St Martin, anchor for lunch and speed off.

The walk, more of a hike, from the beach over the hills along the Atlantic coast is magnificent. It is an excellent nature trail for children and leads to Anse des Flamands, where you can buy croissants and ice cream. (A few cruisers hitchhike into Gustavia from here.) Depending on the conditions, large dinghies can drive to Gustavia to check in or check out the town.

Gustavia is a good place from which to sail the 28 miles to Saba. It is 40 miles to Basseterre, St Kitts, and 45 to Charlestown, Nevis.

ST MARTIN & ST MAARTEN

St Martin is divided into two countries, the French Saint Martin and the Dutch Sint Maarten. The story goes that the division was decided when a Frenchman with a bottle of red wine and a Dutchman with jenever (gin) set off in opposite directions. The French secured more of the island (55sq km) because the gin hit the Dutchman (35sq km) harder and faster.

St Martin is an excellent island on which to carry out boat maintenance and provision. Superyacht skippers often sail to St Martin from expensive islands such as Antigua or the British Virgin Islands.

On the Dutch side, Philipsburg is a free

port, so offers more streets of electronics, cameras, sparklies and scent. Everyday shopping for cruisers is also good. Just outside there is a large Le Grand Marché, one of many supermarkets on the island. It can be disorientating to walk into a French supermarket on the Dutch side of a Caribbean island and be faced with piles of Gouda.

Simpson Bay has a bridge opening three times a day. It is in Simpson Bay that you will find engineers, sail lofts, refrigeration, radar, engines, teak, anything boat related.

Budget Marine and Island Water World, the two largest chandleries in the Caribbean, have dinghy docks that seem continually in use. Local minibuses drive over the hill to Philipsburg for any shopping not available in Simpson Bay (e.g. the toy shop). Bobby's Marina out near the International Airport caters for cruisers, as does Lagoon Marina (Lagoonies) at the other end of Simpson Bay in Cole Bay. Most of the other marinas are aimed at and priced for superyachts.

For crazy tourists who have drunk too much, one of the thrills of St Martin is to go to the beach at the end of the runway and (illegally) grab the fencing as a jumbo takes off. If they can stand the heat and force of the jet engines and hang on to the fence, they are blown horizontally as the plane heads down the runway. Others are blown across the road and onto the beach. A bar beside the beach plays the St Martin air traffic control on speakers and the flights are chalked up on a board. Apparently, the KLM jumbo gives the best 'ride'.

The Heineken Regatta is held in March, a popular date on the Caribbean calendar. Several yachts are chartered in Antigua and sail up to take part.

The morning cruisers' net keeps cruisers informed of the latest social gatherings, offers, haircuts at Lagoonies, bands and events.

If you don't want to save yourself for all the French cuisine, the Dutch side offers a wide variety of dining. There is also a small Chinatown in the Cole Bay area. Marigot Bay on the French side is perfectly positioned for provisioning and yacht facilities. It is open to the sea, so not as dirty as Simpson Bay. Numerous restaurants line the quayside beside a tourist market. Enoch's has been open for lunch for 40 years – get there early, the locals do. There is a US supermarket full of French food and fresh produce that is flown in regularly. Save your haircuts for the French side.

BRITISH VIRGIN ISLANDS

These breath-taking islands are a highlight and a see-before-you-die experience. However, long-term cruisers should be cautious of some of the charterers whose credit cards outbalance their seamanship. From experience I know that four visits of thirty days each is just enough to begin to know the British and US Virgins. Here are a few recommendations.

Road Harbour is not pretty, but it is the main town of the BVIs, so it can be useful. Most of the charter companies are based in and around the harbour. The town offers most services including yacht facilities, supermarkets such as Bobby's and Village Cay Marina, where crews from the superyachts congregate in the bar.

Virgin Gorda is so named because to Columbus it looked like a fat virgin, lying on her side. You can anchor off the main town, Spanish Town or, if you are feeling flush, take a berth. If you have come from St Martin it is advisable to use up the food you have on board. The Virgins are not cheap, especially Spanish Town. The Baths, an iconic round rock formation, is the place everyone heads for. It is possible to anchor in good conditions. There is a trail through the rocks that is perfect for stunning photographs. As always, try to avoid the times when cruise-ship folks are visiting. If you dinghy in, remember that the surf can become quite rough, making getting in and out of the dinghy a trial.

Leverick Bay in Gorda Sound has numerous anchorages. If you want a Caribbean-resort hotel, the Bitter End at the far end of the bay is for you. While there you can walk around to the even more exclusive Biras Creek Hotel and Resort.

The following are places that you should make an effort to get to:

- Cooper Island for the Painkiller cocktails from the Cooper Island Beach Club.
- Little Harbour off Peter Island, which is not an easy anchor but is an idyllic spot and, if the weather has not been too rough, a great place for snorkelling.
- Jost Van Dyke and Little Jost Van Dyke, which are slightly less busy than Tortola. Foxes is a famous beach bar and restaurant attracting numerous charter boats for dinner.

- Brewers Bay if you are heading from Tortola to Jost Van Dyke. The coral around the entrance can make it tricky, but it is far lovelier than the usually crowded Cane Garden Bay, next door round Du Bois Point.
- Other get-the-t-shirt haunts on Tortola are Soper's Hole, West End, Nanny Cay, Trellis Bay and the Willie T (William Thornton Floating Bar and Restaurant), living off its infamous reputation on the Bight at Norman Island.

There is also Anegada, which means the 'drowned island'. After the Great Barrier Reef and Belize, it is the third largest reef in the world. The island is only 28 feet high, making landmarks hard to distinguish from the sea. Coral heads, the surrounding reef and over 300 sunken vessels along with hazardous currents make this a destination only for experienced yachts. Taxis pick up from any of the hotels off the main anchorage. The flamingos in the salt ponds can be a side trip en route to Loblolly Bay with its glorious beach and snorkelling, on the other side of the island.

IN A HURRY TO LEAVE

Little did we know as we entered Simpson Bay that we would spend so long in the olive-green water. We were there four weeks and became pretty scratchy after a month trapped in the bay. There are yacht services on the both the Dutch and French side. Dutch St Martin is more overtly touristy than the French side of the island. *Moonshine* went through a transformation, though, from rather beaten-up Atlantic boat to rather enchanting yacht.

Although we had been in the bay desperate to leave, our actual time to go caught us by surprise. A whirlwind day of last-minutes stalled when I was kept waiting in the bank for an hour and a half, John went spare running from customs to all sorts, all over, presuming kidnap, road kill but not the obvious, that Caribbean banks are very, very slow. Time against us, we rattled around the boat throwing provisions into the fridge, wrapping up cups and precious things, and wishing that, yet again, the deadline wasn't beating us. Our friends' boats raised anchor and circled, waiting for the bridge to open. By the skin of our teeth we were away and spun through the bridge to sail through the night north to the British Virgin Islands.

Source: *Moonshine* blog

US VIRGIN ISLANDS

Yoga on Pomato Beach, Anegada, British Virgin Islands

You will be on American soil in the US Virgins so, if you require a US visa, make sure you have one before landing. Rumours that you can catch a ferry from the BVIs to the US Virgins, acquire a US visa and return with your yacht are not true. The regulations concerning yachts-people and cruising permits for their boats entering and leaving the US Virgins, as well as entering and leaving Puerto Rico and arriving in the United States, are complex. Be clear that you, the immigration officer and the customs officer you are dealing with fully comprehend the overall view. Officers may have different interpretations of the regulations, even between Miami and Fort Lauderdale.

Charlotte Amalie, the capital of the US Virgins, is on St Thomas. You can anchor in Long Bay, with the cruise ships towering

Green Cay and Tortola viewed from Jost Van Dyve Islands, British Virgin Islands

above you. In this free port and cruise ship destination, Main Street is another place for electronics, cameras, sparklies and scent.

Taxi prices from the Waterfront (the tourist shopping centre), around Long Bay Road, round St Thomas Harbour to the cruise-ship terminal area escalate fast and exorbitantly as the time of a sailing draws closer. Don't get stung.

Near the cruise-ship quay is a Filipino restaurant and supermarket where cruise-ship personnel phone home and shop for specialities. It's a funky place and great for cheap phone calls. K-Mart is one of two supermarkets 15 minutes from the cruise-ship dock. If you are running out of St Martin provisioning, it's the best place before Puerto Rico.

A particularly enchanting anchorage if you want to get away from the tourists and are heading towards the Spanish Virgins, is tucked behind Water Island, in Honeymoon Bay, also called Druif Bay.

The sail between Tortolla (British Virgins) and St John's (US Virgins) through Sir Francis Drake Channel is spectacular. Two-thirds of St John's is a National Park. For rules and regulations concerning where you can anchor and where you can hike, consult the National Park Service Visitors' Centre. If you want to take in the beauty of this island, pick up a mooring (or anchor if permitted) in anchorages away from Cruz Bay, the main town and tourist hot spot.

Beware: Cruz Bay is not a place to be when American students descend on spring break.

For pilot books, Chris Doyle's books on the Leeward and Windward Islands are more cruiser-owner orientated than the more charter-market-focused *Cruising Guide to the Virgin Islands*, by Nancy and Simon Scott. There is also *Grenada to the Virgin Islands*, from Jacques Patuelli.

THE US VIRGINS NORTHWARDS

The US Virgins are where yachts heading north to the USA say their final farewells to those leaving their yachts in hurricane holes in the Caribbean or heading back to the UK. Physical goodbyes could have been made several weeks and islands before. This is where the hard graft north begins and paths divide. There is more on this route in Chapter 10.

When sailing from the Virgins to the USA, use *The Gentleman's Guide to Passages South* by Bruce Van Sant (www. thornlesspath.com). It has quirky English but excellent advice.

ATLANTIC CIRCUIT

The Atlantic Circuit is usually completed in a year, leaving the UK in June. Cruisers explore the Caribbean for four months then sail home from the BVIs or the USA, across the North Atlantic via Bermuda and the Azores in spring.

Those completing an Atlantic Circuit usually want to return for a longer trip. Shipping the boat from Newport in the north east USA is a way of gleaning another month. Chapter 10 includes information on rallies to and from the USA and the Caribbean.

ATLANTIC FROM WEST TO EAST

West to east across the Atlantic is acknowledged as the more difficult of the two crossings. Boats set off from the Caribbean or USA. Beaufort, North Carolina is a popular departure point for the sail to Bermuda, then north to the Azores and on to Falmouth, or Gibraltar and the Mediterranean, or even north to Scotland and the Baltic.

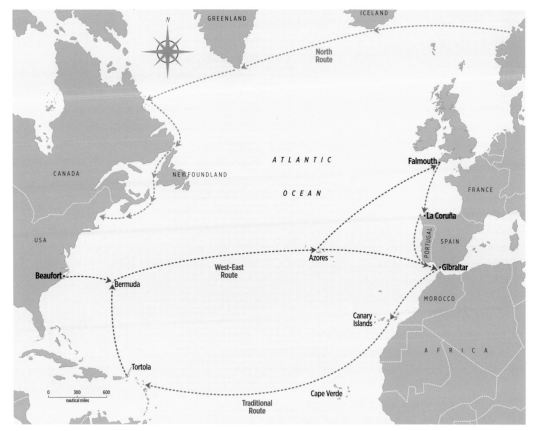

Common Atlantic crossings

Before considering this passage, more than most, research and review the problems. As ever these are not reasons not to go, but reasons to be careful:

- You can experience summer thunderstorms.
- If you are setting off further north than the Cape Cod / Newport area, coastal fog can be a problem. (If you are as far north as the Grand Banks there could be the possibility of ice.)
- If you leave the east coast too late in July or August you could face hurricanes, particularly in the corridor between Bermuda and the USA.

The Atlantic Crossing Guide and Jimmy Cornell's *World Cruising Routes* should be on the navigation table. If you decide to join a rally back to the UK, ARC Europe starts in the BVIs and the Chesapeake, East Coast USA in early May, crossing to Bermuda and the Azores.

WESTERN CARIBBEAN

The Western Caribbean includes Cuba, Jamaica and the Cayman Islands. It reaches from the Texas US border around the coast to Mexico, Belize, Guatemala, Nicaragua, Costa Rica, Panama, Colombia and Venezuela, the ABC Islands and San Blas. These are not the safest of areas. Below are recommended highlights and suggestions.

Pilot guides include *Cruising Ports: Florida to California via Panama*, John Rains and *A Cruising Guide to* the Northwest Caribbean, Stephen Pavlidis.

CUBA

Of all the islands you could sail to, get to Cuba as soon as you can before it changes too much. As the political situation alters so will the island: better for the Cubans, not so good for cruisers in search of cultures and islands unaffected by MTV. It is not easy, but it is worth it.

Cuba appeals more to cruisers who want to immerse themselves in an island where time, in many ways, has stood still; it is also a place where corrupt officials and lengthy paperwork can make the experience frustrating. We had one or two officials

---

POSTCARDS FROM THE KEDGE

Al and Mel, with their daughters, Ayla 9 and Molly 6, set off on an Atlantic Circuit aboard *Troubadour* (Al's parents' boat), a Pocock 45 commissioned by the discerning owners to satisfy a very open brief for the perfect blue-water cruiser: 'capable of sailing to windward properly while making long-distance passages and being self-sufficient while cruising in remote areas.'

Dear Nicola

Here are our favourite Caribbean anchorages:
- Petit Tabac, Grenadines – the perfect tropical island dotted with palm trees, long white sand beaches and gently sloping coral reef shores to explore.
- Saline Bay, Mayreau – a peaceful, sheltered bay, perfect for the safety of the girls independent play and a lovely beach peppered with places to take refuge from the scorching sun.
- Port Elizabeth, Bequia – we were lucky to be there during the annual music festival which saw this colourful bay bursting into lively life day and night.
- Jamesby Island, Tobago Cays – an incredible location on the planet, teeming with turtles, sting rays, trunk fish and eagle rays this was a quiet, sheltered anchorage compared to the popularity of the rest of the Cays.
- Pine Cay, Turks and Caicos – quite honestly the best stretch of beach we discovered on our trip.

Nicola Rodriguez
The Yacht Moonshine
Las Olas Marina
Fort Lauderdale
USA

Best wishes
Al & Mel

THE SEA & STARS

Charles Tongue, a retired businessman, crossed the Atlantic, cruised the Caribbean and returned home. En route west to east, he wrote:

To have the opportunity to sail across an ocean in a small boat is definitely a privilege. As the days pass, the emptiness, *the isolation and the wild beauty of the surroundings touch the senses and then at night, sooner or later, creation puts on one of its most spectacular shows – a moonlit sea and a clear sky filled with millions of stars, stretching without interruption, from horizon to horizon in every direction, as far as the eye can see.*

who asked for gifts, such as one taking all of John's razors and another emptying all our Diet Cokes into his briefcase. As Cuba opens up, the problem is decreasing. The people themselves could not be more welcoming and friendly.

Cuba can be approached from the south if you're sailing north from the Caribbean or from the north into Hemingway Marina, Havana if you're sailing from the Florida Keys. The Gulf Stream flows between north Cuba and Florida and must be taken into consideration when planning any trip to north or west Cuba.

Some cruisers base themselves in Havana and tour the country by hire car or bus. For example, Trinidad in the south is a UNESCO World Heritage Site and a music centre. It is possible to eat and stay in Cuban houses, a form of bed and breakfast (for which the government charges tax).

Pilot guides include *Cuba: A Cruising Guide*, Nigel Calder, and *A Cruising Guide to the Northwest Caribbean*, Stephen Pavlidis.

From the south of Cuba, you can drop from Santiago de Cuba to Jamaica and on to the Cayman Islands, or from Cabo San Antonio on the western tip across the Gulf Stream to Isla Mujeres, just off the Yucatan Peninsula, Mexico. From Florida it is a three-day passage for Mexico, but, wait, wait, wait for the right weather. Never underestimate the effect of the Gulf Stream and also make sure that you understand the north-flowing Yucatan Current that flows along the Yucatan Strait, between the Yucatan Peninsula and Cuba, and the Gulf Loop Current that flows around the Gulf of Mexico, which both feed into the Gulf Stream.

THE YUCATAN PENINSULA, BELIZE & OUTLYING CAYES

If you sail from Cuba to Isla Mujeres you will be six miles from Cancun, a massive tourist centre where you can check in, have a good meal, provision and head off south towards Tulum. Mayan ruins are found throughout the Yucatan, Belize, Honduras and Guatemala. Mexico's Chichen Itza is the most famous of the scores of ruins along the Ruta Maya, the Mayan Trail following the ancient culture that reached its peak 1,000 years ago. If you have taken a road trip and are 'ruined out' there is Agua Azul, an amazing waterfall near Palenque in Chiapas.

The largest of the Cayes of Belize, Ambergris, is 25 miles long. A 6-foot channel divides Ambergris from Mexico, along the Yucatan border.

Belize (www.belize.com) was once called British Honduras and remains a Commonwealth country. The story goes that Belize City was built on a foundation of

The picture of Havana, Cuba

OCC Rally boats at Placencia Marina, Belize

mahogany chips and broken rum bottles. The faded grandeur of British rule can be seen in the cathedral and government buildings in Belize City, such as the Culture Museum that was Government House, the Governor General's residence. If you like zoos, there is one. Xanantunich (Maiden of the Rock) is the nearest Mayan site to the town. Go to a pub, shop and provision in the town before heading to the islands off Belize, the Cayes.

Along the coast of Belize lie 174 miles of the world's second-largest reef, providing spectacular diving and snorkelling. Caye Caulker (www.gocayecaulker.com) is a good base from which to explore other Cayes such as Chapel, Long and George. The 'Acquarium' is said to be a go-to for divers near Caye Caulker. If spending any time in the Cayes, check out the Marine Reserves, for example Caye Caulker, Hol Chan and Sapodilla Bay. The Great Blue Hole is a 120-metre-deep hole, the top of many divers wish lists. After diving and snorkling, if you want bars and restaurants, head for nearby Ambergris. If you are interested in birds, look up the Red-footed Boobies on Half Moon Caye at the Belize Audubon Society, www.belizeaudubon. org. Boats with deep drafts may find some of the anchorages around the Cayes too shallow.

Belize is considered by most visitors to Central America as comparatively pristine and organised. Once in Guatemala you are entering the real Central America, so the political situation and the infrastructure are less stable.

GUATEMALA

The Rio Dulce in Guatemala is freshwater, hence the name, 'sweet river'. It is a popular river in which to spend hurricane season. Livingston is the village at the mouth of the river that carries you through a spectacular gorge with 300-foot limestone cliffs surrounded by dense tropical undergrowth. Further up river is the marina district, where cruisers spend hurricane season, using it as a base to learn Spanish or explore inland Guatemala or Belize.

The Rio Dulce is not *Heart of Darkness* territory, but it is a place to remain aware. Although there have been attacks and shootings, these have been among criminals. There are marinas that are fairly secure. From the Rio Dulce most cruisers sail directly to Panama or to the San Blas Islands and on to the ABCs.

COLOMBIA

The ancient city of Cartagena in Colombia is a favourite of many cruisers, especially those who have taken part in the Christmas or Easter celebrations. Rosemarie Smart-Alecio who has sailed in the Caribbean,

Pacific and Far East chose an anchorage in Colombia as one of her favourites, Guayraca Bay, North Colombia: 'Fjord-like, within the highest coastal range of mountains in the world (5,000 metres) and the only place to see snow in the Caribbean. We try to forget the katabatic winds!'

The western Caribbean is in flux and there have been reports of violence and thefts. Once in the Caribbean, talk to those who have just returned and research what the real situation is, not urban rumour.

VENEZUELA

This applies particularly to Venezuela. During Chavez's time the country became increasingly unsafe and anti-cruiser. Cruisers who left their boats for hurricane season moved north or back across the Atlantic. The offshore islands such as Los Roques, Margarita Island, Los Testigos, Aves de Barlovento and Aves de Sotovento are a rewarding cruising area, however again there have been attacks on cruisers. Cruisers used to take trips inland to the Angel Falls or further to the Andes. Find out from people who have just returned how the land and the waters lie.

Santa Marta, Columbia

10
HURRICANE SEASON

June too soon
July stand by
August come it must
September remember
October all over.

Mariners' rhyme

The verse above is a useful guide but cannot be relied on: most experts now agree that October (and even November) can see hurricane activity. The most likely times hurricanes will form are between 15th August and 15th October and cruising sailors need to get out of their way or prepare for the carnage that they can cause.

The accepted hurricane belt is changing, so aim for north of Cape Hatteras, North Carolina, USA (Lat 35° 13' 29"N and Long 075° 31' 48"W) and south of Grenada (Lat 33° 78' 38"N, Long 089° 80' 22"W). Not that they screech to a halt at the border: hurricanes happen as far as New York and the Maritimes. It is important to understand fully the hurricane belt as defined by your insurer, and what your responsibilities are if you are remaining in that belt.

The National Oceanic and Atmospheric Administration (NOAA, www.noaa.gov) is extremely useful providing information on where tropical storms and hurricanes are forming and their predicted track. The Hurricane Zone (www.hurricanezone.net) is also worth keeping an eye on.

The distress caused by the direct hit on Grenada by Hurricane Ivan on 7th September 2004 was intense. The National Hurricane Centre described its rapid strengthening as unprecedented. Along with the true devastation for the local people, there were also smashed yachts and broken dreams. Scores of those who had joined the 1% club (without insurance), who really had sailed away, were beaten up. Cruisers had flocked to Grenada because there had been no direct hit for many years. Worse, still the catastrophic damage caused to the Caribbean islands in 2017 by Hurricanes Irma and Maria.

So hurricanes happen and you have to be prepared to run or secure yourself. If you choose to remain in the Caribbean, find a reputable marina of which your insurer approves, and be prepared. And beware, the closer the hurricane season the more unstable the weather. Lightning storms are a danger in the spring. One boat that risked an ill-advised weather window from the Bahamas ended up with its electrics in a pile of fried wires on the dock in Charleston, South Carolina.

HURRICANE ISABEL

In September Hurricane Isabel struck the Eastern Chesapeake. This is my experience.

We sailed north for 1,200 miles from St Marten in the Caribbean to Chesapeake Bay, USA, where 'hurricanes hardly happen' – only to be thumped by Isabel, a once-in-25-year phenomenon.

Our departure from Puerto Rico was hastened when Tropical Storm Ana came six weeks early, in April. All the way north through the British and US Virgins and the Bahamas we had muttered, 'June too soon. July stand by. August come it must. September remember. October all over.' We motor-sailed up the Intracoastal Waterway (ICW) from West Palm Beach to Norfolk and into the Chesapeake Bay.

In July we'd stood fast as the remnants of Tropical Storm Claudette bashed about us. At the beginning of September, we took shelter in a lightning storm in Solomons Island, Maryland, one hour south of Washington, DC. We had anticipated completing our end-of-first-year sort-out-fix-it in Annapolis, three days' sail away. We found that Solomons suited all our needs, and was cheaper. One week after our arrival on 7th September, Tropical Storm Isabel grew to hurricane strength. By 11th September she was a category five with 155mph winds.

On Sunday 14th September, Hurricane Isabel was north of the Bahamas, heading towards us in the USA. She was still category five but weakening. We were amazed. Isabel was forecast to track above the usual points of landfall such as the Bahamas, Florida and South Carolina, to hit *Moonshine* in Maryland on Thursday 18th September in the afternoon. Wednesday we were flying home for a visit – or rather, not. *Moonshine* was to have been berthed in the Hospitality Harbour while we visited the UK.

Three anchors in a protected area, versus secured in a spider's web of lines on a dock? Would the anchors hold? How to configure the lines? Would we be able to stay? We knew of one marina in the south that ordered all boats out during hurricanes. In February St Margarets doubled *Moonshine*'s insurance premium and reduced the cover, no longer insuring against damage caused by named storms even if we were out of the designated hurricane belt (north of Cape Hatteras, North Carolina and south of Grenada). Searches for alternatives offered no better for new clients.

By Monday 15th September Isabel had reduced speed to category four. With a $200 fee to change each ticket, I argued with British Airways that we were not 'choosing' but being forced to change our flights because our home was in danger. My 'special circumstances' was met by supervisors quoting 'policy'. We decided to wait until Tuesday for a BA thaw. The genoa, the main and the sail bag were removed. Most of D dock were in denial. Dave on *Island Girl* changed the oil.

On Tuesday 16th September John walked the dock and made the first attempt on the spider's web of lines that would be *Moonshine*'s safety net. Fighter jets flew out of the Naval Air Warfare Centre (NAWCAD) 5 miles away, to airbases out of Isabel's path. Ships in the US naval fleet sailed out from Norfolk, Virginia, to the safety of the Atlantic Ocean. British Airways relaxed its policy for those flying on Thursday and Friday, but they couldn't accommodate us. Spitting, we paid out the $200 each.

The tensions grew. Our usually healthy appetites died. Diet Coke kept us going. Bill Glascock has owned the Hospitality

Marina, our chosen hurricane hole, for 17 years. Isabel was his first hurricane. While fielding anxious questions he emptied his floating, wooden office of electrical equipment and placed giant fenders between it and the dock. Greg von Zielinski and Bill had been friends since high school. Greg lives aboard a lifeboat from a naval warship, converted for his 'ocean ministry'. I nicknamed him Spiderman. Greg used to import yachts and his knowledge and advice on knots and spider's-web strategy were invaluable.

The dock was full of discussions on the weather channel's latest and the perfect cat's cradle. Trawlers, motorboats and yacht skippers compared knots. The clove hitch with two half-hitches was deemed best. If it wasn't knots it was second guessing the height of the surge, the seawater that the strong winds would pile up ashore. If the lines were not tied tightly enough at the top of the pilings the surge could float the boat off, free to smash itself on pilings and neighbours. One of the empty berths next to us belonged to *Best Pals*. Like numerous keel-less motorboats it had been lifted out then blocked 1 foot off the ground about 200 yards inland. Another powerboater wondered if a flimsy tarpaulin would help keep his seats dry. He wrapped his four puny lines, cracked open a beer and lumbered off. Perhaps clueless was better than the gnawing threat we felt. Perhaps not.

John spent the night following Isabel's relentless flight on the NOAA website and researching the best spider's-web configuration. Across the dock was *Island Girl*, a Cape Dory 37 and Dave and Cindy Foss's only home. After seven years of planning they had set out in July from Michigan, in the northern US. Dave's mother-in-law was

The spider's web John created with Greg to hold Moonshine during Hurricane Isabel

dead against cruising. Her name? Isabel.

The joke went around that the Floridians had put out huge fans to blow Isabel north. It was working. Again, we chewed over whether to stay on the dock or head for a creek. Local knowledge suggested St Leonard's Creek, where the high sides gave good protection. The berths either side of *Moonshine* were free. We gave black looks to those entering the D dock channel. In the adjacent Spring Cove Marina, the boats were crammed in.

As with the discussions on spider's webs, so with the anchor debates. Danforths were considered best for the mud of the Chesapeake. Some dismissed the Bahamian moor V formation because the boat can twist in the wind, winding the two chains around each other. If one knew the wind direction, two anchors on the same side could pull against it; however, this is risky as the final track of the hurricane is unpredictable. The triangle method was considered best. Whether at anchor or on a dock, everyone viewed other people's boats as potential liabilities.

In their mid-20s, Dan and Carol on *Alona*, an ancient trawler, had been anchored in St Leonard's Creek for two days when older cruisers set their one (!) anchor over *Alona*'s anchor line, and refused to move it. *Alona* was forced to reset. Captain Seaweed (think Ben Gunn), 83 years old, plumbed the depth of the furthest end of Cuckold Creek. Using a triangular configuration of three anchors, he wedged his steel boat with its 4-foot draft into a nook. He had a fourth anchor spare just in case.

Solomons Island is on the Patuxent River, along which there are dozens of creeks offering hurricane holes. Those on *Trooper*, a Hillyard 37, were unsure about the dock they were offered in Mill Creek. They dropped a lead line and discovered a Hillyard 37-size hurricane hole. Three anchors and a web of 20 lines, some over 100 feet long reaching to the dock and surrounding trees, ensured that the only movement could be 6 inches down into the mud below. In June in Pipeline Canal near Southport, North Carolina, during a vicious lightning storm, we had dragged for the first time onto a beach and bent our CQR. It knocked our confidence and swayed our decision to stay on the dock.

On Wednesday 17th September the fear of the unknown gripped dock masters and cruisers alike. Isabel was now category two with winds of 110mph at the eye wall. Sleep was fitful and disturbing. At 2am John could not sleep. The thumping noises on the cabin roof turned out to be him taking the barbeque and the liferaft off the stern railings and the wind generator from the gantry, removing all items that added windage. The bimini was dismantled, the spray hood strapped down, even the pegs from the clothes line. The fishing rods, boathook, brush and dan buoy were stored in the forward cabin with the bimini canvas, sail bag and sails. The mainsail battens lay on the salon sole. The outboard motor, horseshoe life preserver, empty jerry cans for water and fuel joined the windvane in *Moonshine*'s cavernous cockpit locker. Fenders were hung around bow and aft.

The governors of North Carolina, Virginia, Maryland and Delaware declared states of emergency and mobilised the National Guard. West Marine and other shops were boarded up.

Still no one came to secure the 40-foot Beneteau next to us. Bill and Greg worked tirelessly securing boats abandoned by their owners. It seemed surreal to see them tying a rope rail lifeline along the walkway on a sunny day with blue, cloudless skies. *Moonshine* sat in her web of 16 5/8" dock lines attached to 11 pilings, her 45lb CQR set on chain just off her bow and her spare anchor rode wrapped around the windlass, then tied off 100 feet away to a pile on the other side of the channel.

Greg and Bill worked tirelessly securing boats abandoned by their owners

Would the cleats hold? The preparations kept the stress at bay. John extended the web around the Beneteau. The owner's dockside tub of roses was lugged into the cockpit. The intention to stay onboard *Moonshine* during the storm seemed foolhardy; a room in the hotel overlooking the boats was the answer. We cut the cost by sharing with *Island Girl*.

On Thursday 19th September at 5am we tied *Moonbeam*, the dinghy, on a diagonal between two piles. If she was blown anywhere it would be into the mud around the edge of the mini cove. The sky was grey. High tide at 9am did not go down. Grim predictions filled the paper. US boats detached the shore power and the batteries to power the bilges were charged by running the engine. The lines from the windlass stretched across the channel were raised, thereby allowing skippers to haul their boats away from dock. No more boats could enter C or D docks. It was blustery and spitting. We checked into the hotel with a marina cart full of waterproofs, torches, cameras, laptops, picnics and our most important possessions. The weather channel remained on until the power failed later that night.

Isabel made landfall in Kill Devil Hills, North Carolina at 11am. Cars were turned upside down in the 9-foot storm surge. The Outer Banks and North Carolina coast took the full force. Houses were swamped, and some washed away in nearby Kitty Hawk. It was estimated that 300,000 were without power in Virginia Beach. We thought of our friends in Belhaven, North Carolina, where the waters from Pamlico Sound, just inside the Outer Banks, would flood the town, just as it did during Floyd in 1999. Floyd hit less-populated areas after a drought; Isabel was aiming for metropolitan areas such as Norfolk, Annapolis, Washington, DC and Baltimore after a rainy summer.

We experienced the first effects of the bands (or spirals) of the system along the Patuxent River at 5pm. Isabel's now increasing speed meant there was less rainfall. The water had risen 4 feet and lapped at the base of the finger pontoons, just under the walkway. John and the other skippers raised the lines even further up the pilings. By the time the winds reached Solomons Island they were down to a mere sustained 40 knots with gusts of storm force 11, not the estimated 74 knots, hurricane strength. By 7.30pm they lulled, which gave us a false sense of security. We thought we'd got away with it.

Replete from our Chinese takeaway, we watched the boats from our fifth-floor hotel room. Suddenly Dave's cap was blown across the room. It was 9.30pm and the winds had returned with a vengeance: up by 20 knots. We were now in the northeast quadrant (or RFQ, right front quadrant) where the winds are at their highest and the surge highest too. All hell broke loose. We hadn't got away with it at all: the eye wall was coming.

On the fifth floor the windows shook. Huge trees arched and crashed. Below, the masts tilted at an acute angle. The rigging screamed. We recalled our first days out in the Atlantic, 200 miles offshore, in a 40-knot storm with gusts of 55. At least this time we were up a dogleg, at the back of Back Creek, protected by trees and a large hotel. This was a far more menacing situation. The extra 20 knots felt like 40. With the darkness and rain obscuring their vision, the skippers used the rope rail along the walkway to pull themselves against the wind through the waves washing over the dock, which was now two feet deep under water. Strangely it was 70° F, quite warm. There were several explosions and flashes in the distance. The sky turned green. The town's power transponders had blown.

The boat's lines on D dock were secure. It was way too hazardous for any more changes to be made. Reluctant and feeling helpless in the face of such severe conditions, John and Dave returned to the hotel warning other skippers not to go out.

Isabel stomped north to Annapolis at the top of Chesapeake Bay, causing extensive flooding and wind damage.

By Friday 19th September at 4am the winds were abating. The dock was still 2 feet under water. Nonetheless, all was well in Hospitality Harbour. Our new D-dock family had survived remarkably intact.

At 8am it was a beautiful morning with clear blue skies, and hardly a breath of wind. We sloshed along the dock. *Moonshine* floated above us. We motored

After the hurricane, all's well that ends well

with Greg a mile down Back Creek to the opening into the Patuxent River where the damage was heaviest. The front line of onslaught from Isabel left pilings stripped of their walkways and docks broken up. The bowsprit of a Cabo Roca had been smashed against its pilings. The portside hull of a Swan 42 was splintered and completely separated at the hull deck join; a chilling site. Shredded sails flapped in the light breeze.

In Spring Cove Marina, next to us, a boom had torn through a bimini. Its autumn newsletter seemed ironic: 'If everyone is prepared, I'm sure the hurricane will miss!' The power was still out. The marina shop fridge was defrosting. Cruisers slurped free, melting ice cream. Several metal strips in the roof of the large boat 'garage' had been ripped up. Nails in the sheet had gouged holes in a sleek motorboat's gelcoat. Captain Seaweed motored past, wrinkled and toothless as ever, his sixth hurricane under his keel with no ill effects. *Alona* was re-anchored near the picturesque Drum Point Lighthouse and Dan and Carol were re-attaching their makeshift red check tablecloth awning. In St Leonard's Creek a massive oak had fallen towards *Alona*; it had landed on her lines.

By 4pm the water was under the dock. Bill re-activated the power. Air conditioning flowed into the trawlers. We were able to climb up to *Moonshine*, still high in the water. It was good to be back on our home.

The Beneteau's owner never showed. The rose bush was a bit the worse for hurricane wear. The reparations took a day, much faster than the fearful preparations. The D dockers celebrated with Bill and Greg in Solomons Island Yacht Club, before a D-Day barbeque.

ROUTES NORTH FROM THE CARIBBEAN

BRITISH VIRGIN ISLANDS TO THE USA VIA BERMUDA

If you're leaving the Caribbean you can sail from Tortola in the British Virgin Islands to Bermuda, wait for weather, and thence head to the USA. The ARC USA (formerly known as the Atlantic Cup) run by the World Cruising Club is a rally that leaves Tortola in early May. The Atlantic Ocean route via Bermuda can be rough both north in the spring and south in the late autumn. It takes approximately 9 days for a 40-foot boat compared with six weeks hopping island to island.

US VIRGIN ISLANDS TO PUERTO RICO TO DOMINICAN REPUBLIC TO TURKS & CAICOS TO BAHAMAS

The alternative route north from the British Virgins, through the US Virgins if you have a US visa, to Puerto Rico, Dominican Republic, Turks and Caicos, the Bahamas to the USA, is a long haul but one full of discovery and revelations.

The Atlantic from the US Virgins, through the Spanish Virgins to Puerto Rico and the Dominican Republic is difficult to navigate. The seabed is mountainous with numerous shelves, changing rapidly from thousands to twenty feet under the keel, and from smooth waters to confused and steep waves. Violent currents sweep yachts off course which, when negotiating small islands and coastlines, is hazardous. *The Gentleman's Guide to Passages South* is the most useful pilot guide.

SPANISH VIRGIN ISLANDS

Some cruisers leave the Caribbean chain early in order to spend extra time in the comparatively unspoilt Spanish Virgin Islands. Culebra and Vieques lie between the US Virgins and Puerto Rico. Many feel that these islands and the east coast of Puerto Rico are what the British and US Virgins were 30 years ago. Vieques is particularly untouched, as until recently it was a naval range and off limits.

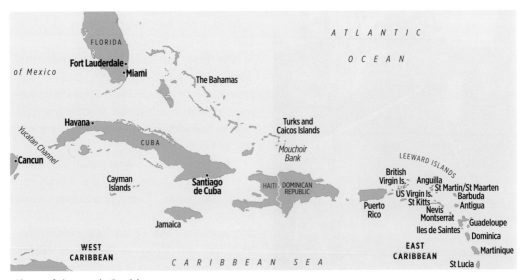

Chart of the north Caribbean

ESCONDIDO

One of our favourite anchorages is found along the northern coast of 'DR', for the beauty and the memories. John and I were sailing south from the USA to the Caribbean, on our first boat, *Moonshine*. I was three weeks pregnant, having just conceived Jack in Conception Island, Bahamas.

After a long 48-hour sail, we anchored in Escondido, one of the most spectacular tropical backdrops we had seen. It was John's birthday and at 8am whales surfaced twenty feet from the boat. Happy Birthday spumes, and they were gone.

PUERTO RICO

While in Puerto Rico you could hire a car and head off to the Arecibo Observatory (www.naic.edu), the world's largest single-aperture telescope. The drive up to the radio telescope takes you through spectacular rainforest. Bond fans will remember Roger Moore scaling the 1001ft (305 metre) telescope.

If you are running low, you can re-provision in Puerto Rico, where you can find American supermarkets and chain stores.

On the south coast, Ponce is a good stop, if for no other reason than to see the bizarre fire station – think *Wizard of Oz*. On the west, Boquerón is the best anchorage from which to cross to the Dominican Republic. Take a taxi to Mayagüez for shopping and customs.

HAITI & THE DOMINICAN REPUBLIC

Haiti and the Dominican Republic make up the two elements of the landmass of Hispaniola. It is worth stopping in the marina in Punta Cana on the east coast of the Dominican Republic, before heading along the north coast.

If you time your journey to cross

Punta Cana, east coast of the Dominican Republic

between the Dominican Republic and the Turks and Caicos between January and March, you can see whales that have swum for thousands of miles to breed on the Mouchoir Bank.

TURKS & CAICOS

Big Sand Cay in the southern Turks and Caicos is where the real superlatives start. Idyllic, paradise, heavenly – all applied as we worked our way to and through the Bahamas.

Plana Cay is heaven on earth. It is surrounded by at least 40 miles of Atlantic Ocean which, in the best conditions, forces an arduous passage; however, it is worth it once you get there.

WORTH THE WAIT

From the blog of *Seraphim*, heading north, March-April:

The Mona Passage has a fearful reputation, however our crossing from Puerto Rico to the Dominican Republic was not so awful. To greet us on the east coast of the Dominican Republic was Punta Cana, a huge new marina, which was almost empty. Luxury apartments overlooked swimming pools measured by the acre, which overlooked a long Caribbean beach. Rest day's toughest choice was which pool next. They even had their own lifeguard and, dull but essential, free laundry.

Covering the miles from the Virgins north to the Turks meant a lot of engine hours. Twelve-hour days of pounding engine is exhausting. But at the end we have powder sand and crystal waters, pretty much every day, unless it is Ocean World when we have dolphin shows, seal shows, shark shows, parrot shows, lovebirds and tigers. A totally different experience to Luperon, the third-world anchorage that is the usual jump-off from the Dominican Republic to cross the Mouchoir Bank to the Turks and Caicos Islands.

Heaven on earth
Turtles come to lay their eggs on Big Sand Cay. Behind us stretched the Turks and Caicos, to the southwest, our destination, the Caribbean chain. But for now, this remote, uninhabited island was ours. Miles from up-market hotels, it is a blissful rest from the wearisome bash into the easterlies on passage from the Bahamas to the Virgins. The sandy anchorage was deep and well protected from the trade winds, although sometimes open to swell.

Snorkelling near the boat, sharks and rays circled 20 feet below us. Our fellow travellers on Seafever had a hydrophone. Fascinated, we listened to whales courting. Half a mile away one breached. Amazing.

My arrival on paradise's blueprint was undignified: I misjudged the extremely steep beach and fell out of the dinghy. Spoilt in the Exuma Islands, blasé about stunning beaches, we were taken aback by these glistening, almost iridescent stretches.

Feeling our footsteps were the first, we took a long walk along the island's two sides. On the Atlantic shore we found a lion – well, driftwood that we dressed with a seaweed mane. Pricked by cactus on the direct route back to the dinghy, we retraced our footsteps, in and out of the surf.

With time and winds against us, we only stayed a day and a night. But Big Sand stays with us as one of our most magical anchorages.

Big Sand Cay, Turks and Caicos

THE BAHAMAS

The Bahamas are achingly beautiful, however coral heads in shallow waters can make them treacherous. It is essential to follow the charts and take your time. Most cruisers dash through heading north, then take their time tracking south to the Caribbean. Some spend the whole winter cruising the Bahamas – easily done. If you are considering two years in the Caribbean it is worth rethinking and spending your first winter season in the Caribbean chain and your second in the Bahamas.

If you are in the Bahamas on Boxing Day or New Year's Eve, there is a carnival, a 'jump up', called Junkanoo. The biggest is in Nassau and lasts all night. Make every effort to be there. The rivalry between the different teams such as the Valley Boys and the Saxons is intense. Each team takes a year from the end of one Junkanoo to the next to create their spectacular costumes. Cowbells are rigged onto bicycle chain contraptions worn on the chest and played

Junkanoo, the Bahamian Carnival celebrated throughout the Bahamas at Christmas and New Year

by turning the pedals with the hands. The noise and rhythms keep you dancing all night.

While sailing through the Bahamas look out for an evening of 'rake and scrape', when all the locals turn up to the bar to play their instrument, be it washboard or guitar. These are some of the best nights you can have.

In Thunderball Cave, Staniel Cay, Jack and 'James Bond' Rodriguez swam in the cave in which 007 struggled against underwater villains. It was also featured more recently in *Into the Blue*, a feature film about treasure hunting, shot in Nassau. It was slightly surreal watching the movie anchored at Rose Island, off Nassau.

Hog Cay is a real pirates' lair, *Seraphim* anchored where Anne Bonny and others used to hide before sweeping out on unsuspecting ships. In this part of the Exuma Land and Sea Park we were visited by a large barracuda, parrot fish and manta rays. Established for over 50 years, the area contains a wide range of species and strives

to keep the land and sea as unpolluted and untouched as possible. The motto is: 'Take photographs, leave bubbles.'

At Warderick Wells the boys had a temporary beach that appeared during low tide, 20 feet from the boat. Following in the footsteps of tradition, we laid a driftwood plank with our boat name and details on the top of Boo Boo Hill, where it is claimed the voices of those drowned at sea can be heard. Or maybe it is the wind through the blow holes in the porous rock.

The friendly Black Island in the Exuma chain has an excellent laundry, and an extraordinary garden of wood shapes grown from 30 years of William T's imagination. Strong and lean and fit, this 72-year-old guides visitors around, revealing in a few words the bizarre collection, creating the garden as he speaks. William told us he looks into the clouds, sees a shape and walks into the woods to find it. Dolphins, whales, eagles, a cobra, a woman washing her hair, a drunk guy falling over and scores of others are found in the Garden of Eden – as well as papayas, bananas and John's sweet-and-sour favourite, tamarind.

From Rose Island, Nassau glitters in the distance. At the end of the elegant necklace of green and yellow lights is a gold chunk with red beads, Atlantis, a vast resort on Paradise Island. The height of kitsch and hideous taste, it is a must.

On Grand Bahama, Port Lucaya is one of the main tourist centres. Presently times are hard, so the marinas, usually full of sports fishing boats, are offering deals that make them affordable for sailing boats. The Port Lucaya market sells all kinds of tourist knick-knacks. Local buses can take you to the supermarkets. At low tide, visit the long Lucaya Beach – at high tide it is nothing, at low tide it is breath-taking. Another must is the Garden of the Groves, an enchanting series of tropical gardens

Lucaya Beach at low tide, Grand Bahama

with a maze.

The Ocean Reef Yacht Club and Resort (www.oryc.com) is a hidden gem, and most cruisers who know try to keep it a secret. The entrance is difficult but at high tide is navigable with caution. If you are visiting Grand Bahama, keep your boat here.

Bimini, 47 miles from Florida across the Gulf Stream, has a strange captivating charm. As one local said, 'There ain't no time zone here.' These tiny islands on the edge of the Bahama Banks have attracted sports fishermen for decades.

Looking out from North Bimini towards the Gulf Stream, the stairway to heaven

BROWNS MARINA, NORTH BIMINI

From the blog of *Seraphim*, April 2010.

Browns Marina is next to the Government Dock, both mentioned in Hemingway's Islands in the Stream. From the cockpit we watched the loading and unloading of the large ferries and boats, and the local water taxi. It's quiet now, after the influx during the Easter celebrations.

Ashley Saunders writes books on Bimini. His house, The Dolphin House, has a small museum and displays his inventive mosaics. Boat building has been in his family for generations. His brother Ansil built the Bimini Boatfisher, an exquisite craft made from various woods, including horseflesh wood and mahogany. It is almost too beautiful to launch in seawater.

On Dr Martin Luther King's first visit to the island he wrote his acceptance speech for the Nobel Prize. His second visit to the island was at a more sober time. Saunders felt that King knew the end was near and spoke movingly of his experience with King, whom he took to a tranquil place in the mangroves to write his final speech, three days before his death. While out on Saunders' boat, fatigued King asked Ansil to talk, saying he was tired of talking. Saunders recited a psalm he had written. We were blown away when Ansil gave an impassioned recital of some of the poem. The air stood still. High energies surrounded him.

Still wowed by Saunders, en route home I met Philippa, who runs Browns Marina, and Tammy, the baker at Taste of Heaven. I booked four guava duffs, all-time melt in the mouth. Locals call the bakery 'Tammy Souse Souse' because of the lunchtime souse (pickled) dishes she serves.

Walking past the long wall of the Big Game Resort with a sea painting by Bennet Davis, past Jontras, my grocery, past our first marina, the Bimini Blue Waters Marina, the Anchorage Hotel and back to Browns, several locals greeted us and chatted. Bimini was becoming home and more and more difficult to leave.

THE GULF STREAM

The Gulf Stream must be approached with caution. With the right winds and the right conditions it is a great sail, or even motor. With a northerly, the wind over the north flowing tide, it is dangerous. Locals talk about the waves looking like 'elephants' holding trunk to tail.

Fishing in the Gulf Stream between Bimini and Florida

POSTCARDS FROM THE KEDGE

The Gohlkes bought *Liberty*, a Morgan Out Island 416, their first and only boat, after Nancy foolishly rejected Dave's midlife crisis request for a '68 Camaro. Just 361 days later, David and Nancy left Kemah, Texas, with their sons Christopher and Joshua (ages 8 and 5 at the time), on their six-month sabbatical cruise.

They were in Isla Mujeres, Mexico before they realised they really didn't know how to sail. After cruising Belize and Guatemala, they returned to Texas. On the way home, they realised they were ready to trade life in the 'burbs for the cruising life. After two-and-a-half years of saving and boat work, they set sail on their current cruise. The past three years have seen the Gohlkes on *Liberty* along the Gulf coast, in the Bahamas for three winter seasons and up the US east coast for two hurricane seasons, with a recent several-month trip back to Texas for work to fill the cruising kitty, work on the boat and family visits.

Liberty left Texas again in March, bound for the Caribbean. With just over 15,000 miles under the keel (including several long offshore passages), the Gohlkes report that they may even have learned how to sail at this point.

David, Nancy, Christopher and Josh Gohlke, Johnson Cay, Ragged Island, Bahamas

---

Dear Nicola

We recommend the following anchorages:

- Double Breasted Cay, Ragged Islands, Bahamas – deserted protection most of the way around, beautiful beaches, shallow anchorage (not to be overcrowded), lots of reefs for snorkelling and hunting, lots of lobsters.
- Lighthouse Reef, Belize.
- Conception Island, Bahamas.
- George Town, Exumas, Bahamas – we usually anchor at Volleyball Beach. If we want to get away from the hubbub of Volleyball Beach and create a little hubbub of our own, we anchor at Hamburger Beach, where the kids can wake board around the neighbouring boats.
- Double Breasted Cay, Abacos.

Nicola Rodriguez
The Yacht Moonshine
English Harbour
Antigua
West Indies

Best wishes
The Gohlkes

THE USA

FORT LAUDERDALE

When sailing in daylight the 50 miles across the Gulf Stream from the Bahamas, the first sights of America, from up to 10 miles away, are the skyscrapers of Miami and Fort Lauderdale. Both cities have excellent Class A inlets that can be entered in most conditions. We chose Port Everglades in Fort Lauderdale, as it is a port of entry for customs and immigration and gave access to the canal system of Fort Lauderdale, the 'Venice of America'. Once through the entrance of the inlet, turn to starboard and head north to Las Olas Municipal Marina, where buoys can be taken for $45 a night, noon to noon.

Seraphim wintering in New River Marina, Fort Lauderdale

There are dozens of marinas with prices ranging from $3 to $10 a foot, with every kind of marina service a cruiser could wish for. From small fishing boats, to mega-yachts and cruise ships, Fort Lauderdale caters to all (www.fort-lauderdale-marine-directory.com). There is an anchorage in Lake Sylvia, however a sandbar makes the entrance tricky and officially boats are only allowed to stay one day per year. As ever, Skipper Bob's *Anchorages Along the Intracoastal Waterway* is a useful guide.

In the middle of the canal system is the New River, with yet more marinas and yacht facilities. *Seraphim* tied up alongside the Riverwalk, at the New River Municipal Marina, which at $1.20 a foot is one of the cheapest marinas in an expensive city, although there are no showers or laundry; those are 1-mile up river at Cooley's Landing. Our two-week stop stretched to three months of boat repairs. It was easy to stay: Lauderdale is known as Lingerdale.

Marina Mile (State road 84) caters for every boat requirement. Regular stops for John were chandleries such as West Marine, Boat Owners' Warehouse (BOW) and a huge second-hand shop, Sailorman, all within blocks of each other. The excellent Diesel Services of America assisted with some minor engine problems. Solar and wind specialists Emarine supplied a new wind generator. During our stay our plans for 'where next?' changed repeatedly, ranging from the Bahamas to Panama, hence we had to get new charts and a library of western Caribbean books from Bluewater Books and Chandlery.

The Floridian on Las Olas Boulevard is a tradition, a 24-hour restaurant that is great for breakfast. Lester's is an old-fashioned diner on Marina Mile, near the chandleries, good for outstanding burgers after hunting down a gadget. The best kebabs in our America were five minutes from the boat at the American Turkish Restaurant, run by Eric, who cooks the lamb to succulent perfection.

Cruiser traffic is constant year around. Up-and-down island conversations thrive on the docksides, laundries or in the supermarket, whether heading north in the spring or further south on the Thorny Path in January.

When returning in the autumn, push to arrive in Fort Lauderdale for the Winterfest Boat Parade in mid-December. Las Olas Marina buoys give front-row views of a spectacular evening of boats decorated in Christmas lights.

Source: Cruising Notes, Practical Boat Owner

THE INTRACOASTAL WATERWAY (ICW)

The Intracoastal Waterway takes you from Miami 1,090 miles north to Mile Marker 1 in Norfolk, Virginia, and then unofficially on to New York City and Maine. It also runs along the west Florida coast up along the Gulf of Mexico to Texas.

The Americans call the ICW 'the Ditch'. It is a series of interconnecting rivers and man-made canals running pretty well parallel with the east coast of the USA. At 50 miles a day it can be covered in three weeks but can take six depending on how many places you visit.

The US Corp of Engineers, fresh from building the Panama Canal, worked on the channels connecting the rivers. There are numerous buoyed channels, known as inlets, that run out into the Atlantic. In places where the waterway meanders, for example parts of Georgia, it is worth coming out into the ocean if the weather is clear for a three- or four-day run. It is a slow motor, a gentle slalom between the green day markers. Do not try to travel at night, you will run aground and might be hit by a barge. If you run aground in the day, you can radio an upcoming motor cruiser asking them to power up, providing a large wake to help lift you off. Be careful what you ask for – you can be swamped.

It is wise to buy insurance, for example from Seatow or Towboat US, for towing you out of trouble if you do run aground. If you do not have towing insurance and someone offers to haul you off, establish how much it will cost, and insist on using your lines (ropes). If they use their own lines, they could, within maritime law, claim salvage rights, in which case they own your boat, which could become costly. This is worth remembering in all rescue scenarios.

The controlling depth of the ICW is officially 10 feet. Realistically, it is between 5 and 6 feet. Most of the bridges have a minimum clearance of 65 feet, except Julia Tuttle in Miami. Other bridges open on request or keep to a rigid timetable. Many is the time cruisers have cursed when a bridge will not stay open the extra two minutes required to help them on their way. That extra time can cost the boat an extra half an hour waiting, sometimes in strong currents, for example in Beaufort, South Carolina. Everyone who has motored in the ICW has stories about unhelpful bridge operators. Keep an eye on the tides, particularly if you are near an inlet where the outgoing and incoming tides affect the ICW.

Maptech charts and *Anchorages Along the Intracoastal Waterway* by Skipper Bob are required cockpit reading. The Maptech charts show the route, page after page, up the ICW. *Anchorages Along the Intracoastal Waterway* is a navigation aid providing information concerning the route. It also gives suggested anchorages marks out of five for Holding, Wind Protection, Current Flow, Wake Protection, Scenic Beauty and Ease of Shopping. In Daytona the holding was described as black jello. There is also a dog icon for where you can walk your dog. Places of interest – such as Buckshot on the beautiful Waccamaw River, in South Carolina, where a local shop sells excellent sausages – are mentioned along with overnight docking. There is also a Skipper Bob marinas book: *Marinas Along the Intracoastal Waterway.* Bill Moeller's guide, *The Intracoastal Waterway, Norfolk to Miami*, has useful descriptions and backgrounds, with vital bridge-opening times.

As a keen radio listener, whenever we came to a new area I searched the dial for National Public Radio (NPR), an American cousin of BBC Radio 4, which illuminated and humoured our journeys north and south.

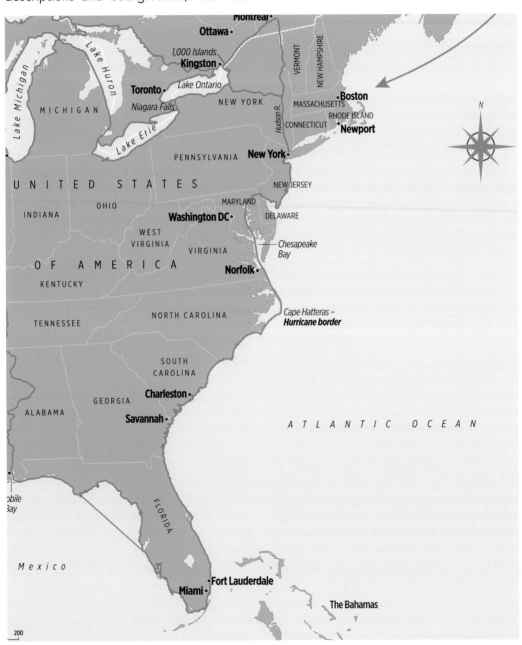

The Intracoastal Waterway

THE THORNY PATH: SOUTH FROM FLORIDA TO THE BRITISH VIRGINS & THE CARIBBEAN

In October most boats start heading south using the Intracoastal Waterway; some head offshore via Bermuda. From the Chesapeake south on the Intracoastal in the Fall can be full of magnificent scenery. However, it can be extremely cold. Wise boats put up an awning around the cockpit to protect them from the elements.

As we saw in Chapter 9, the 600 islands in the Bahamas chain are a series of diverse treats waiting to be explored. Some cruisers spend winter after winter in the Bahamas, others spend one winter in the Bahamas so that they are ready to explore further north into Maine and Nova Scotia, even Newfoundland, in the summer.

The Thorny Path leads from Florida through the Bahamas and Turks and Caicos to the Dominican Republic, Puerto Rico and the Virgins. It is called the Thorny Path because you are sailing into big seas blown up by the east winds. It is do-able if you leave early in the flat calm of 4am and sail until 10am, when the east winds begin to blow. Then you stop, anchor, explore and start again, pretty much every day, cold fronts allowing, for six weeks. It can be as arduous or relaxed as you wish. If you follow Bruce Van Sant's *Gentleman's Guide to Passages South* you'll have a good run; if you don't, you will, as we discovered, get thumped.

As with the ARC USA heading north in the spring, the World Cruising Club runs the Caribbean 1500 (www.worldcruising. com/carib1500/event.aspx) south from Portsmouth, Virginia voyaging 1,500 miles to the Nanny Cay, Tortola, British Virgin Islands. The ARC Bahamas (www. worldcruising.com/arc_bahamas) sails from Portsmouth south to Harborview Marina,

Marsh Harbour, Abacos in the northern Bahamas.

In early November, Offshore Passage Opportunities runs the North American Rally to the Caribbean (NARC), which leaves Newport for Bermuda, then south to St Martin. The organisers are contactable via www.sailopo.com. This is also an opportunity for people looking to crew to find a ride.

Beaufort in North Carolina is a popular jumping-off point for boats sailing across to Bermuda and south. Unofficial rallies form in the anchorage as boats are waiting to leave. When the weather window comes a dozen boats will leave together.

FLORIDA

The two most memorable experiences of our second ICW sojourn were seeing the launch of Space Shuttle Atlantis from our viewpoint on the deck of *Seraphim*, and our entry into Manhattan, New York.

Sadly, the Space Shuttle is no more, however the John F Kennedy Space Center is a great day out. It is on Merritt Island, in the middle of 'mother nature's SWAT team': alligators, ten types of poisonous snakes, boars, huge mosquitoes and impenetrable jungle surrounding Cape Canaveral.

Try the Space Shuttle ride, view the earth from the Space Shuttle via an IMAX film, walk under and around the massive Apollo rocket, which is a surprisingly emotional experience, meet a Space Shuttle astronaut, walk through the Rocket Garden and be inspired by the pioneers of space.

While in Florida, be a tourist. Take a berth and hire a car. Head off to Orlando and the numerous theme parks: Disney, Universal, MGM plus the other hoopla. After about five days dizzying nausea will strike and it's back to the boat.

Whilst staying at the Harbour Town Marina near Cape Canaveral, Jack (pictured) and James were intrigued by a manatee and her calf

GEORGIA

The grasslands of Georgia are breathtakingly beautiful but are very windy. It's the scenic route, so take it easy. An overnight sail from St Augustine in the north of Florida up to Charleston in South Carolina can save five days of chugging.

If you choose to sail outside in the ocean past Georgia, then still take time to visit Savannah by road from Charleston, having read the ubiquitous book *Midnight in the Garden of Good and Evil* by John Berendt.

CHARLESTON

Among those who have anchored in Charleston there are wry smiles in reply to 'What did you pick up?' The answer varies from logs, to trees, chunks of roots and chain. The current is fast and the anchoring poor, but Charleston (with its antebellum houses, pivotal 'first shot fired' point in American history, South Carolina Aquarium, excellent Children's Museum of the Lowlands, USS Yorktown (aircraft carrier) museum and good provisioning) is a great place to stop. Another plus for those with children is Brittlebank Park playground, not far from the anchorage. 4th July is pretty spectacular, with 360-degree fireworks from the anchorage. If the fast currents are too much there is charming Wappoo Creek, south of the city and a bus ride in.

In the sections below are excerpts from our blogs kept as we headed north and south.

THE AMERICAN DREAM

Charleston, South Carolina, 5th June
From Florida into southern Georgia we motored on, dolphins, oystercatchers, ospreys and pelicans entranced us along the way.

One night in a creek Jack watched egrets yanking worms from the mud at low tide, washing and gulping them.

McClellanville, South Carolina, 6th June
Heading north in the South where they talk slow and call me 'ma'am'.

Right now, we're in Forrest Gump territory, hiding from lightning storms, on a dock. As Jack said, "not much of one", with dozens of shrimpers down the way. Nowhere is miles away let alone the middle of it, not good to be the only boat with a 53-foot sticky-up thing in miles of grassland...

Once the weather cleared a walk discovered a 'labyrinth' (maze) in bricks in a side street. Anyone was invited to walk or dance the circle of bricks, use it as a meditation exercise, prayer circle or fun thing.

Last trip up the ICW yielded a terrifying night in Cape Fear, and this afternoon's ICW was pretty bad. The storm turned back towards us and John on the helm was forced to motor through driving rain in a stretch of the ICW that is becoming notorious for being un-dredged, the first place the funding dries up.

Waccamaw River, South Carolina, 7th June

Heading north in the South in the Waccamaw River where the Spanish moss hangs down and the tree roots reach up from the water.

After the stressful time of lightning storms yesterday, this Sunday was a soothing recovery along an intriguing, beautiful stretch of waterway. Either side is a wide diversity of green and silver trees, some tall and elegant, others straight out of Dr Seuss, while others seem to be the forms witches take when hiding in a hurry.

As the sun sets huge dragonflies appear. An osprey nest overlooks our anchorage. John and I take turns with the binoculars, awed by these hunters in flight. To Jack, it's another osprey, which he sees all along the rivers. I wonder if he'll ever realise how fortunate he is?

A highly-charged day, one may say, with high-explosive shells from US Marines exercising in Camp LeJeune, through which the ICW passes, landing on the banks and lightning, again at night. Helicopters had been doing Apocalypse Now a mile from the marina the previous day when the waterway had been closed. John re-checked and it was re-confirmed that the waterway was open, aka safe. We felt a mile was a lot too close. But all was fine, and we chugged on past the twisted metal wrecks of yesterday's war games.

A long day along 'the Ditch' came to an end in Southport Village Marina with the Southern welcome from Bill Gregory, an ex-detective Yankee from Detroit with a great deal on dockage, $1.30 a foot, yehaa! (Usually upwards of $2.00.) And it got better: a playground down the road that was even better than Brittlebank in Charleston, which we'd voted no 1.

It was here, with the no-see-ums nibbling, that we met broken-hearted George, who used to sail nuclear submarines, or rather fly them because 48 knots is fast. George is my height and wiry, with a tan mark that stops at the top of where his socks usually are. He named his boat *Christina*, after his Greek girlfriend who left him.

John and he discussed the Bahamas and the book *Blind Man's Bluff*, about the secrets of nuclear subs. Predictably George steered, elegantly, off the subject. George made the world smaller, knowing our friend Bill Glascock, 'the big cheese', in the Chesapeake, and would have talked longer but he really needed a smoke.

As we carried Jack home and James gambolled along the pontoon, the moon was full and 'awsum'. We smiled and smooched and knew that those folks and this evening are why we go cruising.

POSTCARDS FROM THE KEDGE

Gary Naigle and Greta Gustavson live in Norfolk, Virginia. We met them in St Martin, West Indies. They sponsored our membership of the Ocean Cruising Club.

Dear Nicola

Here are our favourite anchorages:

- East River, Mobjack Bay, Mathews County, VA – a short sail for us but a million miles from the middle of the city. Our favourite getaway spot.
- Pretty Marsh Harbor, Mt. Desert Island, ME – we came across this quite by accident. We were the only boat in the entire bay.
- Peter Island, Little Bay, BVI – I was mesmerised by a gigantic school of fish swimming next to us when Gary and I were snorkeling. The other side: Yikes! Barracuda, with really big teeth.
- St George's, Bermuda – our very first blue-water adventures were from and to Bermuda. Truly a gem and a very welcome sight after a short ocean voyage.
- Tobago Cays – this small island epitomised what I thought was so grand and glorious in the Caribbean. Perfect beaches, crystal-clear water, palm trees.

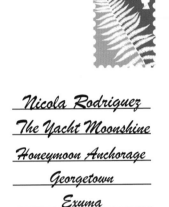

Nicola Rodriguez
The Yacht Moonshine
Honeymoon Anchorage
Georgetown
Exuma

Best wishes
Gary & Greta

WASHINGTON, DC

Mile Marker 1 in Norfolk, Virginia is the official start of the Intracoastal Waterway and the entrance to Chesapeake Bay. Two days north from Norfolk and two days' sail up the Potomac River lies Washington, DC, where boats can anchor in the Washington Channel near the centre of the nation's capital for up to two weeks. Call the Harbour Patrol on Channel 17 on arrival. The Capital Yacht Club and the Gangplank Marina are adjacent to the anchorage. Further out, where the Anacostia River joins the Potomac, is James Creek Marina.

It is possible to tie up a dinghy for free at the Poseidon Dock by Whites Restaurant; however, it is advisable to pay one of the marinas a daily fee. The Capital charged $15, which included a key to the dock, showers, laundry and use of the air-conditioned Club House, which in the hot, muggy Washington summer is a treat. It also includes a discount at Jenny's, the Chinese Restaurant, the upstairs neighbour. On Saturday mornings the Capital members welcome guests for an excellent $5 breakfast.

Both 20 minutes from the yacht club are supermarket Safeways and, on Sundays, an open-air farmers' market at the Ministry of Agriculture. At the end of Washington Channel, under the bridge, is a chandlery in the Washington Marina.

The nearby Smithsonian Institution includes several 'must-see' museums, for example the Air and Space Museum and the Natural History Museum. The docent tours, which are free, give a good overview if time is short. The Smithsonian Castle is 15 minutes from the Capital Yacht Club.

Exhume your bicycles for a ride

around the monuments and the White House. For longer distances the Metro at L'Enfant Plaza is just a short 10 minutes' walk from the CYC. Try Visitor Information for brochures galore, and check on www.washington.org for festivals, open-air concerts and city-wide information.

We couldn't tour the White House because we hadn't applied in time. British visitors should contact the British Embassy seven weeks in advance (www.ukinusa.fco.gov.uk). When the Supreme Court is in session it is possible to sit in on the arguments.

If you're not museumed out, a good excursion is the Udvar-Hazy Center, the aircraft hangar extension of the Air and Space Museum, near Dulles Airport.

Helicopters regularly use the Potomac as their flight path. An anchor light is required at night.

Winters are cold, but the National Cherry Blossom Week in spring is beautiful. When planning the trip, remember that Washington, DC is the end of the river and there is no loop back to the Chesapeake. It's two days up, two days back, but worth doing.

Source: Cruising Notes, Practical Boat Owner

BALTIMORE & NORTH

In the north of the Chesapeake is Baltimore, where you can anchor right in the middle of the city, which has the excellent Port Discovery children's museum and aquarium. Just outside, in Canton, there is a Safeway right next to the anchorage. Annapolis was sail, Baltimore is power, so be prepared to be severely 'waked'.

In Tuckerton, on the New Jersey coast, there is the Jacques Cousteau National Estuarine Research Reserve, visit www.jcnerr.org to find out more.

ANNAPOLIS, MARYLAND

In the north of the Chesapeake Bay on the western shore is Annapolis. It is similar to Dartmouth in Devon, UK, with a Naval Academy, weekly racing and an enchanting, historic town (www.annapolis.com).

Annapolis City Marina buoys in Spa Creek offer more protection than in the harbour for $30 a day or $190 a week, although it's further from the City Dock. There are dinghy docks at the end of the streets leading into Spa Creek. These can be useful but use a map – it could be a long walk.

As a sailing centre there are all kinds of yacht shops. Chuck at Doyle Sails repaired our mainsail. The Eberspacher heating unit was overhauled by Ocean Options. A new fire extinguisher and a hydrostatic release for the liferaft were supplied by USA Services and Electronic Marine sold us a Raymarine fluxgate compass. Numerous shops in the historical district sell excellent yachtie bounty, from humorous t-shirts to exquisite glass yachts and paintings.

There is a great playground for the children five minutes from the city dock. Connector Buses provide eight routes around the area. Take the Brown route from near the city dock for the supermarket, chandleries such as West Marine and Fawcett Marine, and the laundry.

Annapolis can become crowded, particularly around 4th July and the Boat Show. Other anchorages nearby include Back Creek in Eastport and Weems Creek up the Severn River.

Source: Cruising Notes, Practical Boat Owner

Back Creek, Annapolis, Maryland

NEW YORK, NEW YORK

The way to New York is north out of Chesapeake Bay, through the C&D Canal, across Delaware Bay and out into the ocean, where the Atlantic shoals and can be hazardous. Sandy Hook is a convenient and safe anchorage in which to recuperate after plugging into the New Jersey coastal waters, before entering NYC. There is also an anchorage in the Liberty State Park, near the Statue of Liberty.

Sailing up the Hudson River past New York City was thrilling, with hundreds of skyscrapers and upmarket apartment buildings putting their best façades forward, competing for light and status. From the Statue of Liberty up the Hudson River to the George Washington Bridge is a spectacular sail.

There are numerous marinas, but they are expensive. One at Chelsea Piers, at $5 a foot plus $20 electric per night, has access to a golf driving range and skating rink for an extra fee. Buoys at the 79th Street Yacht Basin are a much more reasonable $30 a day on a first-come, first-served basis (www.nycgovparks. org). Pedro, the dock master, is extremely helpful. Beware of the strong current through the anchorage; at 3.6 knots it can make boarding from the dinghy a problem. If the mooring field is full, anchor and wait, or dinghy around the field searching for buoys with yellow markings, which are only visible at water level.

79th Street Yacht Basin is on Upper West Side, an excellent location for walking to museums, or catching buses or the subway up or down town. It is near delightful playgrounds for the children, with several others in Central Park. Ten minutes up the hill on Broadway are supermarkets such as Fairway, which, as it claims, 'is like no other', and the eclectic Zabars. Nick's Place (Broadway and 77th) is a memorable breakfast place. The American Museum of Natural History and

Central Park are a half-hour walk away.

As ever, a double-decker tour bus is the best way to see the city. In addition to the scores of museums, sights and shops, if you're downtown, go to the South Street Sea Port.

Chandlery West Marine (12 W 37th Street) is a $15 taxi ride and located in the Garment District. The manager quipped that 37th and 5th Avenue 'has all you could need: clothes, marine shop, porn and psychics.'

East out of the City towards Long Island one has to negotiate Hell Gate. Afterwards, rest up in City Island, a quaint town with British pubs and fish and chips.

Source: Cruising Notes, Practical Boat Owner

Sailing into New York City was a high point

POSTCARDS FROM THE KEDGE

Greg von Zielinski moved from the Chesapeake and now lives in Florida. He describes himself as a preacher who lives on board *Ocean Ministries*, his 54' ketch, between the Chesapeake and the Caribbean.

Dear Nicola

My favourite anchorages are:

- Mystic Connecticut
- Block Island by the Coast Guard station
- Christmas Cove off St Thomas USVI
- Sampson Key in the Bahamas
- Highborn Key in the Bahamas

Nicola Rodriguez
The Yacht Moonshine
Newtown Creek
Isle of Wight
UK

Best wishes
Greg

LONG ISLAND SOUND & NORTH TO MAINE

Through Hells Gate in New York's East River, past funky and quaint City Island, on up to hundreds of bays and inlets and the enchantments of Long Island Sound (the Museum of America and the Sea in Mystic Seaport), Nantucket (Martha's Vineyard and the Hamptons), Cape Cod, Boston and finally Maine, with its lobsters and sometimes fog. Maine is a place to visit during the summer months.

Acadia National Park, Maine, NE USA is a special place worth making the stretch for. If you sail this far you could consider the route around Nova Scotia, New Brunswick into the St Lawrence Seaway.

Pilot guides to the area include *Embassy Cruising Guide: Long Island Sound to Cape May, NJ*; *A Cruising Guide to Narragansett Bay and the South Coast of Massachusetts*, Lynda Morris and Patrick Childress; *A Cruising Guide to the Maine Coast*, Jan and Hank Taft; and *A Cruising Guide to Nova Scotia*, Peter Loveridge.

ST LAWRENCE SEAWAY

For those contemplating a long, northern circle route, the St Lawrence Seaway involves sailing around the Maritimes, the coasts of Nova Scotia, New Brunswick, Prince Edward Island into the St Lawrence River, down to Quebec and Montreal (from where you can visit Ottawa). Ships and large barges use this route. (See Clive Woodman's account in *Roving Commissions* or on the Royal Crouising Club's website.)

The Rideau Canal and Lake Champlain take you through locks and canals to

Kingston, where you enter Lake Ontario and the charming Thousand Islands.

Useful websites include the Canadian Parks Service, www.pc.gc.ca, www.skipperbob.net (*Cruising the Rideau and Richelieu Canals*), www.greatlakes-seaway.com and, for the New York section, www.canals.ny.gov.

Toronto is a few days west from Kingston along the lake shore, or you could head south to enter the canal system leading to Albany on the Hudson River, and down to New York City, from where you can sail in the Atlantic Ocean south, either staying on the 'outside' (ocean) or taking the C&D Canal route to Chesapeake Bay. At Norfolk you can re-enter the ICW.

The pilot guide is *Cruising Guide: St Lawrence River and Quebec Waterway*s. If heading up around Nova Scotia, you may also like to read *The Shipping News* by Annie Proulx, which is set in Newfoundland but gives an insight into the Maritimes. The knots at the beginning of each chapter are intriguing in themselves.

THE GREAT LAKES

From Lake Ontario, the Welland Canal takes you into Lake Erie and the Great Lakes. Research it at www.glc.org, www.wellandcanal.com or www.skipperbob.net.

If you are considering this route read a children's book, *Paddle to the Sea*, written in 1941 by Holling C Holling, which follows the journey of a wooden canoe made by a boy of the First Nations from the winter snow of Lake Nipigon through the five lakes to the St Lawrence River and the ocean. Alternatively, from Lake Ontario you could take the Trent-Severn Waterway to Georgian Bay, part of Lake Huron.

The lakes are small freshwater seas and should not be underestimated. Storms and bad conditions can blow up very fast, so speak to knowledgeable locals before you sail.

Caution: if you venture too far, be clear that, although these northern parts are hot in the summer, they become cold in the autumn and freezing in the winter. Boats heading south from Canada should be en route by September. It is a long and taxing haul down through the canals and rivers to New York City. Then there is the ugly stretch of the New Jersey coast, which entertains hazardous conditions from late summer, Delaware Bay, the C&D Canal and down through Chesapeake Bay, then on through Virginia, the Carolinas, Georgia and Florida.

THE GREAT LOOP

The Great Loop is sometimes called the Circle Route. There are several variations.

You could head up the east coast from Florida via the Intracoastal Waterway and into the Great Lakes via New York City and the Hudson River. Or you could take the really long way via the St Lawrence Seaway in Canada. Or you could approach the Loop from the Gulf of Mexico up north to Illinois and Chicago, then out into Lake Michigan.

This loop and the other inland routes are covered by Skipper Bob (www.skipperbob.net). The latest information on the Great Loop can be found at the Americas Great Loop Cruising Association (AGLCA, www.greatloop.org).

Before you start this route, you must consider how you feel about motoring and more motoring, being landlocked for at least a month, and how many hours you want to add to your engine.

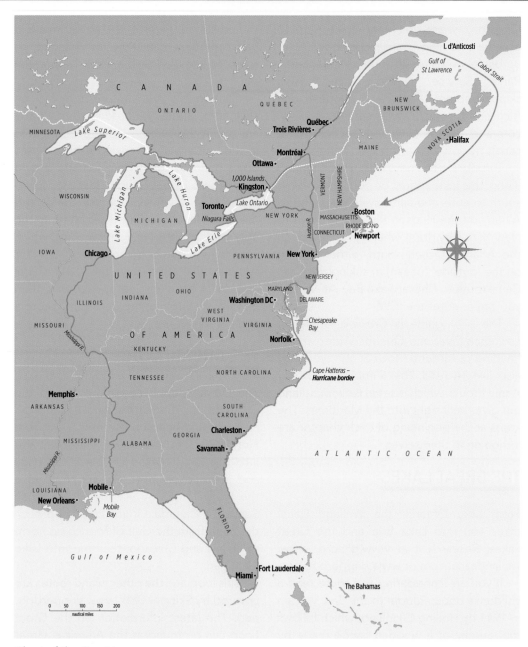

Chart of the Great Loop

TRUCKING ACROSS NORTH AMERICA

There are several firms that truck boats from the west coast, after a Pacific Circuit, back to the east coast, from whence they sail back to Europe, or are shipped from Newport, Rhode Island.

Some cruisers sail from the Caribbean to the Gulf of Mexico and truck their boat to the Pacific coast. It is an opportunity for a land trip across America. Many cruisers hire RVs (recreational vehicles) or buy a camper van and spend hurricane season touring.

11
HIGH & LOW LATITUDES

High and low latitudes refer to the Northern and Arctic waters, and, the Southern and Antarctic waters. Since the first edition of *Sail Away*, global warming has made the North West Passage a more viable option. Listening to veterans of high latitudes discussing the different types of ice, and the patterns of ice floes on ice charts is awe inspiring. Research and preparation are essential for sailing in these areas.

I am very grateful for the contributors in this section from experts Andrew Wilkes (who writes the RCC Pilotage Guide for *Arctic and Northern Waters*) and Ellen Massey Leonard (who has written extensively on these waters). Victor Wejer and Bob Shepton's experiences should also be included in your research. (See below.) If you are thinking of Antarctica, have a read of Pete Hill and Annie Hill's Kindle RCCPF Pilot Guide: *South Georgia*.

Ellen Massey Leonard grew up sailing in San Francisco Bay and British Columbia and has been voyaging offshore since

The Leonard's Celeste in brash ice, Beaufort Sea near Barrow

aged 20 when she and her husband Seth set off to circumnavigate the world aboard a 40-year-old small, classic, and – some would say – primitive cutter. Following their circumnavigation (Maine to Maine via New Zealand and Cape of Good Hope), they upgraded to a 30-year-old small, classic, wooden cutter and sailed to the Arctic Ocean. Seth and Ellen have also cruised extensively in Alaska as well as both the East and West coasts of North America, and have just crossed the Pacific again to Polynesia, celebrating 50,000 total miles en route. Ellen is a frequent contributor to sailing and adventure magazines in the USA, UK, and Canada, and she chronicles their adventures at http://gonefloatabout.com.

Ellen Massey Leonard wrote this contribution about sailing in high latitudes, whilst in the South Pacific, a true blue-water explorer.

Even with all the technology and 'mod-cons' that make sailing today a whole lot easier and more comfortable than it was even just a few decades ago, high latitude voyaging is still a challenge. With the short summer season, the volatile and often rather exciting weather, and the cold air and sea temperatures, the stakes are higher. Risk is inherent in sailing offshore anywhere, of course, but when the water is so cold that you'd live only about 15 minutes in it, the risk is that much greater.

Obviously, a boat and her crew venturing to the polar or sub-arctic regions need to be extremely well prepared, both physically and mentally. There's a lot that's been written on preparing your boat for high latitudes and on creating plans and contingency plans for polar voyages, but while the outfitting and planning can be difficult and time-consuming, it's arguable that mental preparation for the challenges and discomforts (despite all those mod-cons!) might be harder.

Managing your expectations is part of it; for example, a friend of mine who's a scientist on the North Slope of Alaska once mentioned that the waves created by a 20-knot wind at 0°C are steeper than those created by the same wind at 25°C because of the increased density of cold air and consequent increased force upon the water. So, expectations formed from years of Caribbean sailing about what 20 knots feels like are in for a bit of an adjustment in the far north or the far south.

Being ready for lasting rough weather, sleep deprivation, anchor watches, hazards such as ice, and the like is all part of being mentally prepared, but I think the most important part is to know why you're going, and to be honest about it, especially to yourself. If you are going to the high latitudes to be able to tell your friends – or Instagram followers – how rugged you are, it's probably best not to go. You wouldn't enjoy the actual process of it, the daily experiences – good and bad – of the sailing itself. If you are going for yourself – whether for the remote places, the unique landscapes and wildlife, and / or the challenge of sailing in these harsh regions of the world – and you couldn't care less if anyone ever knew you went, then everything will feel worth it.

ICE, ICE, ICE

David and Linda Hughes, with their crew Mark and Charlie Durham sailed their Oyster 66, across the Atlantic to the Caribbean, then south to Chile and the Antarctic. Whilst exploring these southern waters they took *Miss Molly* into a hollow iceburg. A few months later Linda's physio gave her an incredulous look when Linda described a shoulder injury, incurred punting floating ice away from the yacht.

SAILING ALONG THE PACIFIC COAST OF NORTH AMERICA

Andrew Wilkes is veteran of high latitude sailing. He writes the RCC Pilotage guide *Arctic and Northern Waters*. This passage, undertaken by Andrew is a bridge between Alaska and the Pacific. (In this small world whilst preparing this edition we sailed past one another in Solent!) You can also read his account, 'A Cruise around Iceland and to Scoresby Sound, East Greenland' in RCC *Roving Commission, 58*.

We sailed to Alaska by way of the North West Passage and our first landfall was a fleeting affair at Barrow on the North Slope. We had to land a crew member and did so by dinghy on the beach in the middle of the night. It was calm but bad weather was expected so Máire stood offshore with the mainsail still set whilst I rowed our friend ashore. It had not been easy to get in touch with the right person at U.S. Customs and Border Control, but we had eventually done so, and they could not have been more helpful. This set the scene for our subsequent cruising in Alaskan waters: sailing along the Pacific coast of North America.

We went on to sail through the Baring Strait into the Pacific, Dutch Harbour in the Aleutian Archipelago and on to Kodiak where we over-wintered. The following year we sailed to Prince William Sound and then south to the Inside Passage of 'Passage to Juneau' fame.

Our first port of call on the Inside Passage was Elfin Cove. We had not seen any other boats or people for a while and the tiny village seemed buzzing with fishermen and float planes. The first fisherman we met threw a huge salmon onto our deck as a welcome gift. Glaciers swept down to the sea and humpback whales cavorted nearby. Alaska was wild, empty and beautiful. Brown bears took the place of polar bears and huge forests replaced barren tundra.

We cruised south, anchoring every

Stunning Arctic views

night in a beautiful bay or off small settlements. Tides were fierce. Eventually we came to 'civilisation' in the form of Vancouver and then Washington State. Port Townsend is populated with artists and wooden boat fanatics – much more 'us' than nearby Seattle.

The Strait of Juan de Fuca marks the border between Canada and the U.S. Washington State gave way to Oregon which passed into California. The air got warmer and people more populous until we arrived at San Francisco where we over-wintered the boat in the Napa Valley. We thought the people of San Francisco were friendly, cultured and fun.

Both the temperature and the tempo of life ashore got hotter as

Andrew Wilkes' yacht, Marie, in the Arctic

we sailed south from San Francisco. We sailed over the border into Mexico in a pre-Trump era but, even then, the U.S. Customs and Border Control helicopters were very active.

We logged some 3,500nm sailing from San Diego just north of the Mexican border to the entrance to the Panama Canal. For us, it was very much a 'passage' and we went ashore infrequently stopping at Cabo San Lucas, Puerto Vallarta, Acapulco, Puerto Angel in Mexico, and Jiquilsco in El Salvador. The police in Acapulco patrol their patch

in an armoured jeep with a machine gun mounted on the back – something of a culture shock to those more used to seeing a Bobby on a bicycle.

For several days we sailed through large numbers of sea turtles who were swimming north. We made excellent speed under sail as we sailed past the coasts of El Salvador, Nicaragua, Costa Rica and western Panama. However, when we altered course to the northeast in the Gulf of Panama a strong head wind encouraged us to motor-sail to windward. The beer in Panama tasted good.

POSTCARDS FROM THE KEDGE

John Ridgway describes his sailing history: 'Fresh from rowing across the Atlantic with Chay Blyth in 1966, I rather rushed to seize the "opportunity of a lifetime during the lifetime of the opportunity" by entering the Sunday Times Golden Globe Race in 1968: trying to become the first person to sail alone round the world non-stop in *English Rose IV*. With considerable chagrin, I ended up in Brazil. I spent the next 40 years sailing all over the place, in *English Roses V* and *VI*, including 3 circumnavigations by way of the Southern Ocean, often with my wife, Marie Christine, and daughter, Rebecca.'

Dear Nicola

Our 5 favourite anchorages are:
- Stella Creek, by the Wordie Hut, Antarctica: which we visited in January 1995 aboard English Rose VI – the most southerly yacht in the world at the time!
- Kilronan, Inishmore, Aran Islands, Galway, West Ireland: where Chay Blyth and I landed after rowing across the North Atlantic in 93 days in 1966.
- Chiquito Guayabo, SW Panama close to Colombia: time spent with a Choco Indian family in 1994.
- Raroia Atoll in the Tuamotus, the Low or Dangerous Islands in 1994: this is where the Kontiki balsa raft was smashed on the reef in Aug 1947.
- Cape Farewell in Greenland in Aug 1999: during a voyage to catch Arctic Char on Scottish wet flies.

Best wishes
John & Marie Christine

Nicola Rodriguez
The Yacht Moonshine
Simpson Bay
St Martin
West Indes

English Rose VI in Stella Creek, Antarctica 1995: safe – for a while   209

POSTCARDS FROM THE KEDGE

Clive Woodman and Angela Lilienthal are presently sailing in Alaska. They have extensive experience of high latitude sailing, and have come across Bob Shepton (*Addicted to Adventure*) often.

Their accounts of their favourite anchorages were too long to fit on a postcard, but they are worth printing in full:

Clive Woodman and Angela Lilienthal

Our 5 memorable anchorages are:

- *Woodfjord, North Spitsbergen – at almost 80 degrees north and only just over 600 miles from the north pole, possibly the northern-most anchorage in the world. Memorable because it lay beyond the edge of the world as far as our GPS plotter was concerned, an iceberg grounded on top of our anchor, we ran aground whilst leaving (because we were too busy watching polar bears on the shore rather than our echo sounder!) and our engine gearbox failed at a point where we were over a thousand miles away from the nearest place to get it fixed – and all these happened within 30 minutes of one another.*
- *Fogo Harbour, North Newfoundland – the clarity of the light on Fogo Island is unbelievable and has attracted artists and photographers from across the world. To have a gin and tonic in the iconic Fogo Island Inn whilst looking out across the bay is an unforgettable experience.*
- *UUmmannaq Harbour, NW Greenland – to sit drinking a beer in UUmmannaq's 'nightclub' at 0300 in the morning, dancing with the local Innuit and looking out of the tinted windows at the countless icebergs floating past the mouth of the harbour in the light of the midnight sun, whilst Cosmic Dancer lay safely at anchor behind a protective wire boom across the mouth of the harbour which stops these ice behemoths from coming into the anchorage – simply our most surreal sailing related experience ever.*
- *Puilladobhrain (Pool of the Otter), near Oban, west coast of Scotland – for the row ashore and then walk across the peninsula to the inn by the 'Bridge over the Atlantic' where we have enjoyed some very special evenings.*
- *Tobermory, west coast of Scotland – for the classic view across to the distinctive Tobermory waterfront followed by an evening of convivial drinking and listening to Celtic music in the Mishnish Inn.*

12
THE PACIFIC & BEYOND

If you ask circumnavigators and sailors of the many seas where the most beautiful anchorages are to be found, the answer is the Pacific, with the odd one or two in Thailand. The Mediterranean, Caribbean and Bahamas become a distant memory, physically and metaphorically, once the sailor is exploring the Pacific. It is not an easy option, but this is where you are most likely to fulfil your special hopes... and special dreams.

In his book, *Riding Rockets*, Astronaut Mike Mullane, describes flying at five miles a second looking out over the Pacific from the Space Shuttle:

I was looking to a horizon more than a thousand miles distant and could see only the unrelieved blue of the Pacific. In each passing second, that horizon was being pushed five miles to the east but nothing changed. There was no vapor trail of jetliner, or wake of a ship, no cities, no glint of sun from a piece of glass or metal. No signature of life on earth.

Whilst in conversation with Jeanne Socrates, the oldest lady to circumnavigate solo un-assisted, I asked how it was she came to circumnavigate. Jeanne casually replied, "it was more by 'default', you start by crossing the Atlantic, go around the Caribbean, go through Panama." At this point I called her out, on just 'go through Panama', pointing out many bottle it at Panama. Jeanne's surprised reply? "But going through the Canal is a wonderful experience."

Having lost and found yourselves many times in Pacific places too idyllic for words, it will be time to explore exquisite seas in the Far East. Then it will be time to think about going home, wherever that might be now.

In this chapter, once through the Panama Canal, we look to the South Pacific Islands, New Zealand, Australia, Indonesia and the Far East. Once again, these are broad brushstrokes to fire your imagination and guide you at the start of your journey of further research.

Before we start, a few words of advice on keeping boat and body in good condition.

DOING IT FOR YOURSELVES

The World ARC reiterates that in the Pacific it is important to use as many alternative power generators as possible, such as solar panels and wind turbines.

If cruisers rely on a single generator, it can break, and often in the Pacific it is difficult to find spare parts. It means boats with watermakers that are reliant on a generator to start them are reduced to rafting up to other boats and transferring water. Redundancy and self-sufficiency, and even 'double redundancy', are worth keeping in mind in the Pacific. This extends to health and there are some useful books shown in the appendix.

SAN BLAS ISLANDS & PANAMA CANAL

Most cruisers visit the San Blas Islands (or Kuna Yala, Land of the Kuna), east of the Panama Canal. Some winter in the islands, sailing to mainland Panama to provision, and return. Part of the charm of the San Blas is that they are remote. Cruisers come

away with molas, fabric squares made by the Kuna Indians who sell them from their dug-out canoes.

Colón is the nearest city to the Panama Canal, but it is dangerous. It is recommended that you take a taxi directly to the supermarket and directly back, and even then, muggings can happen.

ARC boats anchored at Chichime, San Blas

CHAGRES RIVER, PANAMA

Stuart Ingram's memories of the San Blas Islands.

As one gets closer to the Panama Canal, anxieties about the passage through come to dominate one's thoughts; sometimes this leads to yachts neglecting to cruise the Atlantic coast of Panama. This is a mistake. The San Blas Islands with their unique culture should not be missed, nor should Portobello with the remains of the great fort from the period of the Spanish Empire. It was from Portobello that the annual fleet set out to carry the South American gold back across the Atlantic to Spain. Sir Francis Drake died when planning an attack and his coffin lies somewhere below the sea near the entrance.

Just to the north of the Canal is the entrance to the Chagres River. This river

was dammed higher up to create the Gatun Lake, the top waters of the passage across the isthmus. However, one can still enter it from the sea and go to anchor 4 to 5 miles up deep in the jungle.

Here there are parrots calling in the trees and on the boat, we had two Golden Orioles perched on the pulpit and little swallows on the guardrails.

Later a group of five monkeys suddenly appeared on the river's edge just by the boat, climbing around in the trees. The monkeys howl. During the day it is not too noticeable, but at night it adds a tension to the environment; they seem particularly vocal about 5am, just before dawn.

Paddling the dinghy through the surrounding creeks we saw toucans with their large multicoloured beaks and a woodpecker which had a great red plume.

TRANSITING THE PANAMA CANAL

Shelter Bay Marina (shelterbaymarina.com) is found at the entrance of the Panama Canal. Cruisers find it a useful departure point for the Canal.

Once cruisers arrive in the marina or nearby anchorages they sign in with the authorities and have their boat measured. They then anchor and wait or secure a marina berth and wait. Tankers and cruise ships are given priority. Some independent cruisers complain that, when a rally comes through, they take up the few places allocated to yachts for at least three weeks.

If you are transiting the Panama Canal go to www.pancanal.com and obtain the *Customer Form Procedures for Securing a Handline Transit of the Panama Canal.* Under 'required equipment' on the site (or Autoridad del Canal de Panama) the following are listed:

All handline vessels are required to be equipped with 4 ropes, of adequate strength for the size of the vessel to maintain it stable in the lock chamber under strong turbulence. These ropes must be a minimum of 125 feet (38 metres) long.

The guide provides illustrations and information on picking up mooring lines and types of lockage, for example 'Centre Chamber', where the boat is held in the middle of the lock by lines, or 'Sidewall', where the boat is 'nested' against the wall. Some cruisers recommend using an agent, others prefer experienced line handlers and taxi drivers. If you hire a pilot and land handlers, be prepared for them to ask for extra money during the transit. Negotiations are fluid.

In order to experience how the operation progresses and to help fellow cruisers, some people act as crew for other yachts transiting the Canal. You can see boats transiting on the webcam of the Miraflores Lock (www.pancanal.com/ eng/multimedia). It's quite a kick to see your friends going through: I found myself waving wildly at my laptop!

It is intimidating sharing confined waters with massive ocean-going ships. There

have been horror stories and pictures of yachts being crushed, but such incidents are very, very rare. www.noonsite.com has useful information and the latest costs, in 'Procedures for Transiting the Panama Canal'. Consult the pilot guide *The Panama Cruising Guide* by Eric Bauhaus.

ARC fleet in Miraflores locks – just about to enter the Pacific!

SOUTH AMERICA

You've transited the Canal, sailed under the Bridge of the Americas and the Pacific awaits.

If you want to venture by land inland into South America, this is the time to do it. You can sail south through the Gulf of Panama to Ecuador and see the Andes, Ecuadorean Indians and Inca temples. Further south and inland in Peru there are Machu Picchu, Cuzco and Lake Titicaca.

EQUADOR

Near Quito, Equador, there is the Mitad del Mundo – the middle of the world –

where a monument has been erected to those who, between 1735 and 1739, took part in the French Geodesic Expedition to measure the earth's great girth and to calculate the length of a line of longitude. Rosemarie Smart-Alecio has had many experiences of crossing the line of latitude in several longitudinal positions. She wrote of her visit:

Comparatively most of the Equator is on land, and most of that is inhospitable, being either mountainous or thickly forested. The selected area, just north of what is now Quito, the capital of Ecuador, was one of very few accessible areas. Here by measuring arcs of curvature at the Equator – over a huge area between Quito and Cuenca in Peru – they verified the earth's magnetic declination precisely and, from this, worked out its size... It was one of the highlights of our land travels... And of course, like children, we had fun standing on the Equator and crossing several times between the north and south hemispheres.

Rosemarie is one of few queens of the high seas who can ask her husband and skipper Alfred: "How many times have we crossed the Equator in the last 14 years?"

Bringing in the catch, fishing boats in La Libertad, Ecuador

CHILE

For those with a few thousand miles under their keel who do not mind cold weather, exploring Chile is an option.

During their years of circumnavigating, John and Fay Garey took in over 40 countries, but Chile was their favourite. In this part of their travels they sailed in big seas across the hundreds of miles from Mexico through the Pacific to Easter Island and saw the gigantic moai statues. Then they sailed the 2,000 miles to Chile. Fay Garey described the voyage:

With wind, it always seems to be a matter of too much or too little. The sea was indescribable, raging as if bent on our particular destruction, the sky a sinister mass of steel-grey clouds. Huddled below in all the warm clothes I could muster, I pictured the bluebells, peonies and early roses of an English May, and vowed never to go to sea again! But, as an introduction to the southern hemisphere winter, we saw our first albatross, unmistakably with its majestic wings, pursued by Pintado Petrels in their chequered black and white livery.

Andrew O'Grady wrote the pilot guide Chile, and he and Pete Hill have written the RCCPF / Imray pilot guide Argentina.

THE PACIFIC

The Pacific islands are among the most breath-taking and remote, you can sail in and out of sublime, remote anchorages for weeks. Three weeks of sailing, 3,000 miles from the Galapagos to the Marquesas, thins out the Caribbean crowds. The Mediterranean and Caribbean were the nursery slopes and foothills, now we're stepping up to the mountains. The Pacific is vast. Physically, time and distance at sea are longer. Intellectually, navigation and pilotage will demand more of you. Spiritually, you will find that the white light becomes luminescent.

Island after island after island – it would be pointless (and you would lose points from other cruisers) if you tried to tick off the list. A great part of this journey is the getting there. Once the stretch to the Marquesas has been met and won, then, as, Michael Pocock said, "the cruising between islands that form such magical stepping stones is all possible in relatively short stages." Relatively, don't forget – relative for the Pacific can be four or five days. The pilot guide for the Pacific region is The Pacific Crossing Guide, published by the RCC Pilotage Foundation with the Ocean Cruising Club. It is the go-to guide on this vast area. There are local guides such as Charlie's Charts however, this deeply researched, and knowledge-full book should be kept at your nav station. (We, the Navigators by Dr David Lewis is a favoured book on Pacific navigation.)

Although the Pacific Ocean was named by Ferdinand Magellan in 1521 'Tepre Pacificum', the pacific or peaceful sea, there will be troublesome weather. Arrivals are sweeter nevertheless because the islands are incredibly beautiful – and because over the miles and miles the anticipation grows.

Those who have sailed across the Atlantic in November and rush straight through the Panama Canal in March complain that, by the time they reach French Polynesia, they are utterly exhausted and feel that it is really 'uphill' to Australia or New Zealand. If you can, spend a year in the Caribbean then head into the Pacific. Several boats

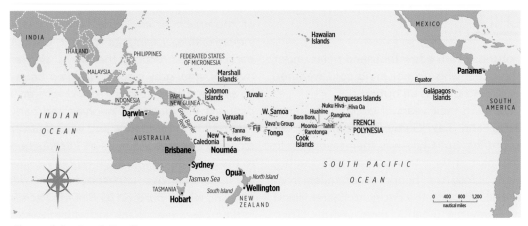

Chart of the South Pacific

on the World ARC take time out from the rally to spend two years exploring the Pacific, Australia and New Zealand before re-joining, heading back to St Lucia via the Cape of Good Hope (South Africa).

The traditional circumnavigation used to continue from the Panama Canal, taking in the Galapagos Islands, to French Polynesia, Society Islands and Fiji, then south to New Zealand or Australia. Then Indonesia, Singapore, Malaysia, Thailand into the Indian Ocean to India, the Maldives or Sri Lanka, Oman, the Red Sea and the Mediterranean. With the pirates in the Indian Ocean, long-distance sailors are reviewing the situation. There are alternative destinations in the Pacific, one of which is Chile, as already mentioned.

GALAPAGOS ISLANDS

Once in the Pacific, most cruisers sail to the Galapagos Islands. If you wish to visit the Galapagos National Park, yachts require permits which you need to organise before leaving Panama. Of the 13 islands, Isabela, San Cristobal and Santa Cruz are the largest, and where yachts must present their permits. All who go are enthralled and say it is a 'must' and a high point of the trip, although some complain that it

is extremely expensive to visit the outer islands. It is possible to anchor in one of the main islands and take guided tours. This skipper's comment is echoed by many:

These semi-mystical islands... are amazing! Despite the fact that everything is geared to relieving you of your hard-earned pennies, the wildlife, so far, has been incredible!

Kicker Rock, Galapagos Islands

THE COCONUT MILK RUN

From the Marquesas this route takes boats through the Tuamotu Archipelago to Papeete on Tahiti in the Society Islands. Then, westward to the Cook Islands, Tonga and Fiji. A regular route is Fiji south to New Zealand. For those aiming for Australia it is west to Vanuatu.

FRENCH POLYNESIA

If you're sailing from the Galapagos, Atunona on Hiva Oa is the Port of Entry to the Marquesas. Taio Hae Bay on Nuku Hiva is many cruisers' favourite on the Coconut Milk Run. As is Hana Vave (Bay of Virgins / Baie des Viege) on Fatu Hiva.

Tanya and Graham Leech sailed in the Pacific in their Westerly Corsair. Tanya writes of the Baie de Vieges: 'The tall sheer cliffs of dense greenery encircling this safe anchorage would, on their own, rank this anchorage highly. But it is the fact that one arrives at the Bay of Virgins after a typical passage of three weeks from the Galapagos (usually) that simply adds to the drama. Ocean crossing is a life lived in constant motion and shades of blue. Arrival at Fatu Hiva brings rest from the swell and a full-on explosion of green from this tiny, remote speck of land.'

Rosemarie Smart-Alecio who cruised the Caribbean, Pacific and Far East extensively, agrees: 'Perhaps because it was our landfall in the Pacific, after a passage that takes on average 20-30 days from Galapagos. Spectacular rock formations.'

Other suggested reading for this region is Paul Theroux's *The Happy Isles of Oceania*. Since you will be sailing in the wake of Captain Cook, read as much as you can on Endeavour. *The Ship: Retracing Captain Cook's Endeavour Voyage* by Simon Baker is pertinent.

Papeete (on Tahiti) is the capital of the French Polynesian islands. As with the rest of French Polynesia it is expensive, although cruisers have reported that if you 'shop smart' it is affordable. Missing Carrefour? The supermarket chain is here. It is also a major hub for air routes, so a good place for friends to visit.

Moorea is a smaller island nearby. *The Pacific Crossing Guide* describes it as 'the first island on the passage across the Pacific that has high dramatic scenery and a fringing reef'.

Most Pacific cruisers agree that Bora Bora lives up to its reputation as the most dramatic and exotic of the islands. Some are disappointed that it has become too commercial. Raiatea and Taha'a provide sheltered cruising in the lagoon although charter boats can make it busier than nearby (in Pacific terms) less sophisticated Huahine.

The pilot guide is *Charlie's Charts of Polynesia* by Charles and Margo Woods.

Gambier Islands, French Polynesia

Moorea (Tahiti), Society Islands

POSTCARDS FROM THE KEDGE

Mark and Charlie Durham are a skipper and hostess couple who sailed the Atlantic with Mark's father and were offered a plum crewing job on their arrival in Antigua. They have sailed extensively in the Mediterranean, Caribbean, Pacific and Antarctic.

Dear Nicola

Our favourite anchorages are:

- Gambier Islands, French Polynesia – such a wonderfully memorable visit after our time spent with its people, especially a small group of children who spontaneously decided to give us a guided tour of their island on our day off.

- Cala Brecknock, Chilean fjords – in Chile there were so many amazing anchorages it is difficult to pick just one. Brecknock and Yvonne were similar in their isolation and wildness.

- Huahine, French Polynesia – Huahine and Rangiroa (along with Bora Bora and Moorea) are typical reef paradise anchorages with incredible diving.

- Deception Island, Antarctica.
- Rangiroa, French Polynesia.

Best wishes
Mark & Charlie

Nicola Rodriguez
The Yacht Moonshine
Marigot Bay
St Martin
West Indes

TONGA

Tonga, officially the Kingdom of Tonga, is made up of 176 coral atolls and volcanic islands forming three groups: Vava'u in the north, Ha'apai in the middle and Tongatapu in the south. Most of the population live on Tongatapu, whereas most of the tourists head for Vava'u. The King's Palace is in Nuku'alofa, on Tongatapu. Captain Cook's welcome here prompted him to call these, the Friendly Islands.

It is wise to remember that the Tongans seriously observe Sunday as a day of rest. If in a tourist centre, such as Neiafu, the capital of the Vava'u Group, find out the location of the next Tongan feast, it's worth experiencing.

The pilot guide is *Ken's Comprehensive Cruising Guide for the Kingdom of Tonga* by Kenneth Hellewell.

In her favourite anchorages Tanya Leech includes Minerva Reed which lies between Tonga and New Zealand: 'There is absolutely no land to be seen at all, just a submerged reef. A very welcome stop on a challenging passage and surreal experience of mid-ocean anchoring!'

FIJI

The islands that make up the Fijian archipelago are spread across a vast expanse of the Pacific. (1.3 million square kilometres, or 501,932 square miles of the South Pacific.) Many cruisers can only stop at a couple and visiting others can involve complicated pilotage in areas where charts cannot always be trusted.

The Royal Suva Yacht Club is the place to head for in Suva, the capital of Fiji, on the island of Viti Levu. It is a great meeting place for yachts sailing the Pacific. Some cruisers remain in Fiji during cyclone season, but most sail south to New Zealand and back in between cyclone seasons. Other continue west towards Australia.

There are numerous other islands and reefs. To the east is the Lau or Eastern Group, with the Exploring Islands, and, to the west through the Koro Sea, the Yasawa Group. Michael Pocock reminds cruisers that in the less sophisticated outer islands such as the Lau Group, the Ministry of Native Affairs insist on 'rigid standards of dress and behaviour.' If cruisers wish to visit island villages, they must present the Chief with a gift of kava roots. This ceremony done, the welcome is warm.

Levuka, the old capital, is the smallest of the Ports of Entry for Fiji and is considered a hidden gem, the most charming with a quaint air of Old England. You can get an amazing view by climbing the 199 steps up Mission Hill. The whitewashed clapboard Ovalau Club welcomes visitors. Jason and Fiona sailing on *Trenlley* said of Fiji:

Musket Cove at the bottom of the chain is an ideal cruisers' rest up. Full of surfers on yachts. The real Fiji up the chain is wonderful cruising – often we were the only boat in the anchorage. We managed to swim with huge manta rays and had some good snorkelling... Not a huge amount of wind for sailing, but interesting day sails between small islands, reefs and rocks keep you on your toes, especially as you often have the sun in your eyes. We had several hairy moments, but it was always worth the effort. Towards the end of our time in Fiji we found that cruisers were exchanging tracks to help them through the reefs. Wish we'd had those!

One of the cruiser rest ups is Vuda Point, where they bury your boat during Cyclone season. I asked one family about whether they came back to a cockroach infestation; they said the geckos had kept them at bay – lots of gecko poo though.

POSTCARDS FROM THE KEDGE

Rosemarie Smart-Alecio has cruised the Caribbean, Pacific and Far East extensively.

Dear Nicola

My favourite anchorages are:

- Bay of Virgins, Marquesas, French Polynesia – perhaps because it was our landfall in the Pacific, after a passage that takes on average between 20 and 30 days from Galapagos. Spectacular rock formations.
- Moorea, Tahiti, Society Islands.
- Almost anywhere in the Bay of Islands, New Zealand.
- Phang Nga Bay, Phuket Island, Thailand.
- Guayraca Bay, north Colombia – fjord-like, within the highest coastal range of mountains in the world (5,000 metres) and the only place to see snow in the Caribbean. We try to forget the katabatic winds!

Best wishes
Rosemarie

Nicola Rodriguez
The Yacht Moonshine
Potomac River
Washington DC
USA

Musket Cove, Fiji

NEW ZEALAND

Most cruisers experience a bumpy ride from Fiji to Opua, a Port of Entry in north east North Island, New Zealand.

But once you get there, this area, the Bay of Islands, is a popular and beautiful cruising ground. Also, south of here, off Auckland, lies the Hauraki Gulf where you can explore numerous islands in the Marine Park amongst them Great and Little Barrier Islands, Kawau and

Motukorea (Browns).

June to September is considered, even by New Zealanders, too cold to go sailing, so you may want to take a trip home, or go and explore the amazing inland area of New Zealand.

New Zealand's Yachting governing body, Sail New Zealand, is based in Westhaven Marina, Auckland (www. yachtingnz.org.nz).

The pilot guides are *New Zealand's The Hauraki Gulf Boating Atlas* by David Thatcher and *Coastal Cruising Handbook* from the Royal Akarana Yacht Club.

VANUATU

If you are heading towards Australia from Fiji, the island chain of Vanuatu is on your horizon. Previously known as the 'New Hebrides', both English and French are spoken in addition to the 130 local languages, of which Bislama (a form of Pidgin English), is the most common. While among the people of Vanuatu, the Ni Vanuatu, try to see kastom dancing. Even better, if you befriend a local, see if there is a wedding coming up.

Tanna island is towards the southern end of Vanuatu. One Pacific sailor, spoke for many when he said of Port Resolution (Tanna) "the anchorage is good, but it's the friendly people ashore who make it, and there's the chance for an unforgettable trip to watch the active volcano (Mount Yasur) erupt during a sunset visit." Lonely Planet describes it as 'one of the world's most accessible volcanoes.' Beware of the scalding pools where streams from the volcano run to the water's edge.

POSTCARDS FROM THE KEDGE

The Gifford family spent eight years circumnavigating: www.sailingtotem.com. They say they have 100 top ten favourite places! But managed to narrow it down to 5 for me:

Dear Nicola

Our favourite anchorages are:

- Baie du Contoleur, Nuku Hiva, French Polynesia. Lush mountains drop sharply towards the sea, but what made this anchorage most stunning was bioluminescence like we've not seen elsewhere.
- 'Teacup anchorage', Raja Ampat, Indonesia. Our name for the otherwise unnamed hideaway near Misool island in eastern Indonesia; too deep to anchor, we tied off on four sides and jumped off Totem and into the most vibrant marine life we've ever seen.
- Liberty Island, New York, USA. As the sky darkens at dusk, the buildings off Manhattan first glow reflected sunset shades, then twinkle golden hues as night-time lights come up and shine on the statue of Liberty.
- Banda Neira, Indonesia. History has drama here: lightning flashes over the volcano to your west at night; to your east is a 17th century fort.
- Spencer Bay, Namibia. Mountainous sand dunes look down at Antarctic-chilled current. Fur seals swim by, the island adjacent teems with penguins, and the bay you just left has a flock of flamingos on shore.

Nicola Rodriguez
The Yacht Moonshine
Island Harbour
Anguilla
West Indes

Best wishes
The Gifford Family

POSTCARDS FROM THE KEDGE

Jeremy Wyatt, Director of the World Cruising Club, describes his favourite anchorages but needed two postcard!

Dear Nicola

My favourite places to visit by boat:

In the Pacific there is just so much to see that a lifetime cruising would hardly be sufficient, so here are a couple of pointers:

- The stunning sandy beaches of Fulaga in Fiji – the stuff of paradise dreams.
- The Kingdom of Tonga. Whilst the beaches may be better elsewhere, they are a 'must see' for the genuine warmth of the welcome justifying their name as the friendly isles. Whilst there, go and swim into Mariners Cave in the Vav'u group if you are brave enough.
- New Zealand simply has to be on any true cruiser's wish-list. For me, the area around Picton at the north end of the South Island is truly stunning.

Nicola Rodriguez
The Yacht Moonshine
La Savina
Formentera
Spain

In Northern Europe, I love cruising on the west coast of Scotland where, if the weather is kind, you can enjoy some of the cleanest water, the most inspiring wildlife and scenery of awe-inspiring beauty:

- For the simple pleasure of a perfect sandy white beach, a romantic castle and clean clear water try Loch Breachacha, on Coll.
- The anchorage at the Sound of Ulva on the west side of Mull is the perfect place to lay at anchor watching sea eagles soaring overhead and, on a still dawn, see otters patrolling the tideline.
- And finally, no cruise on the Inner Hebrides would be complete without a visit to Loch Scaviag on the Isle of Skye. Anchor in the pool surrounded by the near sheer black granite slabs of the Cuillin Hills rising straight out of the sea. Watch from you boat as curious seals peer back at you. Make it a magic moment with a dram of Talisker single malt whisky, made just a few miles away at Carbost, and you have the perfect place to reflect on life as a cruising sailor.

Nicola Rodriguez
The Yacht Moonshine
La Savina
Formentera
Spain

Best wishes
Jeremy

PORT RESOLUTION, TANNA, VANTUATU

Stuart Ingram shared his view on this harbour:

Tanna is towards the southern end of the chain of islands that make up Vanuatu, previously known as the New Hebrides. The whole area is prone to earthquakes and volcanic action. When Captain James Cook anchored here in 1774, naming the bay after his ship, the seabed was about 20 metres lower. In 1878 there was an uplift and now the harbour is only suitable for yachts. On entering one can see smoke coming from the crater of Mt Yasur, which is 361 metres high and lies about 4 miles away. The Lonely Planet Guide encouragingly refers to it as 'one of the world's most accessible volcanoes.'

Along the shore there are hot pools where the streams run into the water's edge. An over-curious yachtsman put his foot into one of the pools to see how hot it was; a month later he was still hopping around on the blisters. There are a number of families around the bay but no proper village. One family tends to adopt a yacht, arranging visits to the volcano and setting up meals of local food.

Cargo cults, the idea of riches arriving from beyond the sea, have a long tradition, particularly in Tanna. In the Second World War, the Americans set up an enormous base on an island just to the north and 1,000 men from Tanna were recruited to work there. Here they saw an abundance of riches and also black Americans with whom they could identify. From this grew up the John Frum (or John 'from' America) movement, which believed that John Frum would come with abundant riches for the believers. In some villages, particularly in eastern Tanna, it is the predominant belief. Large red crosses are erected, copied from the red crosses on the wartime ambulances, and in some cases tin cans and wire are strung together in imitation aerials to encourage John Frum to speak to his people. True believers give up all worldly wealth and let their ground become overgrown, as John Frum will eventually provide everything.

On Friday nights, groups from the villages come together to sing, and one can go to listen.

WHAT AN UNFORGETTABLE DAY

Rosemarie Smart-Alecio has been exploring the Pacific for many years. Here are excerpts from her piece in *Flying Fish*, the journal of the Ocean Cruising Club, describing her good fortune to be invited to the pre-nuptial of their guide Alik's nephew, one of the Yassur who lived in the volcano village on Tanna, two days' sail from the ceremony.

The women and girls wore long, brightly coloured shredded 'grass' skirts with characteristic coloured, painted fabric tops, and had tall dyed feathers held on their heads by dried pandanus bands.

The men and boys were bare-chested and wore sulus (skirts) – either the traditional ones, woven from natural fibres, or of bright, printed fabric. Woven pandanus bands held crowns of fresh vegetation on their heads as well as around their legs and arms. As we approached we noticed, their body paint, especially on their faces, mostly in their national colours of red, green, yellow and black.

There was dancing and offering of gifts such as yams, taro and kumara earth covered fresh from the ground – as well as hefty hands of bananas. Woven mats, rolls of printed cottons and beautifully woven bags followed. Another gift was carried down the steep hillside by two young men, on a pole between them a fully-grown pig, its fore and hind hooves trussed together over the pole, its very-much-alive body swinging heavily beneath. A sow was also presented, and the carcass of a cow carried by sixteen men. After some discussion between the fathers and the Chief of each village, there followed welcoming words to and from all, and more dancing.

However, the men from the visiting village could not relax, for it was their job to dismantle the pile of presents and pack them into their boats for transportation back to their island... a human chain lifted and tossed piece after piece into the boats...

Alik was anxious to know whether the dancing had satisfied me. He had just no idea how thrilling our afternoon had been and seemed to find it difficult to comprehend our awe and appreciation of what he had made possible for us. We did our best to indicate how privileged we felt at having been allowed to witness such a special event and asked that he pass on our delight and thanks to the families for allowing us to join them.

POSTCARDS FROM THE KEDGE

Jason and Fiona Harvey on their Oyster 435 ketch *Trenelly* have crossed the Atlantic twice and are exploring the Pacific with their son Dylan and daughter Molly. Jason wrote about his favourite anchorages.

Dear Nicola

My favourite anchorages are:
- Asanvari, Vanuatu – great people, lots of children, great yacht club. Also, superb views, a great beach and a waterfall only improve a great spot.
- Port Resolution, Tanna, Vanuatu – because of the fantastic volcano nearby. Standing on the edge of an active volcano while it thunders and spits fire into the sky high above you is a truly awesome experience.
- San Blas – any or all of the islands because of the isolation and the wonderful people, but one with a small wreck was best of all.
- Bayswater Marina, Bayswater, Auckland, New Zealand – a marina, I know. A great spot, with a 10-minute ferry to the central buisiness district and just a short trip down to lovely Devonport. The sailing options from here are great – we felt they were better than those of the Bay of Islands going out from Opua.

Best wishes Jason

Nicola Rodriguez
The Yacht Moonshine
Marina Del Atlantico
Santa Cruz
Tenerife

NEW CALEDONIA

New Caledonia (Nouvelle Caledonie) offers extensive, uncrowded cruising in lagoons with barrier reefs particularly on the west and south coasts.

Grand Terre is the largest island, with a 'largest insular coral reef in the world', meaning that you can sail around most the island inside the reef.

There are a wide range of yacht services, (Port Moselle), good provisioning, French cuisine, and all the trappings of tourist centres. The 'off lying islands' are formed by the Loyalty Group, the Ile des Pines, the Chesterfield Islands and Belep Island.

Some cruisers spend several cyclone seasons in New Caledonia, using it as a base from which to return to the South Pacific or Indonesia. Ile des Pins and Ile Ténia are considered particularly idyllic.

The pilot guide is *Cruising Guide to New Caledonia*, Joel Marc, Marc Raubeau and Ross Blackman.

AN ALTERNATIVE PACIFIC

In their early 30s Peter and Katharine Ingram bought *Kokiri*, a Pacific 38, in New Zealand and sailed her to Vanuatu, the Solomon Islands, Federated States of Micronesia, Papua New Guinea, through the Philipines to Manila where they spent time on the inevitable maintenance that was required before heading north to Japan where they were given a warm welcome, especially in Tokyo. From Ofunato in north Japan, they sailed through the North Pacific Ocean to the Aleutian Islands, Alaska and British Columbia. This is an arduous route but a thoroughly rewarding one full of variety and beautiful, unexplored cruising areas. From British Columbia they shipped *Kokiri* across Canada and sailed across the Atlantic to Spain. They summarised their adventure: 'We covered over 16,000 miles, visited eight countries and some of the remotest coasts on earth in the course of our 16-month cruise, without serious storms, breakages or mishaps.'

Their descriptions of their favourite anchorages are too big to fit on a postcard, but too good to miss!

■ Loch na h'Uidhe, Taransay, Outer Hebrides: A wonderful sheltered anchorage on sand bottom. Beautiful sandy beaches, fantastic walking and a loch in the middle for freshwater swimming. (Peter proposed here, and Katharine accepted.)

■ Trappers Cove, Adak, Aleutian Islands: As we arrived in the shallow protected Trappers Cove we could see Bald Eagles watching the bay and Caribou wandering on the hillside. The sun was shining, and the place was perfect. Rolling easy hills and shortish, regularly grazed tundra made for lovely walking ashore, but not so many grazing animals that the flowers suffered and so there were still the carpets of purple, green and yellow as far as the eye could see. From the hilltop behind the boat we could see, on the other side of the bay just below the mist line, a tumbling waterfall evidently coming from a lake.

■ Rendova Harbour, Rendova Island, Soloman Islands: A lovely sheltered anchorage with spectacularly friendly people. We were invited into inner bay in 8-metre coral and had the village party to beat all village parties. In the evening, entertainment ranged from the fantastically brilliant traditional pan pipe playing and dancing, all in traditional dress, to the excellent, if slightly raucous, women's singing / dancing groups, to the slightly less brilliant dancing to a ghetto blaster, to the mind numbingly dull men's group parable dramas. The next day there was an astounding feast cooked underground in a custom oven. A custom oven consists of hot stones in the ground, covered with pandanas leaves. The food is then wrapped in more pandanas leaves, put on the stones, covered with more leaves, weighed down with more hot stones and left overnight. There were three ovens. One for pig, one for tuna and one for sweet potatoes and taro. No sooner was breakfast finished than the feast was spread out on leaves on the ground and all 300 Anglicans sat down cross legged and gorged themselves on the most succulent pork I have ever, ever tasted.

- North Cove, Coron Island, Calamian Islands, Philippines: A fantastic cauldron of an anchorage with sheer cliffs of sculptured limestone plunging down to finish with great overhangs at sea level.

- Poluwat, Chuuk State, Federated States of Micronesia: A perfectly sheltered atoll placed in the middle of the most wonderful trade-wind cruising. The island has masses of interest: wonderful sailing canoes, traditionally built canoe houses. Very friendly, interesting locals, some of whom are still traditional navigators (by the stars, swell patterns and changes in sea colour). The island has a fascinating history and was occupied in the war by the Japanese. All the remnants of the war are just lying around, buried in the jungle. We spent three weeks there building our beloved dingy and on Katharine's 30th birthday we set off with the fleet of traditional sailing canoes to fish for tuna on the fringing reef. A wonderful and perfect place, of which we have very fond memories.

Peter and Katharine Ingram's evening cuise off Coron Island in the Calamian Islands

Poluwat, Chuck State, Federated States of Micronesia

AUSTRALIA

If you are heading to Australia go to www.homeaffairs.gov.au to help familiarise yourself with entry requirements.

With the exception of New Zealand citizens travelling on New Zealand passports, all foreign nationals must obtain a valid visa / Electronic Travel Authority (ETA) before arrival in Australia. Visas are available from Australian Missions overseas, www.embassy.gov.au. They are also available, in ETA form, from travel agents and airlines in certain countries. Look also for the Termite Alert, as well as *Operator Guidelines for Vessels less than 25 metres arriving in Australia*. There are legal requirements for the master of

Torres Strait, Australia

a vessel about to arrive in Australia, for example 96 hours before arrival you must email, phone or fax to alert Customs.

If you are spending time in Australia, look up www.downunderrally.com who organise 'East' and 'West' rallies around e.g. The Gold Coast to New Caledonian. John Hemdown describes his rally: 'The Down Under 'Go West' Rally provides westbound yachts with a professional and informative introduction to Australia, and ensures participants receive current and accurate information before departing and on arrival.'

Also look out for the Coral Sea Rally, from Cairns to Port Moresby, Papa New Guinea, organised by the Royal Papua Yacht Club (RPYC) in conjunction with Cairns Yacht Club and Cairns Cruising Yacht Squadron (www.rpyc.com.pg). Another rally worth exploring is a circumnavigation of Tasmania

organised by the Royal Tasmanian Yacht Club. (See below).

Pilot books are *Australian Cruising Guide* by Alan Lucas and *Downwind Around Australia and Africa*, by Warwick Clay. *English Passengers* by Matthew Kneale is a humorous yet moving account of passengers on a voyage to Tasmania, one of them in search of Eden.

Also, whilst in Australia pick up a copy of the Australian sailing magazine *Cruising Helmsman*.

WHITSUNDAYS

The Whitsunday Islands lie off northeast Australia, within the Great Barrier Reef Marine Park. The Reef to the east protects the islands from the ocean swell ensuring relaxed sailing in azure waters, (but with numerous charter boats). The white beaches fringing the islands are internationally famous.

Among the most charming stops in this heavenly cruising ground are Whitehaven Beach, a local describes it as 'a big long open anchorage with a beach of white 'squeaky' sand to run along.' Others include Pudding Island, Hook Island and Butterfly Bay. If you can make it for the Hamilton Island Race Week in the third week of August, you'll see an impressive racing fleet.

Pilot books include *100 Magic Miles of the Great Barrier Reef: The Whitsunday Islands* by David Colfelt and *Cruising the New South Wales Coast* and *Cruising the Coral Coast* by Alan Lucas.

Jason Lawrence wrote an account: 'Australia, ¾ Circumnavigation' in *RCC Roving Commission 56*.

SYDNEY

Sydney Harbour is 19 kilometres (12 miles) long and covers 52 square kilometres (20 square miles) including 70 beaches, numerous inlets and bays, plus the Sydney Opera House. Efficient public transport systems make travel to the sights of interest easy from most anchorages.

The most prestigious of the many yachting spectacles is the Sydney Hobart Race, which starts on 26th December. It is full of challenges. Yachts race 600 miles from Sydney through the Tasman Sea, south along the Bass Strait to Storm Bay, Tasmania, finishing in Hobart. Maxis (79-81-foot boats) take two days. Veterans of this crash through the Tasman Sea (on the edge of the Southern Ocean) describe it as the 'customary pasting'.

AN ALTERNATIVE TO SAILING HOME

An option once in Australia is to sail down the east coast to Sydney, taking in Great Keppel Island, coral atoll Lady Musgrave Island, Fraser Island, Jervis Bay, Eden, even as far as Flinders Island. If you have been awed by the cliff faces in Mallorca or Sardinia, then the Cathedral Rocks on the southeast coat of Tasmania are a treat. Tasmania is temperate, giving a relief from the tropics.

You could try the bi-annual Royal Yacht Club of Tasmania VDL (Van Diemen's Land) Circumnavigation (www.ryct.org.au). From Hobart it takes 35 days visiting amongst other beautiful places, Port Arthur, Maria Island, the Schouten Passage, Wineglass Bay ('bright white beaches and pink granite mountains rising steeply out of the sea'), the Banks Strait, the Gordon River and Port Davey.

A PACIFIC SOJURN

Mike and Devala Robinson tell their tale:

Mike and I did the 'daft' thing in our early 50s – took on the biggest mortgage we'd ever had, bought a beautiful Oyster 46 (the first boat we had ever owned) and sailed off into the sunset. We both left demanding but satisfying careers – Mike as editor of Panorama and Devala as head of physiotherapy at Great Ormond Street

Hospital. We swapped professional lives of decision making where our opinions were valued, where we worked with committed bright people, for crawling round on our knees cleaning, hunting round industrial estates looking for the place to fill a gas bottle or that elusive piece of tubing. Suffice to say the first year was a challenge as we worked out how to live aboard and keep our beautiful boat safe and well maintained.

The plan had been a three-year circumnavigation but, like all true cruisers, our plans were written in the sand at low water and this gradually morphed, by degrees into nine years. Seven of these were spent in the Pacific, a most wonderful cruising ground where, with many others, we joined the 'Pacific Eddy' commuting between New Zealand the Pacific islands and Australia, according to season.

The rewards of the trip have been immense, and we returned with heads stuffed full of the most incredible experiences and memories we will never forget, and some that are already fading – like all that chrome polishing.

Mike and Devala's favourite anchorages can't fit on a postcard:

- Off Lomati on the island of Matuku, Southern Lau Islands, Fiji. This heads the list and we visited many times because of the wonderful welcome we received ashore – we felt we truly became a part of the village. We accepted every invitation, even to things like the island council meeting

Mike and Devala Robinson on Rano Raraku, Rapa Nui (Easter Island)

and did what we could to help – from ferrying people to the capital Suva to typing up, preparing and printing a document for an application to central government for funds to build a jetty.

- Anakena Bay, Rapa Nui (Easter Island). We were one of only four yachts cruising around Easter Island. The moai (the immense stone statues the island is famous for) ashore are unforgettable and so many more (some 900) than we had ever imagined. There is only one town, Hangaroa, where all the tourists stay. This meant we often had anchorages and the moai ashore all to ourselves from late afternoon to mid-morning.
- Fulanga, Southern Lau Islands, Fiji – any one of the myriad anchorages amid water that was every shade of azure blue imaginable with golden sandy beaches. The massive lagoon is littered with rocky outcrops (motus). Fulanga is often described as 'the jewel in the crown' of the Southern Lau islands, which are themselves the Pacific of which you dream.
- Athol Bay, Sydney Harbour. Where else can you anchor for free with a view of the famous Opera House that is to die for, sounds of wild animals in the background (Sydney Zoo is located ashore here) and, on New Year's Eve, the most fantastic firework display you can imagine. All the anchorages in Sydney Harbour are free.
- Grey Isles outside Port Fitzroy on Great Barrier Island, Hauraki Gulf New Zealand. So close to Auckland and yet, get the timing right i.e. anything other than the period between Christmas and New Year, and you can really be by yourself plus you can dive for scallops – 20 per person per day – what's not to love?

DARWIN

If you are heading towards Darwin, in north Australia, try to make time to push further to the Kimberleys, west of Darwin, which is an area of outstanding natural beauty.

The pilot guide is the *Northern Territory Coast. A Cruising Guide* by John Knight. A pilot guide for Western Australia (covering the west coast including Christmas and Cocos Islands) is Fremantle Sailing Club's *Western Australian Cruising Guide* edited by Kim Klaka.

SOUTH EAST ASIA

Looking over the horizon, the Royal Cruising Club's *South China Seas* by Jo Winter covers that area. There is also the *Cruising Guide to SE Asia Vol 2* by Stephen Davies and Elaine Morgan, but this may be hard to come by.

Jo Winter's account in the Royal Cruising Club's *Roving Commissions 56*, 'An Assortment of Islands, a Philippine Circuit', gives a good idea of this area. Similarly, in *Roving Commissions 58* 'North to Japan, A cruise from Port Carmen, Philippines to Taiwan and Japan'.

INDONESIA

Sail Indonesia (www.sailindonesia.net) is a rally that leaves Darwin in July (winter). Many yachts take the Sail Indonesia option to help facilitate the complex bureaucracy involved in sailing through these islands.

Since 2016 there has been no requirements for the CAIT, Cruising Authority for Indonesian Territory Waters. Yachts are required to check in with Indonesian Customs and have AIS on board. The new Yacht Electronic Registration System can be found on yachters.beacukai.go.id.

It is wise to stock up on frozen and vacuumed meat before leaving Australia for Indonesia – and alcohol.

The marinas in Darwin are full around the time of departure, so book early. Over three months Sail Indonesia voyages to Singapore via Kupang in Timor, Rote Island, Lembata, Flores Island, Lombok, Bali, Karimun Java and Belitung. There is a return rally to Australia in April. If participating in the Sail Indonesia Rally you

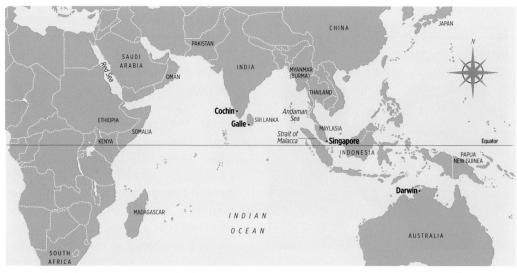

Chart of South East Asia and the Indian Ocean

may want to join the Darwin Dili Yacht Rally, run by Sail Timor-Leste (www.sailtimorleste. org). There are 'co-operative arrangements between the two rallies.'

Some independent cruisers choose to use an agent in Jakarta or Bali.

The Komodo Dragon, the largest lizard in the world, averaging 3 metres long can be found on the islands of Komodo, Gili Montang, and Rinca where you can anchor in Loh Buaya for the Ranger Base. The largest population of dragons is found on Flores, at the Wae Wuul and Wolo Tado Reserves. Look up www. komodonationalpark.org.

A guide that maybe useful is the *Cruising Guide to Indonesia* by Andy Scott.

CROSSING THE LINE

Don't forget that the Equator goes all around, so while sailing in these waters you could cross more than once. As you approach Borneo, Sumatra or Singapore you will cross the Equator, so dig out your shaving foam or whatever you are going to inflict on those who have not crossed, your celebratory libation and feast – well, at least a treat (with some for Neptune) – and stand ready to watch the GPS click over to Latitude 00.00.00. (In the Indonesia–Singapore area, Longitude will read something in the range of 105° 22' 186" East.)

Approximately 300 miles north and

BANDA ISLANDS, INDONESIA

Stuart Ingram described these islands:

This small group of islands are a jewel, beautiful, full of extraordinary history and, with no airport, still well beyond the reach of any but the most determined tourist. If a reason for travelling on your own yacht is to reach the wonderful but inaccessible, then this is the justification.

The islands are dominated by Gunung Api, an active volcano that last erupted in 1988, but steam and sulphurous gases continue to escape from vents on its sides. On the main island of Neira, Fort Nassau and Fort Belgica look down on the anchorage and the faded colonial glory of the Dutch architecture of the small town. Sitting with a Bintang beer and looking out across the waterfront, it is all too easy to forget the terrible history of this small group of islands.

At one time Banda was the only source of the world's nutmeg. When nutmeg was believed to ward off plague and was used to disguise the taste of decaying

meat, whoever controlled the nutmeg controlled a fortune. The islands were fought over, and the Dutch East India Company used a degree of ruthlessness against their European foes and the local population that sickens the stomach even today. Run, a very small island in the group, was held against the Dutch by the English under the inspired leadership of Captain Nathaniel Courthope. Following Courthope's death they surrendered, but in the final settlement the Dutch were so anxious to retain Run that they gave up Manhattan in exchange: New Amsterdam became New York and the rest is history. [See Giles Milton's excellent book Nathaniel's Nutmeg: How One Man's Courage Changed the Course of History.]

The soft outer covering of the nutmeg is used to make a jam or sliced and dried as sweets. The red covering of the inner nut is mace, which is dried and used as a spice, much going into the secret formulation of Coca-Cola. The brown nutmeg kernels in the centre are dried.

south of the Equator is the Intertropical Convergence Zone (also known as the doldrums or equatorial calms), where the opposing trade winds of the oceans come into play – or not. The trade winds meet and cancel each other out, resulting in hot and humid conditions: 90% humidity is common, plus unpredictable weather. Ships, and to an extent their crew, would lie motionless waiting for wind to fill their sails. No doubt they scratched the backstay and whistled for wind.

SOUTHWEST MONSOON

Be aware that the southwest monsoon affects Thailand, Malaysia and Singapore from the beginning of June to the end of September. (The north east monsoon season lasts from November to March.) During the southwest monsoon cruisers often travel inland. Rosemarie Smart-Alecio and her husband caught a train across the high Qinghai-Tibet plateau from Chengdu to Lhasa, capital of Tibet (3,400km, 50 hours) and then on to the Himalayas and Everest Base Camp, Qomolangma, and Kathmandu, Nepal. This included a visit to the Panda Research Base in Chengdu. A stretch of a trip, but amazing.

SINGAPORE

The Singapore Straits are one of the busiest shipping areas in the word. (Sailing in the Solent, between southern England and the Isle of Wight, and / or around Ushant off northern France are all good practice.) Added to the huge tankers, container ships, barges and ferries, if you arrive at the end of January there is also the Singapore Straits Regatta.

Keppel Bay Marina is popular with cruisers (www.marinakeppelbay.com), as is Raffles Marina (www.rafflesmarina.com.sg).

MALAYSIA

Historically the South China Sea and those around Indonesia and Malaysia (for example the Strait of Malacca between Sumatra and Western Malaysia) have been pirate seas. Reports of incidents are fewer, however, and once near Phuket and around the tourist areas where yacht charters abound, you are safer.

Malaysia is composed of Malaya (peninsular Malaysia) and the islands of Sarawak and Sabah (Malaysian Borneo). Johor Bahru is on the east coast of Malaysia and has many pleasures to offer. In the South China Sea there are scores of islands, including Sebana, Sibu and Pulau Timoman, where the film *South Pacific* was shot in 1958.

If you want to see Orang-Utans, go to Malaysian Borneo, to Kalimantan to the Tanjung Puting National Park Orang-Utan Sanctuary. Alternatively, near Kuching, the capital of Sarawak, is the Semenggoh Orang-Utan Sanctuary. It is possible to see the Proboscis Monkeys, particular to this part of the world in the Bako National Park.

If you want to join a rally, www.sailmalaysia.net is supported by Malaysia Tourism, and keen to promote 'marine tourism'.

There are three choices:
- Passage to Langkawi
- Passage to the East taking in the less travelled routes
- Sail Malaysia Rally which voyages from Langkawi to Tawau via Singapore, Anambas / Natuna Islands and Brunei Darussalam.

Cruisers visiting the capital Kuala Lumpur leave their boats at the Royal Selangor Yacht Club in Klang, the port for the capital.

Most yachts head up the west coast of Malaysia through the Strait of Malacca north towards Langkawi, a major tourist destination which most cruisers find a good stop for provisioning, yacht services and the sybaritic.

Cruisers who have sailed in these waters found themselves staying much longer in northwest Malaysia / Thailand. Rosemarie Smart-Alecio said of her many years in these waters, "Not only the delights of cruising between Langkawi and Thailand's west coast, but it is also easy to leave the boat safely and go inland travelling… We have visited China twice, Cambodia, Laos, Thailand and much of Malaysia."

Try to find the *Southeast Asia Pilot*, Bill O'Leary and Andy Dowden; and *Cruising Guide to Southeast Asia, Vol. 2: Papua New Guinea, Indonesia, Singapore and the Malacca Strait to Phuket (including West Peninsular Malaysia)*.

POSTCARDS FROM THE KEDGE

Miles Kendall is the author of *Ultimate Sailing Adventures*.

Dear Nicola

My 5 favourite anchorages are:

- Yong Kasem Bay on the island of Koh Phi Phi in Thailand's Andaman Sea – swimming with dolphins, then fish barbequed on a deserted beach.
- Terre-de-Haut, Îles des Saintes, Caribbean.
- Lavezzi, Corsica.
- Wall Bay, Gocek, Turkey.
- Grebe Beach, Helford River, Cornwall.

Best wishes
Miles

Nicola Rodriguez
The Yacht Moonshine
Osbourne Bay
Isle of Wight
UK

Yong Kasem on the island of Koh Phi Phi in Thailand's Andaman Sea: Miles Kendall's number one anchorage where he swam with dolphins and barbequed fish on a deserted beach

THAILAND

Just across the Malaysian 'sea border', north of Langkawi, are the islands of Ko Lipe, Ko Rawi and the less commercial and loveliest, Koh Butang. From Phuket on the west coast sail out into the Andaman Sea where you will find dozens of exquisite islands such as the Butang group and Phi Phi Island. If you want to visit 'James Bond Island' (previously Koh Ping Kan), head from Phuket around to Phang Nga Bay and the limestone pillars. Just follow the tourist boats to see where Roger Moore in *The Man with the Golden Gun* hunted down Scaramanga's (Christopher Lee) hideout. This is prime yacht charter area so if you want quiet anchorages, sail to the Surin Islands or Similian Islands which are part of Thailands Marine Park. Cruisers who know the west coast of Thailand (as far as Ranong on the border of Myanmar / Burma), have said they prefer the Surins because they are more remote.

If you are considering sailing in the waters off Myanmar / Burma, Cambodia or Vietnam, then refer to the latest information from the Foreign and Commonwealth Office. www.gov.uk/foreign-travel-advice/cambodia.

In surfing, the ICON is the highest level in the Independent Ability Measure, iAMs. It could be the motto of ocean sailors. By the time you reach this part of your circumnavigation, this might be true of yourself.

They are blazing 'Explorers' where their inner spark leads the rest have followed.
Through perserverance and fun they achieved the incredible

THAI TRAVELS

Rosemarie Smart-Alecio, with many seasons in the Pacific and Indian Ocean under her keel, wrote of her travels inland:

This area (northwest Malaysia / Thailand) is a good place to stay for a few years, not only for the delights of cruising between Langkawi and Thailand's west coats, but it is also easy to leave the boat safely and go inland travelling. It is also easily possible to 'return' south in the Malacca Strait to cruise the South China Sea area.
    We leave Ironhorse in the Royal Langkawi Yacht Club and have visited China twice, Cambodia, Laos, Thailand and much of Malaysia, and hope to visit Vietnam and Myanmar (Burma) during the southwest monsoon (not such nice sailing weather!) this year. A number of cruisers do similarly.
    During our first season here, we cruised all of the west coast of Thailand as far as Ranong, on the border with Myanmar, thence to the Surin Islands and finally to the Similian Islands.
    Both sets of islands are part of Thailand's National Marine Park. Rangers and the military control it. Anchoring is forbidden and mooring buoys – well maintained generally, is our impression – are provided, but much sought after by all.
    The Surins are more remote than the Similian Islands and we found the diving / snorkelling there was even better, especially in the variety of colours of the coral. Further from the mainland to make it that much more difficult for the fast boats to visit as they do here in their hordes daily, I guess this could be why the Surins would have my vote if I had to choose!

INDIAN OCEAN, SRI LANKA, INDIA, THE MALDIVES

In January, most yachts in this region start focusing on returning to Australia or heading across the Indian Ocean, through the Andaman Sea to the Bay of Bengal to the Laccadive Sea, and Galle in Sri Lanka, or Cuchin in southern India, or Male in the Maldives.

Before heading East thoroughly research the piracy situation. It can be extremely stressful and expensive making the decision to ship in the Maldives, Seychelles or even Oman.

These are long distances. From Phuket to Galle it is 1,100 miles in the Indian Ocean, and then a 400-mile hop to Male in the Maldives, whose 1,200 islands and 25 atolls cover an area of 500 miles north to south. From Uligan, Maldives to Salalah, Oman is 1,200 miles.

To give you an idea of the length of the Red Sea, from Aden in Yemen to the entrance of the Suez Canal in Egypt, it is roughly equivalent to a diagonal line from the north of Scotland to the heel of Sicily, or from Melbourne to Brisbane, or from Miami to Norfolk, Virginia.

If you are in Sri Lanka, explore the hill country, Nuwara Eliya, and the tea plantations – and have a pink gin on the veranda of a planter's lodge.

A useful guide is the *Indian Ocean Cruising Guide* by Rod Heikell and once you have crossed, there is *East Africa Pilot* by Delwyn McPhun. After the Indian Ocean and South Africa, if you are heading up towards Brazil, take Pete Hill's RCCPF *Brazil*, parts 1 and 2 and 3.

PIRACY INFORMATION

The Indian Ocean is still a dangerous place to sail. It is best to research the situation thoroughly.

Information concerning piracy can be found on the website of the European Union Naval Force (www.eunavfor.eu).

At the time of writing, the British Government advice reads: 'The combined threat assessment of the international Naval Counter Piracy Forces remains that all sailing yachts under their own passage should remain out of the designated High Risk Area or face the risk of being hijacked and held hostage for ransom.'

As ever, check with www.noonsite.com which will give good up to date information, as will www.worldcruisingguide.net.

RYA Cruising Manager, Stuart Carruthers, advises:

While defensive measures and the use of armed guards on commercial shipping have had a clear deterrent effect for them, pirate networks still retain both the intent and capability to conduct piracy. Sailing vessels which are slow and low remain vulnerable from opportunistic attacks and hijackings.

Whilst merchant vessels are able to implement self-protection measures and employ armed guards to protect them, a sailing vessel cannot, and it is the crews that are valuable targets of maritime crime.

We would urge the boating community to remain vigilant and to avoid navigating through waters in which pirates are known to operate.

Theft from boats can occasionally lead to violent armed attacks if the owners are on board with the intruders. Personal security and safety must always be given due consideration – even in areas that are usually frequented by boaters and are widely considered to be safe.

We recommend checking the travel advice on the Foreign and Commonwealth Office website for guidance.

The Maritime Security Centre – Horn of Africa (MSCHOA) (eunavfor.eu/mschoa) provides a service aimed at ships. It 'provides 24-hour monitoring of vessels transiting through the Gulf of Aden, whist the provision of an interactive website enables the Centre to communicate the latest counter-piracy guidance to the Maritime Industry, and for shipping companies.' But there is no real provision for sailing vessels.

The International Maritime Bureau (IMB) has set up a Piracy Reporting Centre, www.icc-ccs.org/piracy-reporting-centre, which maps pirate attacks. Lloyds of London (www.lloyds.com) provides information for the shipping industry by their market marine experts.

The World ARC route takes boats south, around the Cape of Good Hope (South Africa), into the South Atlantic, and north to the Caribbean.

Jeremy Wyatt, Director of World Cruising Club stated:

Security on the World ARC route is something we consider when planning the rally. Traditionally there have been more concerns about shore-side security when in countries such as Brazil where street robbery is a problem. However, recent events have focused attention on security at sea, rather than ashore. The route of World ARC stays well away from the current area of concern, heading well south of the Maldives, Seychelles and British Indian Ocean Territory.

For those few who consider the risk of sailing through these highly dangerous waters is worth taking, the latest thinking is for a group of boats to sail the 12,000 miles from Thailand to the Maldives in approximately 10 to 12 days. In the Maldives they form a loose convoy for the sail to Oman. Once there, the boats form a close convoy in a hexagon shape and sail from Oman via Aden, Eritrea and Egypt up to the Suez Canal.

After their three years aboard, Jason Lawrence put Amanda and their sons on a plane, and chose to take the high-risk option of sailing solo across the Indian Ocean. After a few close calls for Jason, including the night a warship 'parked' itself between him and two threatening boats, they were all reunited in Egypt. (You can read about his journey in *Roving Commissions 52*.)

Before leaving on this leg, check and check again that you and your insurance company understand how long you anticipate taking to do the journey, and how long they anticipate, are the same. It is a hard passage and extra time must be factored in.

As I mentioned there have been pirate attacks in the South China Seas, those around Indonesia, Western Malaysia – the Straits of Malacca between Sumatra, and the Philippines. Reports of incidents are fewer, however, if sailing north to Thailand, once in Phuket and around the tourist areas, where yacht charters abound, you are safer.

ASHORE

We were on Martinique when riots in France sparked tyre burning and unrest on the island, a 'region' of France. We sailed away from the Fort de France, the capital, to the north. It became apparent the sleepy village of Deshayes in the far north was also in flux, so, we sailed to Antigua.

Behan Gifford encountered unexpected unrest in Thailand. I agree with her advice, 'Be Known, Be Friendly'.

This is the time when you call on the 'still small voice of calm'.

13
SAILING BACK

The decision to return to land-based life is a difficult one to make. Illness or lack of funds, young children or an elderly relative, can force your hand. For those who do not wish to explore beyond the Panama Canal, it depends on how long they want to explore the Caribbean and the USA. The situation in the Indian Ocean and the Red Sea discourages many from completing a circumnavigation. The choices are to return the way you came, to sell and fly home, or to ship and fly home or re-join the boat in the Mediterranean.

In 2010 John and I had to decide whether to sail on through the Panama Canal or go home. In the end we felt that the risk of piracy was too great and that the Pacific with two small children was too wide. And, 19 months plus of night-and-day childcare had left us exhausted. We needed a break.

Although life aboard is a challenge, do not underestimate the stresses of returning to shore life. It will be a long and testing time of readjustment.

Many retirees who set off on their dream, find it too hard and return to land, but leave again within six months. However tough the maintenance or grim the weather conditions, you are still free to explore – once you are home that freedom is gone.

John and Marie Christine Ridgway off the white cliffs of Dover – nearly home after 9 months in the Southern Ocean raising awareness to the plight of the Albatross

As the miles bubble under the keel, sailors seem to shed skins one after the other until the scales so necessary for living in crowded cities and towns drop away, leaving just the human creature all but naked under the stars. For most, once those scales are gone, they never grow back quite as thick and hard as they once were.

George Day, *Sailing in Thin Water*

REALITY BITES

When you do come back, expect a time of grieving: at least six months, most probably a year. Just as when you started cruising you found a new identity, it will happen again, and since most people are deeply affected by their time living aboard their yacht, it will take time to, literally, find yourself. You will feel fragile, so do not underestimate the effect your return will have on you physically, mentally and spiritually.

Living on the boat when you are saving to leave is a time of hope and anticipation. While you're in the cruising anchorage, living on the boat for the first few months at home seems a good idea. Once back into shore life, living aboard while sorting out the re-entry necessities can make the experience even harsher. Most cruisers who have been out for more than three years find it too painful, almost raw, to return to their boat for a few weeks or months after they return. Somehow when you are used to sailing across the Gulf Stream to the Bahamas, an afternoon sail to the Isle of Wight doesn't quite cut it. Time will pass, however, and you'll find discovering home horizons rather charming.

During the first few months at home there is a great deal to be organised, and much of it is emotionally draining. This is just the start of a very long list:

- Buying or renting a home
- Organising council tax, gas / electric, doctor, dentist
- Taking furniture out of storage or buying new
- Insuring your home and re-insuring the boat for the UK
- Finding a job and readjusting to routine
- Buying and insuring a car
- Selling the boat, or finding an affordable mooring or berth
- Finding a school for the children

It is helpful to maintain an address on land while you are away, whether it's your own residence which is rented out, your shore support's address or somewhere else. It is difficult enough explaining that you have been off the grid for three or four years without having to re-establish an address and residency in an area. You may have to re-register with the local council, electoral role, doctors and dentists. This is not always simple if you have just appeared out of what to administrators seems to be thin air.

Record-breaking round-the-world yachtswoman Dame Ellen MacArthur has spoken about the experience of being in control on her yacht as she circumnavigated, but once ashore that control dissipated, and she was no longer in control as she had been. Admittedly you're probably not an ocean-racing record breaker racing a high-performance yacht, but the same loss of control happens as you step off the boat and landlubberly life takes over. There was a reason Dame Ellen kissed her yacht as she stepped ashore.

For me, there were days on the school run when I felt I was being buried alive. The enforced return to routine can be debilitating. Whilst living on a boat, cruisers become used to open spaces, physically, emotionally and metaphorically, so going for walks or runs in large open spaces is a great panacea.

Jonny Harrison sailed from Newcastle upon Tyne to Australia. On returning to work in a global accounting firm, he said: "I had to start wearing a watch again (actually I had to buy one as I had lost mine!). It's really hard being 'on time' when you are used to just having 'your time'!"

Whereas on the boat one could wear shorts and t-shirts, old clothes must be de-mothballed, or a new wardrobe acquired, which can be expensive. Stocking up a kitchen can be a gradual process, helped by unloading foodstuffs from the boat.

Every little helps at this time of transition. Lugging laundry to laundrettes that beat up your kit is part of the cruising life. A washing machine is one of the perks of living at home.

Although re-connecting with friends can be a joyful experience, it can also be a drain on your depleted reserves. You will be the novelty treat at dinners, which is fun but also exhausting at a time of change. Some friends may seem interested initially, then glaze over as your expences are beyond theirs. Most cruisers find this and revert to small talk, leaving their extraordinary memories for evenings with other cruisers who can talk up and down 20 Caribbean islands or across 30 atolls in the Pacific in a sentence.

DON'T LET GO OF LETTING GO

For those who sell their boats, whether for the money or to draw a definite line under sailing, it is particularly hard. Some claim that it helps them move on. Most admit it was a financial necessity and they miss the boat profoundly.

One alternative to a complete break for those who can afford it is to leave the boat in a safe marina, be it the Caribbean or Pacific, and spend a month or two at home. If possible, avoid staying with friends. It is best to rent, or house sit, ideally for cruisers who are away.

Six months at home, June to November, six months in the Caribbean, December to May, is one choice, although some with grandchildren complain that this means they miss Christmas with the family. While a family Caribbean Christmas may be a just-crossed-the-Atlantic, one-off treat, an annual event is unlikely.

For most it is an either / or choice: continue or come back. Even so, once they are back, cruisers often set off again. Their experience of long-term cruising has changed them. When we lived on the boat, on the inevitable tough days we would remind ourselves that we were living in a magical world and that we should savour it, which indeed we did. 'Don't dream it, be it.' You have lived the dream, you have been it.

Once you have returned from cruising, for many it is not easy to let go of Narnia, Neverland, Nirvana – whatever is your land of dreams-come-true. An Atlantic Circuit presents a difficult adjustment once back ashore. Anyone who has spent more than three years out will find stepping back into real life far harder than letting go of the lines once more. You realise that, as John Masefield wrote, 'you must go down to the sea again.' As I write, the contributors to this book are sailing oceans or anchored in extraordinarily places all over the world. It's time to follow in their wake. Just start at the beginning of this book and you're away.

Coming back home and letting go is hard

CRAZY BUT TRUE

While I was completing the first edition of this book, I was reminded of a story from Fiona Harvey of *Trenelly*. We had just all crossed the Atlantic:

One of my favourite anecdotes is about mooring up in English Harbour and having this lovely English couple help us tie up. Turns out they were also recently married and crazy enough to buy a boat and sail into the sunset with each other. Both they and us were forced home, they by a hurricane and us by ill health, then we all bounced back and did it again – with babies! Crazy but true.

Thank you for joining me on this journey from saving, to buying, equipping, re-fitting and setting off, to maintaining and exploring, crossing oceans and making dreams come true, through high and low waters. I wish us all fair winds and a following sea.

WITH THANKS TO

With special thanks to:
- John Rodriguez without whom the journey would not have happened
- Jack and James for reminding me of what's important
- Denise Watkins, my mother, 'Shore-sure support'

Thanks to all those who have contributed to this book taking us further in our world explorations and providing detailed knowledge and experience. Many of the contributors have been honoured with prestigious awards from the Royal Cruising Club and Ocean Cruising Club.

To all circumnavigators and sailing friends, earls of the oceans and queens of the high seas – with whom we have shared and with whom we hope to share experiences.

ADVENTUROUS SAILORS OF ATLANTIC CIRCUITS & MANY SEAS

Matt & Liz Abbiss
Rob, Sheila, Elise & Verity Avery
David & Susie Baggaley
Sergej & Isabelle Berendson
Lisa Blore
Dee Caffari
Ed & Megan Clay
John, Sara & Harry Coxon
Oliver Crosthwaite-Eyre
Tom Cunliffe
John Douglas
Lizzie Douglas
Mark & Charlie Durham
Fay Garey
Behan Gifford & family
Trevor & Norma Goodson
James & Carol Grazebrook
Anne Hammick
David & Peter Hughes
Al & Mel Ingram
Peter & Katharine Ingram
Stuart & Annabelle Ingram
Jason & Amanda Lawrence & family
Graham & Tanya Leech
Mike & Sharon Lloyd

Royston & Maureen Lloyd-Baker
Bill McLaren
Bob Parr
Mike Pocock
John & Marie Christine Ridgway
Mike & Devala Robinson
Freddie & Jacqui Rose
Jane Russell
Bill & Nancy Salvo
Sarah Smith
Jeanne Socrates
Maureen Tetley
Martin Thomas
Charles Tongue
Jo Wallace
Honor Westall
Jo Winter
Irenke & Woody Wood

EDUCATION

Fiona Jones
Tamara Onslow

THE BALTIC

Fergus & Katherine Quinlan
Nigel Wollen

THE CARIBBEAN
Andrew Blatter (Antigua)
Peter & Sue Bringloe
David & Suzanne Chappell
Martin Smith (Barbados)

USA
David, Nancy, Josh & Chris Gohlke
Greta Gustavson & Gary Naigle
Greg von Zeilinski

AUSTRALIA, NEW ZEALAND, PACIFIC, INDIAN OCEAN
Beth Bushell
Fay Garey
Jonny & Kate Harrison
Jason & Fiona Harvey
John Hemdown
Misty McIntosh
Graham Shaw
Rosemarie Smart-Alecio
Lorriane Zaffiro

HIGH & LOW LATITUDES
Ellen Massey Leonard
Andrew Wilkes
Clive Woodman & Angela Lilienthal

ORGANISATIONS HELPING THE BLUE-WATER CRUISER
Association for Brokers and Yacht Agents (ABYA): Jane Gentry

Blue Water Rally (no longer operating): Richard Bolt, Peter & Annette Seymour
The Cruising Association
Hamble Marine Surveys: Julian Smith
Ocean Cruising Club (OCC)
World Cruising Club / Noonsite: Sally Logsdon & Jeremy Wyatt
The Royal Cruising Club (RCC)
The Royal Yachting Association (RYA): Stuart Carruthers – Training & Cruising
Sail America
Yachting Australia
Yachting New Zealand

PERIODICALS, EDITORS & JOURNALISTS
Blue Water Sailing: George Day & Valerie Adams Merfitt
Cruising World: Elaine Lembo
Flying Fish: Anne Hammick
Practical Boat Owner: Sarah Norbury & Rob Melotti
RCC Pilotage Foundation: Jane Russell
Roving Commissions: Tom & Vicky Jackson
Yachting Monthly: Elaine Bunting, Paul Gelder & Dick Durham
Yachting World: Elaine Bunting

For her charts: Maxine Heath
For his blessing: Reverend Michael Turner

Miles Kendall, the editor, without whom the first edition of this book would not have been published.

Jeremy Atkins, editor and publisher, whose insights and encouragement have been invaluable for this second edition. Gill Pearson and Daniel Stephen at Fernhurst Books without whom the reprint and this edition would not have happened.

To you all, many thanks

Nicola

PICTURE CREDITS

I am very grateful to all who have generously provided their photography in this book. The copyright for the photos is held by them.

All photos by John and Nicola Rodriguez except:

World Cruising Club: p40 (bottom), 54, 177, 212, 213, 214, 216, 220, 227

Mark & Charlie Durham: p28, 217, 218

Alan & Irenka Wood: p49 (right), 74, 93 (bottom), 136

Miles Kendall: p52 (right), 233

Fernhurst Books: p56 (left)

Al & Mel Ingram: p74

Lizzie Douglas: p75 (bottom)

Behan & Jamie Gifford: p75 (top), 112

Gill Pearson: p91, 92, 93 (top), 94, 95, 96, 97, 98

Alatair Buchan: p105 (left)

Fergus Quinlan: p114, 115, 116, 117

www.marinas.com: p135

James Grazebrook: p137, 138

Kitiara Pascoe: p157

David Chappell: p176

Blue Water Sailing: p187 (top)

Ellen Massey Leonard: p205

Andrew Wilkes: p207, 208

John & Marie Christine Ridgway: p209, 237

Clive Woodman & Angela Lilienthal: p210

Peter & Katharine Ingram: p226

Mike & Devala Robinson: p229

FURTHER READING

Many of these books will be available as eBooks and so easy to have onboard digitally.

SEAMANSHIP & SAILING SKILLS

RYA Manual of Seamanship, Tom Cunliffe
RYA Handbooks for Day Skipper up to Yachtmaster
Complete Day Skipper / Yachtmaster / Ocean Skipper series of books, Tom Cunliffe
The Annapolis Book of Seamanship, John Rousmaniere & Mark Smith
Short-Handed Sailing, Alastair Buchan
The Skipper's Pocketbook, Basil Mosenthal & Sara Hopkinson
Expert Sailing Skills, Tom Cunliffe
Illustrated Seamanship, Ivar Dedekam
Capable Cruiser, Lin & Larry Pardy
Ocean Sailing, Paul Heiney

NAVIGATION

Coastal & Offshore Navigation, Tom Cunliffe
Celestial Navigation, Tom Cunliffe

HEALTH & FIRST AID

The Ship Captain's Medical Guide, Harry Leach
First Aid Afloat, Sandra Roberts
First Aid Companion, Sandra Roberts
Doctor on Board: Your Practical Guide to Medical Emergencies at Sea, Jürgen Hauert
First Aid at Sea, Douglas Justins & Colin Berry
Travellers' Health, Dr Richard Dawood
Where There Is No Doctor, David Werner & Carol Thuman
SAS Survival Handbook, John Wiseman

FOOD & WELLBEING

The Care and Feeding of Sailing Crew, Lin Pardey
Rick Stein's Seafood, Rick Stein
The Boat Cookbook, Fiona Sims
The Beaufort Scale Cookbook, June Raper
The Trade Wind Foodie, Rod & Lucinda Heikell
Morgan Freeman and Friends: Caribbean Cooking for a Cause, Wendy Wilkinson, Donna Lee & Morgan Freeman

MOTHER, BABY & CHILDREN

The Great Ormond Street Baby and Child Care Book, What to Expect in the First Year
The Haynes Manual: Baby: Conception to Two Years
New Complete Baby & Toddler Meal Planner, Annabel Karmel
Voyaging With Kids, Behan Gifford, Sara Dawn Johnson & Michael Robertson
Kids in the Cockpit, Jill Schinas
The Cruising Woman's Advisor: How to Prepare for the Voyaging Life, Diana Jessie

WEATHER

The Sailor's Book of the Weather, Simon Keeling
Weather at Sea, David Houghton
RYA Weather Handbook, Chris Tibbs

BOAT MAINTENANCE

Simple Boat Maintenance, Pat Manley
Boatowner's Mechanical and Electrical Manual, Nigel Calder
The Restoration Handbook for Yachts, Enric Rosello

ENGINES

Diesels Afloat, Pat Manley
Diesel Troubleshooter for Boats, Don Seddon
Marine Diesel Engines, Nigel Calder

ELECTRICS & ELECTRONICS

Boatowner's Mechanical and Electrical Manual, Nigel Calder
Essential Boat Electrics, Pat Manley
Electrics Companion, Pat Manley

OTHER TOPICS

Sail for a Living, Sue Pelling
The Insider's Guide to Choosing and Buying a Yacht, Duncan Kent
Field Guide to North American Fishes, Whales and Dolphins, Herbert T Boschung

PILOT / CRUISING GUIDES

General

Ocean Cruising on a Budget, Anne Hammick
The Atlantic Crossing Guide, Jane Russell (RCCPF)
The Pacific Crossing Guide, Kitty Van Hagen (RCCPF)
World Cruising Handbook, Jimmy Cornell
World Cruising Routes, Jimmy Cornell
World Cruising Destinations, Jimmy Cornell
The Atlantic Sailor's Handbook, Alastair Buchan
Ocean Passages and Landfalls, Rod Heikell & Andy O'Grady
How to Sail on a Budget, Alastair Buchan
Voyaging on a Small Income, Ann Hill
The Voyager's Handbook, Beth A. Leonard

Baltic

The Baltic Sea and Approaches, Nigel Wollen (RCCPF)
Cruising Guide to Germany and Denmark, Brian Navin

The Channel

The Shell Channel Pilot, Tom Cunliffe
Channel Islands, Cherbourg Peninsula and North Brittany, Peter Carnegie (RCCPF)
North Brittany & the Channel Islands Cruising Companion, Peter Cumberlidge

Eastern Atlantic Coast & Islands

Atlantic France, Nick Chavasse (RCCPF)
Cruising the Inland Waterways of France and Belgium, Margaret Harwood & Brenda Davison
South Biscay, Steve Pickard (RCCPF)
Atlantic Spain and Portugal, Henry Buchanan (RCCPF)
Cruising Guide to the Canary Islands, Oliver Solanas Heirricks & Mike Westlin
Atlantic Islands, Anne Hammick and Hilary Keatinge (RCCPF)
Cruising Guide to West Africa, Steve Jones (RCCPF)

Mediterranean

The Straits Sailing Handbook, Colin Thomas
Islas Baleares, David and Susie Baggaley (RCCPF)
Mediterranean Spain, Steve Pickard (RCCPF)
Mediterranean France and Corsica Pilot by Rod Heikell
Corsica and North Sardinia, John Marchment (RCCPF)
Italian Waters Pilot, Rod Heikell
Adriatic Pilot, Trevor and Diana Thompson
Ionian, Rod & Lucinda Heikell
West Aegean, Rod & Lucinda Heikell
West Aegean Cruising Companion, Robert Buttress
Greek Waters Pilot, Rod & Lucinda Heikell
East Aegean, Rod Heikell
Turkey Cruising Companion, Emma Watson
Turkish Waters & Cyprus Pilot, Rod Heikell
The Black Sea, David Read Barker & Lisa Borre (RCCPF)
North Africa, Graham Hutt (RCCPF)

Caribbean

The Cruising Guide to the Southern Leeward Islands, Chris Doyle
The Cruising Guide to the Northern Leeward Islands, Chris Doyle
Sailor's Guide to the Windward Islands, Chris Doyle & Marian Cawley
Cruising Guide to Trinidad & Tobago plus Barbados and Guyana, Chris Doyle
Cruising Guide to the Virgin Islands, Nancy & Simon Scott
Grenada to the Virgin Islands, Jacques Patuelli
The Gentleman's Guide to Passages South, Bruce Van Sant
Cruising Ports: Florida to California via Panama, John & Patricia Rains
A Cruising Guide to the Northwest Caribbean, Stephen Pavlidis
Cuba: A Cruising Guide, Nigel Calder
The Cruising Guide to Abaco, Bahamas, Steve Dodge

North America

Anchorages Along the Intracoastal Waterway, Skipper Bob
Marinas Along the Intracoastal Waterway, Skipper Bob
The Intracoastal Waterway, Norfolk to Miami, Bill Moeller & John Kettlewell
Embassy Cruising Guide: Long Island Sound to Cape May, NJ, Maptech
A Cruising Guide to Narragansett Bay and the South Coast of Massachusetts, Lynda Morris & Patrick Childress
A Cruising Guide to the Maine Coast, Jan & Hank Taft
A Cruising Guide to Nova Scotia, Peter Loveridge
Cruising the Rideau and Richelieu Canals, Skipper Bob
Cruising Guide: St Lawrence River and Quebec Waterways, Michael Sacco

Central & South America

The Panama Cruising Guide, Eric Bauhaus

The Panama Guide: A Cruising Guide to the Isthmus of Panama, Nancy Schwalbe & Tom Zydler

Cruising Guide to Venezuela & Bonaire, Chris Doyle

Charlie's Charts: Western Coast of Mexico, Holly Scott

Cruising Ports: The Central American Route, Pat Rains

Cruising Guide to Belize and Mexico's Caribbean Coast, Freya Rauscher

Chile, Andrew O'Grady (RCCPF)

Argentina, Andrew O'Grady & Pete Hill (RCCPF)

Brazil, Parts 1 and 2 and 3, Pete Hill (RCCPF)

High & Low Latitudes

South Georgia, Pete Hill & Annie Hill (RCCPF)

Arctic and Northern Waters, Andrew Wilkes (RCCPF)

Cape Horn and Antarctic Waters, Paul Heiney (RCCPF)

Pacific

Charlie's Charts of Polynesia, Charles and Margo Wood

Ken's Comprehensive Cruising Guide for the Kingdom of Tonga, Kenneth Hellewell

We, the Navigators, Dr David Lewis & Derek Oulton

Exploring the Marquesas Islands, Joe Russell

Cruising Guide to Tahiti and the French Society Islands, Marcia Davock

Cruising Guide to the Kingdom of Tonga, The Moorings

A Yachtsman's Guide to Ha'apai, Phil Gregeen

South Pacific Anchorages, Warwick Clay

South Pacific Handbook, David Stanley

Australasia

The Hauraki Gulf Boating Atlas, David Thatcher

Coastal Cruising Handbook, Royal Akarana Yacht Club

Australian Cruising Guide, Alan Lucas

100 Magic Miles of the Great Barrier Reef: The Whitsunday Islands, David & Carolyn Colfelt

Cruising the New South Wales Coast, Alan Lucas

Cruising the Coral Coast, Alan Lucas

Northern Territory Coast: A Cruising Guide, John Knight

Western Australian Cruising Guide, Freemantle Sailing Club

Downwind Around Australia and Africa, Warwick Clay

Asia

Cruising Guide to SE Asia Vol 2, Stephen Davies & Elaine Morgan

Cruising Guide to Indonesia, Andy Scott

Southeast Asia Pilot, Bill O'Leary & Andy Dowden

South China Seas, Jo Winter (RCCPF)

101 Anchorages within the Indonesia Archipelago, Geoff Wilson

Indian Ocean

Indian Ocean Cruising Guide, Rod Heikell

East Africa Pilot, Delwyn McPhun

NARRATIVE

General

Flying Fish, Ocean Cruising Club

Roving Commissions, Royal Cruising Club

Casting Off & Untie the Lines, Emma Bamford

Dove, Robin Lee Graham & Derek Gill

The Hungry Ocean, Linda Greenlaw

In Bed With the Atlantic, Kitiara Pascoe

In the Heart of the Sea, Nathaniel Philbrick

Islands in the Stream, Ernest Hemingway

Moominpappa at Sea, Tove Jansson

One Wild Song, Paul Heiney

A Passion for the Sea, Jimmy Cornell

Mr Peacock's Possessions, Lydia Syson

The Perfect Strom, Sebastian Junger

Riddle of the Waves, Steve Price Brown

Robinson Crusoe, Daniel Defoe

Sailing Alone Around the World, Joshua Slocum

Sea Glory, Nathaniel Philbrick

A Sea Vagabond's World, Bernard Moitessier

So Many Islands: Stories from the Caribbean, Mediterranean, Indian and Pacific Oceans, Nicholas Laughlin

Then We Sailed Away, John, Marie Christine & Rebecca Ridgeway

The Story Keeper, Anna Mazzola

Topsail and Battleaxe: A Voyage in the Wake of the Vikings, Tom Cunliffe

The Valley at the Centre of the World, Malachy Tallack

Where the Magic Happens, Caspar Craven

Novels by Sam Llewellyn

Baltic
Northern Shores: A History of the Baltic Sea and Its Peoples, Alan Palmer
Small Boat Through Sweden, Roger Pilkington
To the Baltic with Bob, Griff Rhys Jones

Mediterranean
The Pillars of Hercules, Paul Theroux
Granite Island: Portrait of Corsica, Dorothy Carrington
Black Lamb and Grey Falcon, Rebecca West
Balkan Ghosts, Robert Kaplan
Captain Corelli's Mandolin, Louis des Bernieres
The Dark Labyrinth, Lawrence Durrell
Prospero's Cell, Lawrence Durrell
The Gerald Durrell Trilogy (Corfu)
Novels by Victoria Hislop

Caribbean
Caribbean, James A Michener
From Columbus to Castro, Eric Williams

North America
Midnight in the Garden of Good and Evil, John Berendt
The Shipping News, Annie Proulx
Paddle to the Sea, Holling C Holling
Chesapeake, James A Michener

High & Low Latitudes
Addicted to Adventure, Between Rocks and Cold Places, Bob Shepton
The Man Who Ate His Boots, The Tragic History of the Search for the North West Passage, Anthony Brandt
South: The Endurance Expedition, Ernest Shackleton

Pacific
The Happy Isles of Oceania, Paul Theroux
The Ship: Retracing Captain Cook's Endeavour Voyage, Simon Baker
Nathaniel's Nutmeg: How One Man's Courage Changed the Course of History, Giles Milton

Australasia
English Passengers, Matthew Kneale
Down Under & Travels in a Sunburned Country, Bill Bryson
The Bone People, Keri Hulme
The Whale Rider, Witi Ihimaera
Mr Pip, Lloyd Jones (Papua New Guinea)

FERNHURST

BOOKS

We hope you enjoyed this book

If you did, **please post a review on Amazon**

──── Discover more books on ────

SAILING · RACING · CRUISING · MOTOR BOATING

SWIMMING · DIVING · SURFING

CANOEING · KAYAKING · FISHING

View our full range of titles at **www.fernhurstbooks.com**

Sign up to receive details of new books & exclusive special offers at

www.fernhurstbooks.com/register

Get to know us more on **social media**